Routledge Revivals

The Battle for Tolmers Square

First published in 1976, this book tells of the dramatic struggle between tenants' groups, community associations, students, squatters, intellectuals, political parties, and property developers at Tolmers Square in north London. The author describes how property developers, interested only in maximising profits, attempted to redevelop the Tolmers area for offices, while the local authority, pressurised by local tenants and faced with a housing shortage, tried to redevelop for housing. This book is about the politics of central city redevelopment.

Although this text focuses on one particular case study, the same processes operate in all cities where land is used as a commodity for financial speculation. By tracing the Tolmers case in detail, this text demonstrates the forces which operate in city redevelopment, and shows the affect which various forms of opposition can have.

The Battle for Tolmers Square

Nick Wates

Routledge
Taylor & Francis Group

First published in 1976
by Routledge & Kegan Paul Ltd

This edition first published in 2013 by Routledge
2 Park Square, Milton Park, Abingdon, Oxon, OX14 4RN

Simultaneously published in the USA and Canada
by Routledge
711 Third Avenue, New York, NY 10017

Routledge is an imprint of the Taylor & Francis Group, an informa business

Publisher's Note

The publisher has gone to great lengths to ensure the quality of this reprint but points out that some imperfections in the original copies may be apparent.

Disclaimer

The publisher has made every effort to trace copyright holders and welcomes correspondence from those they have been unable to contact.

A Library of Congress record exists under ISBN: 77368727

ISBN 13: 978-0-415-65892-8 (hbk)
ISBN 13: 978-0-203-07552-4 (ebk)
ISBN 13: 978-0-415-65893-5 (pbk)

The Battle for Tolmers Square

Nick Wates

Routledge
Taylor & Francis Group

First published in 1976
by Routledge & Kegan Paul Ltd

This edition first published in 2013 by Routledge
2 Park Square, Milton Park, Abingdon, Oxon, OX14 4RN

Simultaneously published in the USA and Canada
by Routledge
711 Third Avenue, New York, NY 10017

Routledge is an imprint of the Taylor & Francis Group, an informa business

Publisher's Note

The publisher has gone to great lengths to ensure the quality of this reprint but points out that some imperfections in the original copies may be apparent.

Disclaimer

The publisher has made every effort to trace copyright holders and welcomes correspondence from those they have been unable to contact.

A Library of Congress record exists under ISBN: 77368727

ISBN 13: 978-0-415-65892-8 (hbk)
ISBN 13: 978-0-203-07552-4 (ebk)
ISBN 13: 978-0-415-65893-5 (pbk)

The Battle for Tolmers Square

Nick Wates

Routledge & Kegan Paul
London, Henley and Boston

First published in 1976
by Routledge & Kegan Paul Ltd
39 Store Street,
London WC1E 7DD,
Broadway House,
Newtown Road,
Henley-on-Thames,
Oxon RG9 1EN and
9 Park Street,
Boston, Mass. 02108, USA
Set in Journal Roman
by Dahling Dahling Ltd
331 Gray's Inn Road, London WC1X 8PX
Printed and bound in Great Britain
by Unwin Brothers Ltd
The Gresham Press, Old Woking, Surrey
A member of the Staples Printing Group

ISBN 0 7100 8448 X

Contents

Maps and diagrams

Acknowledgements

Design, artwork and layout: Kate Hepburn and Caroline Lwin, with help from Osvaldo Herrera, Sue Hobbs, Laura Margolis, Barry Shaw, John Tracey-White and Danuta Trebus
Photography: separately credited p. 226
Processing of photographs: Bruce Locatelli and Paulo
Assistance with research: Caroline Lwin and Penny McGuire
Draft Typing: Pam Whitehorn
Draft criticism: Christopher Booker, Bob Colenutt, Frank Dobson, Mike Edwards, Mike Fleetwood, Pedro George, David Goldhill, Bennie Gray, Tom Heron, Brian Loughran, Rodney Mace, Mike Macrae, John Mills, Roy Shaw, Dianna Sherston, Rachel Syers, Bernard, Jeremy, Joanna and Oliver Wates, David Watkinson and Tom Woolley.
Working space for several months provided by School of Environmental Studies, University College London.
Assistance with first part of chapter 1: Jamie Gough.
Appendix written by Tim Wilson.

Introduction

For seventeen years Tolmers Square has been the focus of a struggle involving tenants' groups, community associations, students, squatters, intellectuals, political parties at both local and national level, and property developers. This book is the story of that struggle. It is about the politics of central city redevelopment.

Britain's cities are in chaos. While thousands of houses stand empty there are not enough homes for people to live in. While acres of land lie derelict, many thousands of building workers are unemployed. Transport is congested and inadequate, and unemployment in the city centres is higher than the national average. Yet whole areas are still being destroyed to make way for office developments, which frequently have little social value, and merely exacerbate the problems.

More and more people are becoming directly affected by this situation, and in the past few years there has been an increasing public awareness of the need for drastic change. Frustrated by the inaction of local and central government, people have begun to look for other ways of solving the problems. There has been a rapid growth of community groups, squatters' organisations, the conservation movement, and there have been initiatives within many political parties. Sadly, this has only had a marginal effect on the overall situation. The basic causes remain untouched: the shaping of our cities continues to be determined by private profit rather than by public use.

This book describes the events which have taken place in one small area during the past two decades. These events both demonstrate the forces that operate in city redevelopment, and show how different forms of opposition can be more or less effective. The book is written for anyone who is interested in how cities work, but particularly for the increasing number of community activists, politicians, council officials, planners and ordinary people who are facing the problems created by planning blight, powerful developers, and ineffective legislation. Although Tolmers Square is only one 12-acre site, much the same process is happening all over London, and indeed in all the major cities of this country. As someone once remarked, 'We all live in Tolmers Square'.

A place called Tolmers Square

The place known as 'Tolmers Square' (or 'Tolmers', or the 'Tolmers Square Development Area', or more recently 'Tolmers Village') comprises Tolmers Square itself, plus a number of surrounding streets; about 12 acres in all. It is similar to many other places near the centres of cities, and yet like all such places it is unique.

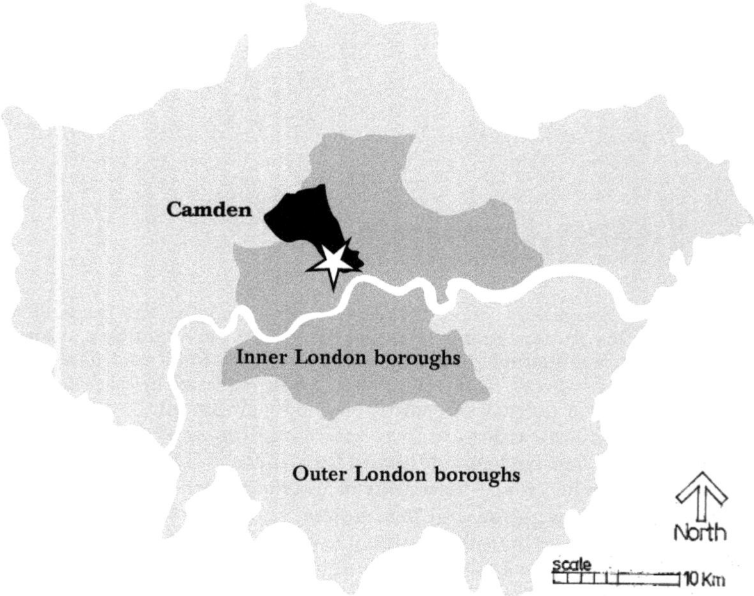

Location of 'Tolmers Square'

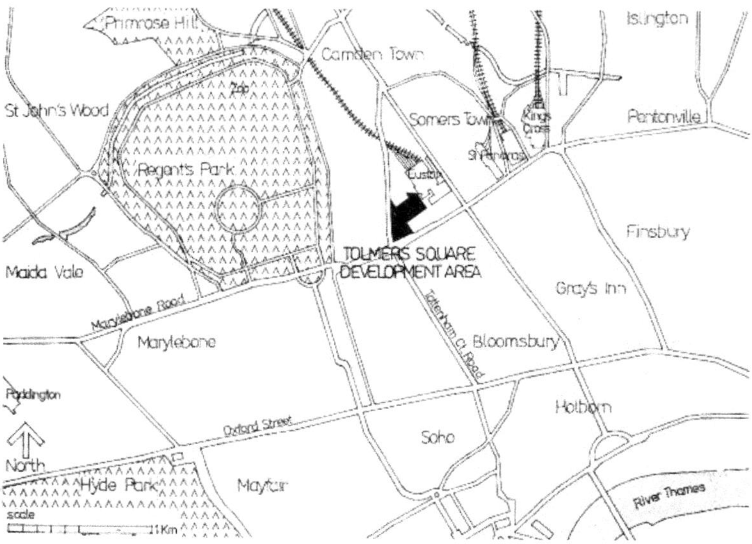

1

2

3

Diversity

During the speculative building booms of the eighteenth and nineteenth centuries, the land was completely built over with Georgian and Victorian terraced houses. Since then there has been

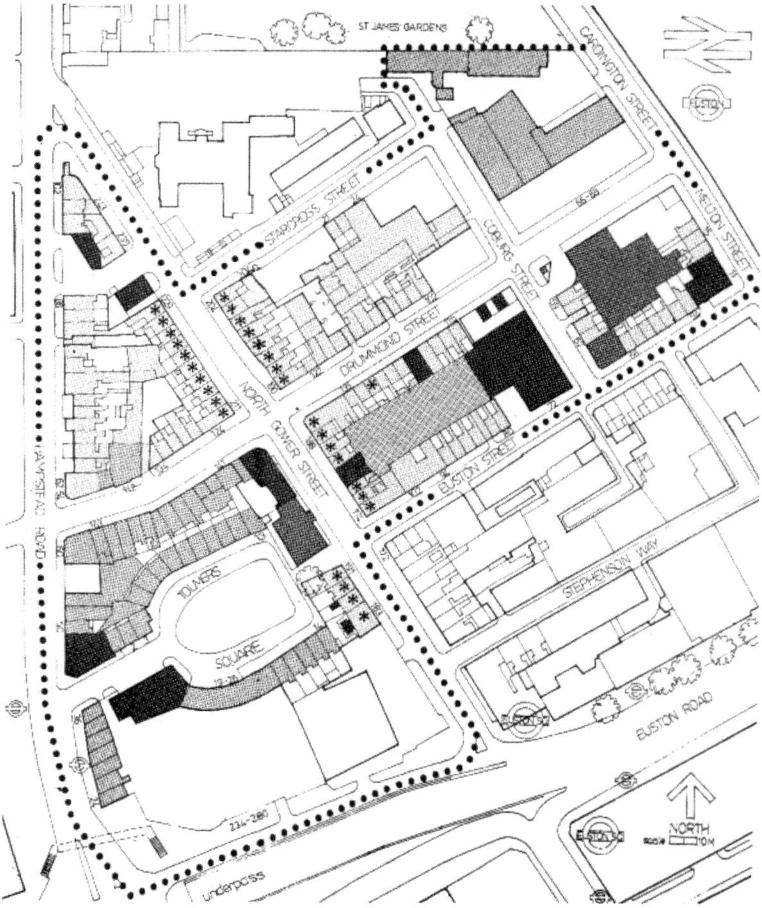

Boundary of Tolmers Square development area, age of buildings, Listed buildings, and street numbering.

• • • • • • boundary of Tolmers Square development area
Note: The precise boundaries of the 'Tolmers area' vary slightly depending on the context. For the sake of consistency, all material in this book relates to the area within the boundary shown above.

c. 1800-50 | c. 1850-1900
c. 1900-50 | c. 1950 onwards

(Source: author's survey)

* * Listed buildings, Grade 2

continual small-scale infilling and rebuilding; with commercial and industrial enterprises infiltrating the area, converting some houses, and building extensions behind others. Over the years a diverse patchwork of buildings and activities grew up.

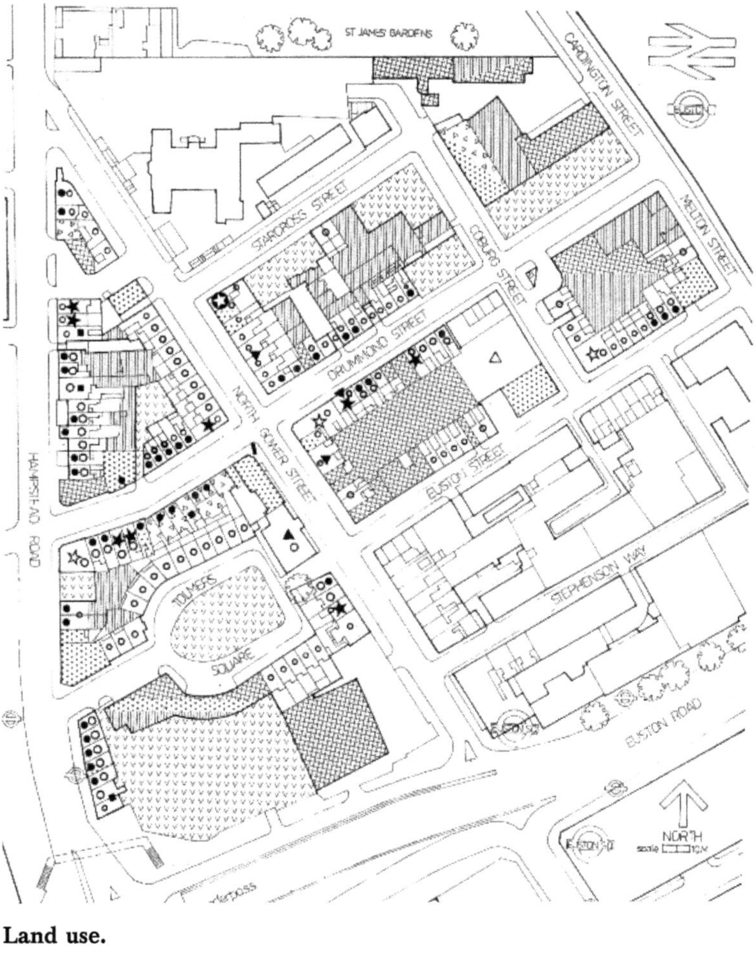

Land use.

Existing or most recent use:

- ° residential
- (vertical hatching) light industry
- (v pattern) vacant land (includes temporary car-parking)
- • shop or other commercial use on ground floor and basement
- ▪ light industrial use on ground floor and basement
- ★ restaurant or cafe on ground floor and basement
- ☆ pub
- ✪ mosque
- △ London Transport generator
- (cross-hatching) commerce
- (dotted) offices
- ▲ hostel, guest house or hotel
- ▵ social club

(Source: author's survey, February 1974)

Who lives there?

Originally built for the middle classes, the housing was soon largely taken over by the working classes. Overcrowding was rampant and was exacerbated by the building of the main-line terminals of St. Pancras and Euston, which displaced thousands of people, and consequently increased the pressure in the surrounding areas. By the end of the nineteenth century it was one of the worst slum areas of London.

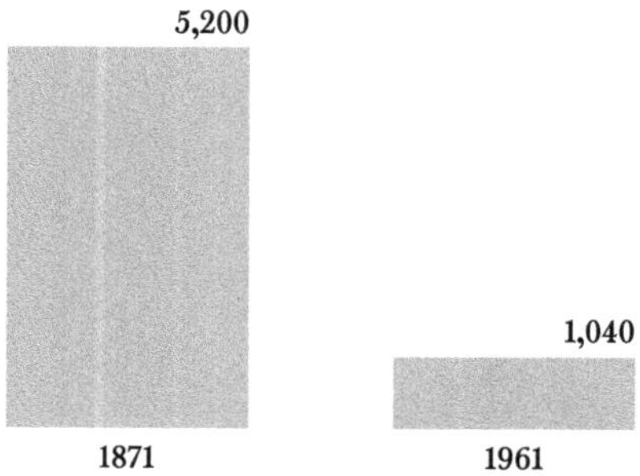

Population decline in the Tolmers area
(Source: Census, 1871 and 1961. See note below)

During the twentieth century, the population steadily declined. In 1871 there were 5,200 people living in the area, whereas ninety years later there were only 1,040. The population decline was partly due to rising space and health standards which lessened overcrowding, but it was also caused by the encroachment of industry, commerce and offices, the expansion of Euston Station, and bombing in the Second World War.

Apart from providing a home for an English working-class community, the remaining housing also had a constantly changing population of many nationalities who were attracted by the relatively cheap rents, and the proximity of employment.

<table>
<tr><th>Birthplace of residents</th><th colspan="2">1961</th><th colspan="2">1971</th></tr>
<tr><td></td><td>number of people</td><td>%</td><td>number of people</td><td>%</td></tr>
<tr><td>England and Wales</td><td>645</td><td>62</td><td>261</td><td>46</td></tr>
<tr><td>Scotland</td><td>43</td><td>4</td><td>8</td><td>1</td></tr>
<tr><td>Ireland</td><td>113</td><td>11</td><td>37</td><td>6</td></tr>
<tr><td>India, Pakistan & Ceylon</td><td>27</td><td>3</td><td>96</td><td>17</td></tr>
<tr><td>Cyprus & Malta</td><td>58</td><td>5</td><td rowspan="2">49</td><td rowspan="2">9</td></tr>
<tr><td>Other Commonwealth countries</td><td>19</td><td>2</td></tr>
<tr><td>Other</td><td>135</td><td>13</td><td>118</td><td>21</td></tr>
<tr><td>Total population:</td><td>1040</td><td>100</td><td>569</td><td>100</td></tr>
</table>

(Source: 1961 and 1971 Census; Note: The Census enumeration districts do not accord precisely with the Tolmers Square development area.)

4 5

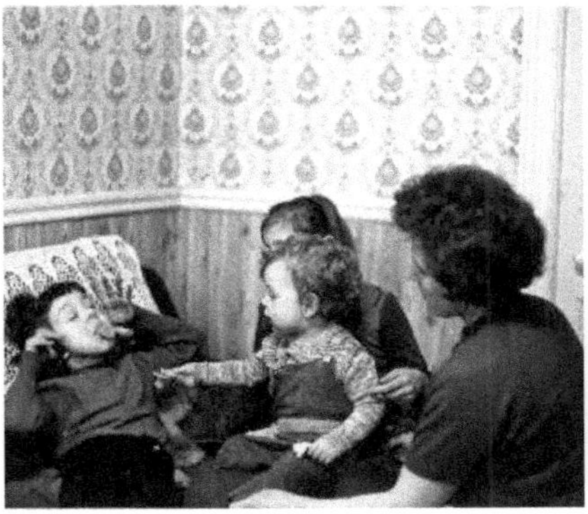

6 7

8 9

Residential rents

Size of accommodation	Number of replies	Range of rent	Average rent
Bedsit	4	£5.00 to £7.50	£6.12
1 bedroom flat	18	£1.59 to £17	£6.20
2 bedroom flat	9	£2.20 to £9	£5.06
3 bedroom flat	6	£2.10 to £18	£8.98

(Source: survey University College London, 1973).

Residential tenure

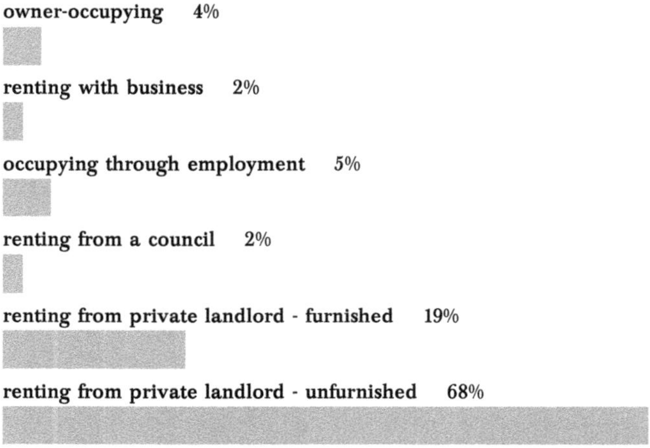

(Source: Census, 1961. See note p.6. Total number of households 399)

Occupation of economically active residents

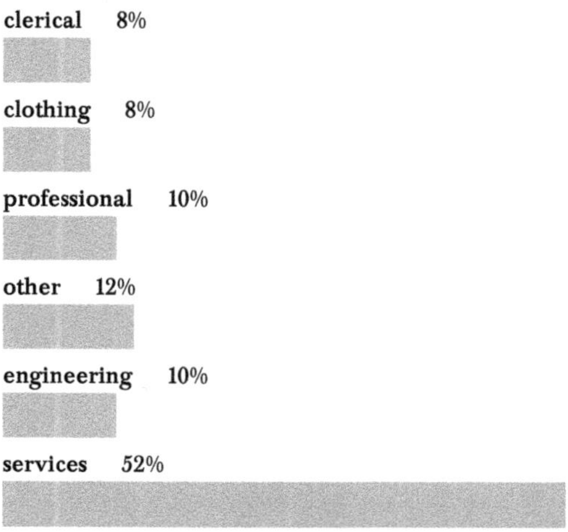

(Source: UCL survey, 1973. Sample of 99)

10 11

12 13

"It was a place with atmosphere, always alive – everyone knew each other" (Teresa Wooten, former resident, Interview).

"There were a lot of prostitutes, not the Park Lane type – they were rough once again catching the passing trade from the station, and they used to use the back of the alleyways" (PC Charles Russell, Interview).

"Dad used to keep chickens in the backyard until they got stolen" (Teresa Wooten, former resident, Interview).

"When they cleaned out the cinema, they swept from one end to the other. The rats would come out of the front door, run round the building, and go in the back door. Every night exactly the same (Pat Richards, former resident, Interview).

"We were really poor...there were five of us in one bedroom. Three in one bed and two in the other" (Pat Richards, former resident, Interview).

"We have to sleep in mum's room. She's got a double bed and I've got a single bed but we have to sleep in the same room" (Michael Holland, resident aged 15, Interview).

Who works there?

Rents were low in relation to Central London, and a fragmented pattern of land tenure ensured that there was always a variety of small units of building to let. As a result, the area provided a 'breeding ground' for a wide variety of enterprises.

The range of businesses

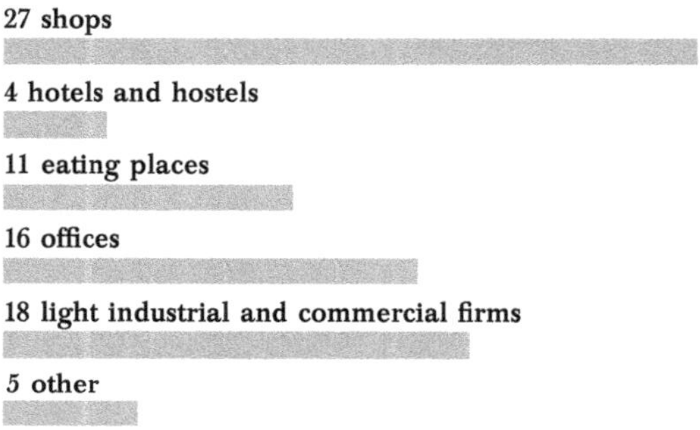

Size of businesses

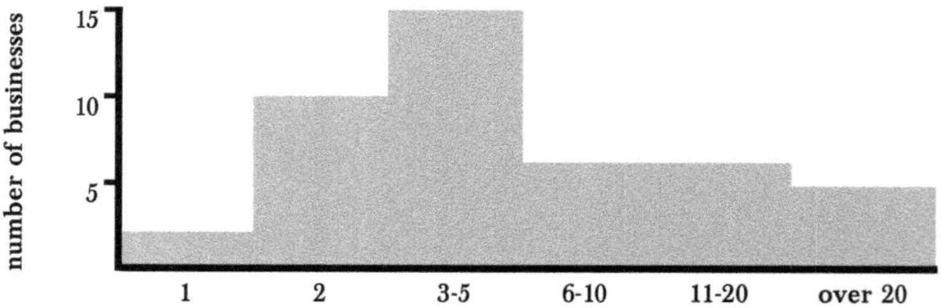

size of businesses by number of employees

(Source: UCL survey, 1973. 53% sample)

Employment in relation to business size

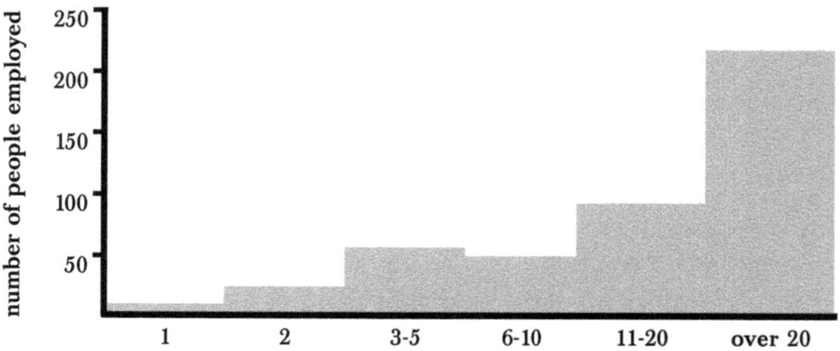

size of business by number of employees

(Source: UCL survey, 1973. 53% sample)

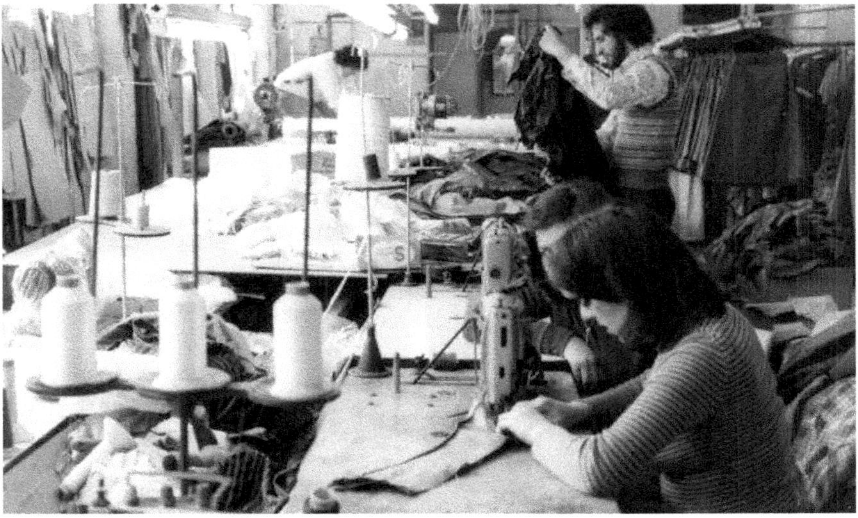
14

15

16

CLEVELAND
JOINERY & CABINET
TANDOOR
SOCIAL SERVICE
INTERCITY
Halal Butchers &
HALAL MEAT
OPTIC
Hot & Cold
FOOD
at the Bar
WINE
LMR
Collectors Corner
OFF LICENCE
RESTAURA
CHARLES
REPAIRS
NO ENTRY
THE LOUIS de SOISSONS PARTNERSHIP BRIGHTON MARINA PROJECT OFFICES 25 TOLMERS SQUARE NW1
BHAVNEETA
SAREES
DIRECTORS CLUB
122a UNIVERSAL HALAL BUTCHERS & GROCERS 122a
GUARANTEED FRESH HALAL MEAT
DR. DAVID PITT
TRAVEL AGENCY
The TEDDERS
H&C WATER IN ALL ROOMS
BED & BREAKFAST
BLANKETS
HOLLANDS
BARGAIN
SHOP
CURTAINS
SHIPS LINEN
PENWAY LTD.
BUILDING & DECORATING SUPPLIES
HOME FREEZER ORDERS TAKEN
THE LONDON C.H.A. CLUB
FRED TALLANT
AVIS TRUCK RENT
Collectors Corner
HIGH TENSION
DANGER
BARBER SHOP
LAURENCE
GOVERNMENT
GENTLEMEN'S HAIRDRESSING SALOON
BERA EXPORT TRIMMINGS
WISE DENTAL SURGEONS
DENTIST
KEBAB
TAKE AWAY
HASSAN
MODERN TAILOR
BASEMENT
INDIAN GROCER

27 shops and services:
- 1 general grocer
- 6 Indian general grocers
- 1 Indian sweet shop
- 1 greengrocer
- 1 betting shop
- 1 fashion boutique
- 2 army and navy surplus stores
- 1 picture gallery
- 1 newsagent / tobacconist
- 1 butcher
- 1 Indian gift shop
- 1 second-hand furniture shop
- 1 optician
- 2 surgeries
- 1 dentist
- 1 travel bureau
- 1 sandwich bar
- 2 barbers

11 Eating Places
- 1 café
- 7 restaurants
- 3 pubs

4 hotels and hostels:
- 2 hotels
- 2 guest houses / hostels

18 light industrial and commercial firms:
- 2 garages
- 2 dressmakers
- 1 wholesale jeweller
- 1 wholesale fruiterer
- 1 wholesale newsagent
- 1 mannequin manufacturer
- 1 rent-a-van service
- 1 second-hand furniture warehouse
- 1 electrical wire warehouse
- 1 tailor
- 1 mechanical engineer
- 1 furnishing contractor
- 1 printer
- 1 antiques restorer
- 1 joiner and cabinet-maker
- 1 electrical engineer

16 offices:
- 1 trade union branch
- 1 chartered accountant
- 1 charity organisation
- 2 architects / engineers
- 1 London Transport
- 1 designer
- 2 import / export companies1 research institute
- 1 mortgage broker
- 1 shipping company
- 4 other companies

5 others:
- 1 electricity substation
- 3 private clubs
- British Rail warehouses, and collectors corner

18

19

20

"There is a . . . meanness about the district of Euston, with it's glut of Bed and Breakfast hovels, expensive retreats for weary Northerners, it's bomb sites from the War, small businesses and impertinent offices (*International Times*, May/June 1974).

"But pause only a few yards on, just before you reach Euston station, and look at the fag-end of the last century around Tolmers Square . . . the sordid jumble of terraced houses and industry east of Hampstead Road (*Evening Standard*, 6 May 1971).

". . . Unsightly tat . . ." (Alan Greengross, Conservative planning chairman, Interview).

"Streets and buildings in our area are small and human in scale, related to the needs of the people." (Tolmers Village Association Exhibition, February 1974).

21

"Tolmers Square is a charming little enclave of porticoed crescents off the Hampstead Road, opposite Mr. Levy's Euston Centre. Behind and around it lie more than a dozen acres of attractive Georgian terraces, Victorian Pubs, small workshops and Indian Restaurants" (*Private Eye*, 9 February 1973).

"Tolmers Square itself was once a very attractive 19th century square which now looks like a graveyard" (*Built Environment*, November 1973).

"If Tolmers Square had been in Paris rather than London, it would be lived in by artists and intellectuals, poor but learned, who would value the proximity of the British Museum and the university, and would live there an industrious life of modest tranquillity. And the church would still be a church. And there would be some trees. And because it is in London it is going to be knocked down." (*Hampstead and Highgate Express*, 5 February 1971).

22

23

24

The Asian Community

Asians are the most recent immigrant group to establish themselves in the area. The first Indian restaurant opened in the early 1950s, and by 1973 there were four other Indian restaurants, eight shops selling various Asian products, a Muslim mosque, and a large residential Asian population. The area was nicknamed 'little India', and became of national importance as a centre of Asian commerce.

The community is a microcosm of the free enterprise system, existing almost independently of the English community. Of the 300 or so Asians living or working in the area in 1973, one-third were Hindus from India, and two-thirds were Muslims from Pakistan, Bangladesh and India (45 percent Pakistan, 45 per cent Bangladesh, 10 per cent India.)

23

"It's become very well known . . . throughout England and Europe that anybody who wants something Indian, they come right to Drummond Street." (Mr Shah, *Tolmers; beginning or end?*).

Before the Second World War, a belt of working-class housing mixed with commerce and light industry stretched for over one mile along the north side of Euston Road, interrupted only by the mainline stations. But Tolmers is now the sole remaining pocket, as the rest has been transformed by redevelopment.

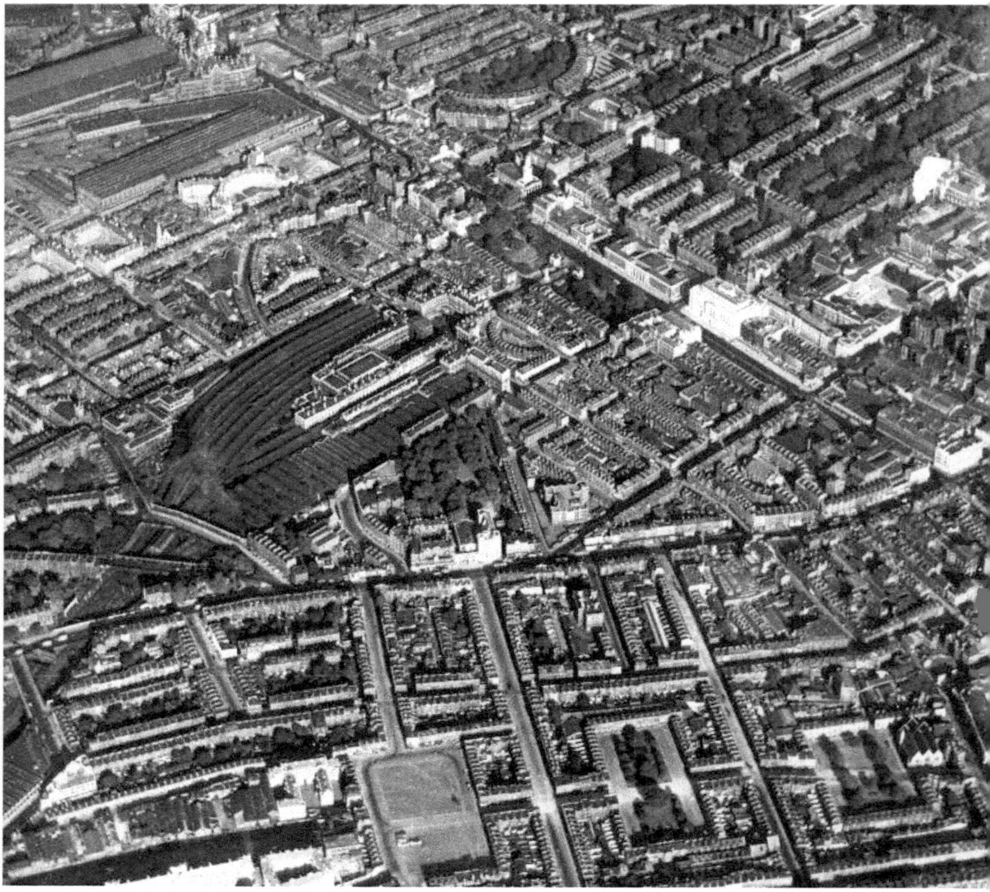

26. 1932

27. 1968

20

Tolmers Village, an improbably last bastion, is almost rural in contrast with Euston Road just around the corner. Were John Waddington & Co. currently designing the monopoly board, they would hardly amalgamate Euston Road with the Angel and Pentonville Road. In every respect . . . Euston Road has eclipsed its lowly associates on the board game and although it's three stations, King's Cross, St Pancras and Euston still contribute to the general sleaziness of the thoroughfare, its property value has lately soared, an elevation shared with its newly-built property" (*International Times*, May/June 1974).

23

...an obsolescent area in an important position (GLC assessment, letter from Ministry of Housing and Local Government to Town Clerk, 2 February 1965).

1.

Conflict of interest

The battle for Tolmers Square came about because of a conflict of interest; a conflict between property developers who wanted to redevelop the area for offices, and various sections of the community who would suffer if this kind of redevelopment took place. As this conflict is a central theme of the Tolmers Square story, this first chapter briefly examines the general forces at work in property development. It examines the mechanics of property speculation, the operation of property companies, and the case against office development in the centre of cities. Anyone who gets bored reading this chapter should turn to Chapter 2 where the real story begins.

The mechanics of property speculation

> The total national stock of office space increased from about 281 million sq. ft. in 1967 to 340 million sq. ft. in 1972, an increase of about 21 per cent in five years . . . if even half of this new office development had been built as housing instead, hundreds of thousands of extra people could have been housed. (*The Property Machine*, p.19).
>
> London has the most expensive office space in Europe, with rents often two or three times as high as those in other capitals . . . From 1960 to 1970, rents increased from 5 per cent to 7 per cent of gross national product (Counter Information Service, 1973).
>
> We live in a society where over 100 people have made more than £1 million each out of property since 1945. We also live in a society where the number of homeless people has more than doubled over the past five years. These two facts are of course interconnected (CIS, 1973, p.2).

Property speculation has become so notorious that many people imagine that it must be some freakish way of making money. The enormous profits must have been made through trickery, inside knowledge, government incompetence and connivance. While these factors are on occasion important, it is vital to realise that property speculation and property booms are fundamental features of post-war capitalist society. They could not (and cannot in future) be avoided by tinkering with government policy in a way which fails to change the underlying causes.

Since the property bubble burst in late 1973, it has become fashionable to assert that property speculation is no longer a problem. This is a useful illusion for property men to nurture, but it is dangerously misleading. However, the boom of 1973 was particularly severe, and a basic understanding of this boom and the consequent slump is essential in order to comprehend the Tolmers situation.

Two important factors lie behind the property boom; a falling rate of profit in the economy as a whole, and a substantial and increasing rate of inflation.

(a) Falling rate of profit:

Since 1945 there has been a steady decline in the profitability of manufacturing industry. This is true for all major capitalist nations, but it has been particularly severe in Britain. Because of this, financiers have looked for more profitable fields of investment for their capital; investment abroad, speculation in raw materials and of course property.

(b) Inflation:

Investment in property involves a high initial expenditure (building) and low subsequent expenditure (maintenance). Manufacturing on the other hand requires relatively constant expenditure. In both cases the money will rise with inflation. Property therefore benefits from inflation in a way that manufacturing does not; the investment is made in the early period with 'cheap money' and the return comes later on with inflated money.

Rising rents

The office boom has been further fuelled by the fact that rents for offices and shops have risen consistently faster than other prices over the whole post-war period. Inflation in property values has been even greater than the general rate of inflation, for a number of reasons.

1. First there is the shortage of suitable sites. Prospective office users naturally prefer, and will pay more for, sites near the core of the city that are already well-serviced by transport systems and other services. These sites are bound to be in short supply, especially in a city like London, which has so many buildings of historical and architectural importance.

Ironically the authorities have exacerbated this situation with legislation. To avoid having to make further costly additions to the infrastructure (roads, sewers etc), the authorities have made restrictions on the location of new developments. In 1964 the Labour Government placed a complete ban on new office developments (The Brown Ban), and in 1965 they instituted a system of permits for offices, called Office Development Permits (ODPs). Any developer wanting to build more than 10,000 square feet of offices had to obtain an ODP from the government. Initially it was extremely difficult to obtain an ODP, although the restrictions were relaxed slightly after a few years. Local Authorities can also exercise control by rejecting planning applications for new development if these applications do not accord with their own 'structure' or 'development' plans (consent being obligatory before building can commence).

These restrictions on development location, whether produced directly by the infrastructure itself, or by 'planning' restrictions, have resulted in the 'under supply' of available land and buildings, thus a steep rise in rents and land values.

2. The second factor has been the chaos of the business cycle. While capital has been pouring into property since the war, it has not done so smoothly, but has proceeded in fits and starts – the business cycle which haunts every market economy. The cycle has been particularly pronounced in the property sector; changes in property company shares have been larger and have taken place faster than in most other sectors, and the pattern of building has been particularly uneven over time.

The sharpness of the cycle happens in the following way. During a downturn of the economy the standard interest rate falls as borrowing for investment declines. The fall, sometimes encouraged by the government as reflationary policy, eventually leads to an increase in borrowing as the upturn begins. As we will see, a fall in the interest rate increases property values and encourages a flow of capital into property. As the upturn proceeds, the demand for property increases very sharply, since businesses generally do not take on new premises on a downturn. As new buildings take some years to reach the market, and as very little new building is started during a down turn, demand quickly exceeds supply, pushing up rents and giving a further boost to property values. The boom ends with the same abruptness as it began. Demand begins to level out, new property comes onto the market, and rents ease. At the same time the interest rate tends to rise. Property companies, with their high rate of borrowing are particularly sensitive to the interest rate, and the combination of stagnant rents and rising interest rates gives a sharp cut-off point when new investment is no longer profitable. Building virtually comes to a standstill, pending the next upturn.

It is by speculating on the timing of this process that huge windfall profits are made. It is also this process, which makes nonsense of any attempts to plan commercial construction.

It must be emphasised that property booms are not isolated phenomena, but are closely tied to other cycles of the market economy. The boom which ended in 1973 was merely a particularly dramatic example: in 1970 the Tories attempted to stimulate the economy by letting the Bank Rate fall from 8 per cent to less than 5 per cent, resulting in a flood of capital into property. At the end of 1973 the interest rate rose suddenly to 13 per cent, wiping out the property companies' profits. By the spring of 1974 the property market had almost completely collapsed.

3. A further factor responsible for increasing rents has been the tendency for property companies to increase in size. The smaller companies have been weeded out by bankruptcies at the end of the booms. The large companies which dominate the market are often tied to cautious institutions which lend them money, and tend to be

rather circumspect in making new investment. This contributes further to under-supply.

4. Finally rents are pushed by withholding of property from the market; by hoarding.

> A lot of office space is held in reserve: buildings nowhere near completion, no one in a hurry to complete them or to start to carry out planning permissions already given; planning applications granted are not being translated into buildings; buildings are not being translated in to lettings (David Eversley, CIS, 1973, p.6.).

This inevitably reduces supply, which then pushes up rents.

Property Companies

> Every year the revulations of property company assets effortlessly create gargantuan surpluses. Through economic boom and recession the men of property have been turning stone into gold (*The Economist*, 18 March 1972; CIS, 1973, p.7).

> The ten largest property companies control assets approaching £3,000 million, larger than the entire gold and dollar reserves of the U.K. Nearly all these companies are de facto controlled by one or two men (CIS, 1973, p.2).

Market Valuation of Property Companies:

1958:	£103 million
1968:	£833 million
1973:	£3,006 million
1975:	£1,881 million

Most commercial property development since the war has been undertaken by property companies. In the early days a property company might consist of no more than a single man operating from a telephone in his flat. But companies have increased in size, and because of the constant need for cash for investment, have become increasingly tied to that imposing network of organisations known as 'finance capital'. Finance capital has been described as 'those companies that make profits out of owning and trading stocks and shares, government bonds, and currencies, and by providing services such as insurance,pensions, hire purchase, and mortagages' (*The Property Machine*, p.41). It contrasts with industrial capital whose main activity is the manufacture and processing of goods and commodities. Many property companies, and incidentally construction firms, are now merely components of institutions of finance capital.

But whatever the size of the company, the mechanics of property development are the same. The company obtains a loan covering the cost of the land acquisition and building construction, which is then repaid with interest over a period of time. The recent trend for the money-lenders to insist on a share of the profits, spreads the gains slightly, does little to change the basic principle.

A company's profit on any building can be looked at from two points of view; its revenue profit and its capital profit.

1. Revenue profit:

The revenue profit is the surplus of rent income over loan repayment charges plus running expenses. In the 1950s and 1960s loan charges were fixed for the whole repayment period (perhaps 40 years) Whereas the rent rose roughly with the rate of inflation, or more as we have seen. The rent income covered the loan payments initially and then far outstripped them later on. Obviously the lower the rate of interest on laons and the higher the rate of inflation, the bigger the revenue profits.

2. Capital profit:

At at a time of boom the property company makes an instant capital profit simply by having the building built. This is because the value of the building on the market far exceeds its construction cost. To look at this in detail, imagine you had an amount of capital to invest and suppose for the moment there is no inflation. You could either loan your capital out and get in return interest payments at the going rate of interest, or you could buy a building, and get the rent payments. The developer who is selling you the building will adjust the price of the building to make these two options more or less equally attractive. For example, if the rent obtainable from a building is £1,000 per annum, and the going annual interest rate (or yield) is 5 per cent then you would be prepared to pay up to £20,000 for the building. In this case the developer would value the building as follows:

$$\text{Price (or value) of the building (£)} = \frac{\text{Annual rent income (£)}}{\text{Annual interest rate}}$$

But if you felt that the annual rent might increase faster than the general interest rate, you would be prepared to accept a lower return on your building investment initially, and therefore you would be prepared to pay more than £20,000 for the building. In these circumstances, the developer will value the building as follows:

$$\text{Price (or value) of the building (£)} = \frac{\text{Annual rent income (£)}}{\text{Going acceptable annual yield for property}}$$

So in the example, if you were prepared to accept a yield of 2.5% instead of 5%, you would be prepared to pay: £1,000 / 2.5% = £40,000.

The important thing to notice is that the price or value is unrelated to building cost, and in a profitable development will far exceed it. We now see how the value of property is closely linked to the interest rate and to predictions as to how it will vary in the future. This is why property is a major area of speculation. The speculator will buy property at a high price assuming a further fall in the desired interest rate. The rise in price encourages further buying, and so on, resulting in spiralling prices. 'The boom is self-generating as rising prices only tend to "prove" that property values always rise, adding to its attraction as an investment' (CIS, 1973, p.4).

Why pick on Tolmers Square?

It is now possible to understand why developers are interested in building offices in places like Tolmers Square. It can be seen from the above that the property system does not look upon land and property as an asset in any environmental or social sense. It is a financial asset, and the location and character of development are not determined by usefulness or social need, but a profit and loss account. The property company will operate where maximum profits are to be found. This will be where land can be assembled cheaply, developed, and rented at the highest rates the market can bear.

Tolmers Square provided an ideal location. The run-down property had little present value, but enormous potential value because of the desirability of the location for future office users, who would consequently be prepared to pay high rents. The rent obtainable for office space in central London was at least three times as high as the rent obtainable for any other type of space, and considerably higher than for office space in other parts of the country. The potential for profit was correspondingly greater.

The benefits for potential office users of the particular locality of Tolmers Square were wet out in a glossy brochure produced by the developers themselves for advertising their neighbouring Euston Centre office complex:

> This site is an exceptionally important one being at the focal point of an area already well established as a commercial office centre with many important companies already in occupation and now beginning to make a forcible challenge as one of London's leading shopping centres (sic). To the South, Oxford Street is only half a mile away, with Soho and Theatreland just beyond. To the west and north there are numerous residential districts ranging from fashionable Primrose Hill to heavily populated Camden Town. The added attraction of Regent's Park is only a few minutes walk away.
>
> The new Euston Centre is located at the corner of one of the most important cross-roads in London. Euston Road forms part of the new East-West through route and Hampstead Road–Tottenham Court Road is a main radial route to the midlands and the north. At this moment, a new high speed underpass system is being constructed and this will result in a rapid flow of traffic as well as bringing added prestige and desirability to the area (sic).
>
> "Five of London's most important main line termini – King's Cross, St. Pancras, Euston, Marylebone and Paddington – lie in a straight east to west line running along Euston Road and the new development is virtually in the middle of this line. This means that all these stations are within very easy reach of the Euston Centre with the rebuilt Euston Station only a few moments away. Thus, railway access to all parts of the east, north and west is extremely good. Underground transport is also excellent with Warren Street on the Northern Line immediately next to the site, and Euston Square and Great Portland Street on the Circle, District and Metropolitan Lines close at hand. The new Victoria Line now under construction, will have a station at Warren Street connecting Victoria to the N.E Suburbs" (*Euston Centre*, c.1964)

Introducing Stock Conversion and Investment Trust

The Tolmers area has received attention from one property company in particular: Stock Conversion and Investment Trust.

"Stock Conversion is a holding company with interests in a large number of property investment and development companies. The Group's main property interests are in Central London area where the Company, its subsidiaries, and associated companies, own a high-class portfolio of mainly office and shop properties. In addition the Group is engaged on a substantial development programme and also holds several important sites in Central London for ultimate redevelopment" (Read, Hurst-Brown and Co., Stock-brokers, report May 1973)

By 1974 Stock conversion was the eleventh largest property development company as measured by their share valuation on the Stock Exchange. 'In financial terms the history of the Stock Conversion group is one of the most remarkable of any publicly quoted company. An investment of £100 in 1954 . . . would now be worth approximately £750,000' (CIS, 1973, p.9).

In 1953 the investments held had a value of £13,155 whereas only 20 years later shareholders' funds were £45,559,000.

"During the entire period the only additions to the share capital have been the subscription of £675,000 in 1962 by various insurance companies for the shares and the issue of 590,000 shares, (less than 10% of the number then outstanding) for acquisitions. The only money shareholders have been asked to subscribe is £5 million for a convertible loan stock issue in 1969 . . .

These gigantic profits have been made by a tiny handful of people; the directors of the company, their close associates, and a few property share analysts. As the *Investors Chronicle* pointed out in 1960, 'The market in the shares has been largely professional, the general public remaining in ignorance of the company's 'performance', and in 1961 the *Investors Chronicle* complained 'It appears to be a policy of the directors who control with associates some three-quarters of the Ordinary capital, to provide no details of the development programme'. Despite the fact that only a quarter of the equity was in public hands, Marriot records, 'One budding stockbroker put his shirt on Stock Conversion and retired on the proceeds, so great were they, at the age of twenty-seven.'

Today Clark's and Levy's (two of the directors) profits on Stock Conversion are approaching £40 million. Even by the standards of post-war property millionaires, these are remarkable sums." (CIS, 1973, p.9)

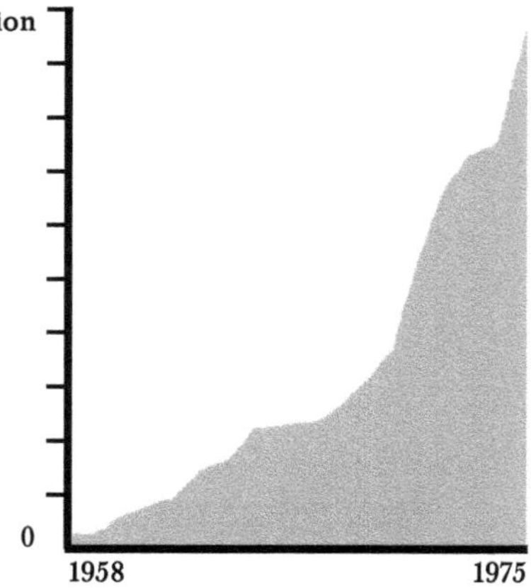

Growth of Stock Conversion's
total investments
(Source: CIS and shareholders' reports)

Stock Conversion has six directors. Between them they own over half of the issued ordinary shares of the company. In addition these men have a total of over 200 directorships of other companies.

The Directors: their business occupations, interests in Stock Conversion, and other directorships.

Director	Business occupation	Interests in Stock Conversion (31 March 1975) 25p Ordinary Shares		5.5% Loan Stock		Total number of directorships
		beneficial	other	beneficial	other	
Robert Clark	barrister	387,624		2,604		38
J.W. Campbell	chartered accountant	14,000	6,217,000	2,900	450,000	55
H.J.B. Cope	actuary	6,000		1,300		32
Joseph Levy	estate agent	2,521,212	1,597,380	290,636	54,800	22
T.A.F. McGee	barrister and chartered accountant	7,980		2,600		27
J.W. Wishart	chartered accountant	600,000	4,170,472	10,000	112,300	32

Note: the total number of ordinary shares issued and fully paid at 31 March 1975 was 29,900,714.
(Source: Company Report 1975, Company Search 23 April 1975)

Stock Conversion is a parent company, and most of its work is done through subsidiaries. It has over thirty-eight major subsidaires, many of which operate from the same address as Stock Conversion, 130 Jermyn Street SW1, and have the same directors. The majority of these companies are straight forward property companies.

In addition these companies have close working relationships with a number of firms of estate agents, who carry out much of the buying, selling and maintenance: For instance D. E. & J. Levy, which operates from the same address as Stock Conversion.

Despite this multitude of companies and firms, the actual work is carried out by very few people; the directors, one or two executives and a few secretaries. For the uninitiated it is extremely confusing at first to ring up several different companies and always get through to the same person. Indeed the effect of this complex structure is to make it very difficult to understand what is basically an extremely simple process.

For the sake of simplicity the name Stock Conversion is often used in this book when it would be strictly accurate to use the name of one of the other companies.

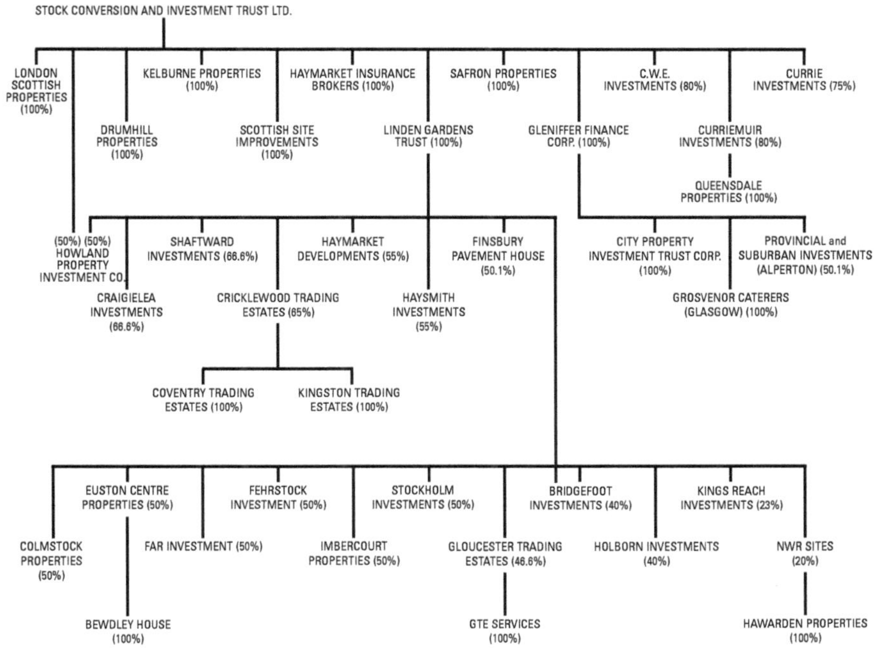

The relationship between the Group's more important subsidiary and associated companies and the parent company

What's wrong with office development

Before we examine the Tolmers Square situation, it is worth spelling out very briefly the general case against office development in the centres of large cities. People frequently ask why there should be such a fuss about a few offices? Surely the nation needs offices, and surely they need to be in the centre of large cities.

The arguments against office development can be grouped under three headings: its effect on employment, housing and congestion; its effect on wealth distribution; and its effect on the use of national resources.

The effect of office development on employment, housing and congestion

If office development takes place in the centre of cities, it almost inevitably displaces housing and manufacturing industry. If the transformation occurs rapidly, this can lead to stresses in a socially balanced community. This can best be illustrated by examining the recent situation in London.

1. Decline in manufacturing industry:

The number of employees in manufacturing in Greater London dropped by 25% in ten years between 1961 and 1971. In inner London the decline was more rapid. In Camden for instance there was a 23% fall in the resident work force in manufacturing in only five years between 1966 and 1971. While a host of reasons can be used to explain this decline (the trend is of course nation wide), soaring land values and redevelopment are two of the foremost.

Skilled workers made redundant as a result of this either had to move out to London, or become unemployed, or take jobs in the lower-paid service sector (restaurants, cleaning, shops etc.). Unskilled workers had less opportunity: 'Unskilled workers either become unemployed, commute to work, or else seek jobs in those activities that are expanding in Camden, notably the lower-paid service industry jobs' (*Camden Scene*, p.33)

2. Decrease in the land available for housing:

Office development uses land and other resources which could otherwise be used for housing, further exacerbating the housing crisis, and the decline in the population in the central area. The population in Greater London has been declining for years and continues to do so. In 1971 there were 7,418,000 people living in Greater London, according to the census. By 1981 the government planners estimate there will be only 6,600,000; a drop over 10% in 10 years. A high proportion of this loss will be from central London. In Camden alone the population fell by 6.3% in three years, from 1971 to 1974. The decline in population is partly the result of rising space standards, and the reduction of overcrowding, but it mainly reflects a fall in the number of houses available, caused by the expansion of the office sector and redevelopment schemes (figures taken from *London, the future and You*, and *Camden Scene*)

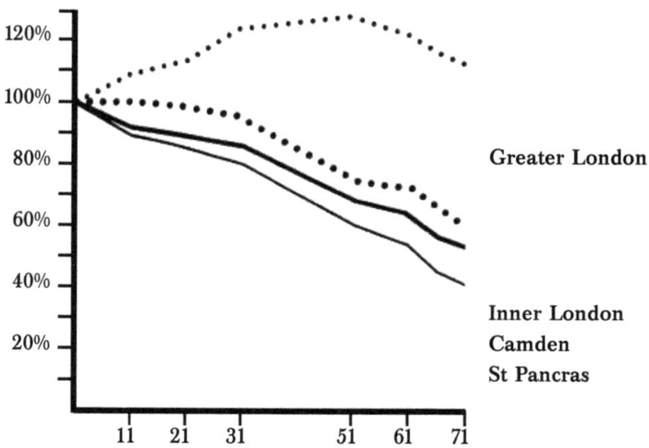

Index of population change, 1901 to 1971 (Source: *Camden Scene*)

The decline in the residential population has a number of adverse effects, one of which is shortages of labour in certain sectors. In 1973 the GLC reported:

> "Many complaints relate to shortages of skilled men in the building and engineering industries. Shortages of labour are also reported in the public sector, particularly where jobs involve shift-work and awkward hours. For example, London Transport has a shortage of 4,200 bus drivers and conductors; the Post Office has 8,0000 vacancies in London and the South East; the Metropolitan Police are short of about 4,500 policemen; British Rail also report shortages; and schools are reporting . . . a drop in the number of applicants for each job." (*Population and Employment*, GLC, 1973).

It also leads to a population imbalance with a high proportion of old people left in the centre, and with young expanding families unable to find accommodation.

3. Increase in congestion:

Industrial employment is replaced by employment of office workers. While some of the manufacturing workers displaced may be able to find employment in the office sector, many will be unsuitable for the jobs and have to commute elsewhere for employment. The new office workers also generally commute from the suburbs or beyond and there will inevitably be a net increase in the number of jobs on the development site. The result is a large expansion in commuting which leads to additional strains on the transport system. The social and economic costs of this congestion are considerable.

As the basis of the economy changes, patterns of employment and living will alter also. The argument is not that change should not take place, but merely that it should evolve at a pace and in a direction determined by the needs of the community rather than those of finance capital.

The effect of office development on wealth distribution.

When discussing the redistribution effects of office redevelopment, the key question is 'who gains and who loses?'

In a normal office redevelopment, the gainers are the owners of the freeholds and/or leaseholds of the land concerned, the professional facilitators (architects, estate agents, surveyors, etc.), the development company, the investing or lending institutions, and the rating authorities who benefit from an increase in rateable value. Because the lending institutions of finance capital are merely channelling the deposits of millions of individual savers, it is often argued that the wealth created by these institutions is spread evenly through society. In fact, of course, this is far from the truth. It would appear that the richest 2 per cent of the population owns 55 per cent of total interest in life insurance funds. In terms of unit trusts, we have moved little from the situation in 1954 when the richest 1 per cent owned about 81 per cent of all company shares owned by individuals. Although institutional holders of shares have increased their share to one-third of total securities, these institutions themselves are contributed to by the richest segment of society as we have just seen. (Figures from *The Property Machine*.) As for the property companies themselves, we have already noted how the wealth created by Stock Conversion is distributed to only a few men.

The losers from commercial development are almost entirely concentrated at the other end of the social spectrum, and their losses are more difficult to measure. First, there are the people who are actually displaced by the development; residents who have to undergo the stresses of moving elsewhere, usually to higher-rent accommodation, where they are likely to have to spend more on travelling to their work; small businesses who may well not be able to afford to set up elsewhere; workers who lose their jobs and have to travel further afield to find work, accept lower-paid work, or even become directly unemployed. Second, there are the people living in the immediate vicinity who are affected by rising land values and rents. Small businesses and shops are forced out, resulting in loss of employment, and loss of useful services for local inhabitants. Poorer tenants may be forced out too, and the rise in house prices means that only the very rich can think of buying their own homes. Third, there are the people who suffer from increasing congestion generally, and those who have to travel long distances to obtain work in the new development, there being little employment where they live.

The increase in rates which accrues to the local authority does little to offset these increased costs for a large segment of the society.

In other words the rich get richer and the poor get poorer. Office redevelopment contributes in no small way to increasing the gap between the rich and poor.

The effect of offices on the use of national resources

In recent years 20-25 per cent of available finance capital has been used for the purposes of developing or speculating in property, a substantial amount of which has been used specifically to finance office redevelopment in the South East. It might well be asked whether this is not a misuse of national resources.

By spending valuable and scarce resources on building offices, these resources cannot be invested in working space, plant, tools and equipment for manufacturing industry; for producing the goods which people need, and on which the wealth of the nation largely depends. Also they cannot be used to solve the housing crisis; a crisis which must in itself be extremely costly for the nation. Instead the resources are used to provide space for activities which in themselves create no surplus value but on the whole merely recirculate it. Many of these activities, ,such as advertising, public relations, and unnecessarily complicated legal transactions, are of dubious social worth anyway. The concentration of human ability and material resources into these activities at the expense of industry is of national concern.

This is not to argue that absolutely new offices should be built. But if offices are required by the nation, they should be located in less crowded regions, where they might help solve unemployment problems, and would not create all the harmful side effects associated with building in the centres of congested cities where buildings which still have a useful life have to be torn down.

While office building is determined by immediate profitability for finance capital, those broader considerations are ignored.

2.

The First Attack

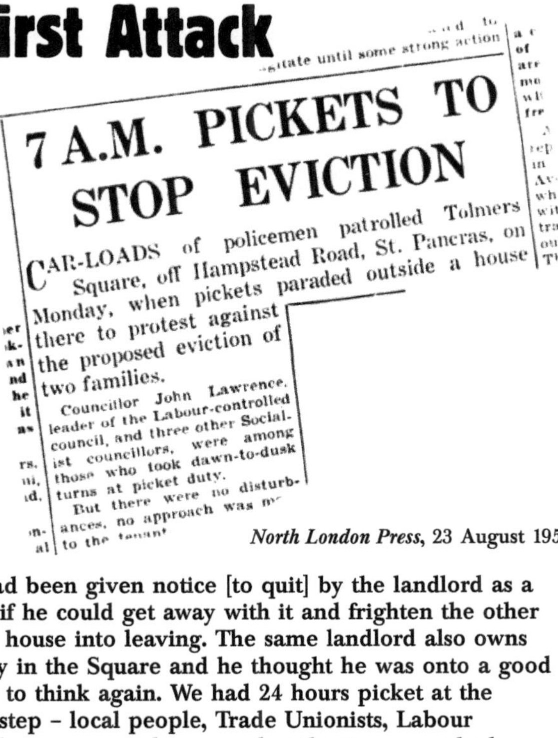

7 A.M. PICKETS TO STOP EVICTION

CAR-LOADS of policemen patrolled Tolmers Square, off Hampstead Road, St. Pancras, on Monday, when pickets paraded outside a house there to protest against the proposed eviction of two families.

Councillor John Lawrence, leader of the Labour-controlled council, and three other Socialist councillors, were among those who took dawn-to-dusk turns at picket duty.

But there were no disturbances, no approach was m[illegible] to the tenant

North London Press, 23 August 1957

This tenant had been given notice [to quit] by the landlord as a try-out to see if he could get away with it and frighten the other tenants in the house into leaving. The same landlord also owns other property in the Square and he thought he was onto a good thing. He had to think again. We had 24 hours picket at the tenant's door step – local people, Trade Unionists, Labour Councillors who represented our ward at the time – we had posters plastered all over the Square telling people that an eviction was intended, we informed the press, and the police obliged by sending a Black Maria, which drew no end of publicity. We won, and the tenant is still in possession of her flat and no other evictions have been attempted in the Square. This was the first of our fights and victories (Rose Gavin, Secretary of the Tolmers Square Tenants Association, speech c. 1960).

This successful defeat of an eviction in 1957 was the beginning of eighteen years of struggle over the future of Tolmers Square.

29. 30. Tolmers Square, 1957

Tolmers Square Tenants win round one

The Tolmers Square Tenants Association (henceforth TSTA) was one of many formed in 1957 in response to the Rent Act of that year; an Act which raised drastically the permissible maximum rents for private tenants. Initially the Association was 70 strong, the core of members being from Tolmers Square itself. It was politically independent though its leading members had close links with the Labour Party, the Co-op Party and the Communist Party, and it gained its strength from fighting primarily local tenants' issues.

Although the majority of members were private tenants, the Association also became involved in the Borough-wide opposition to Council rent increases; a movement which was to become one of the most militant tenants' struggles in Britain, culminating in the famous St Pancras rent strike when 800 police were used to help bailiffs evict rent strikers, and where 14,000 tenants marched on the Town Hall.

The TSTA was consequently established and well-organised when the first property developers turned their attention to Tolmers Square. In August 1959 a property developer applied for planning permission to build a twenty-four storey office block 280 feet high on the south side of the Square. The total development was for 178,000 square feet of office space.

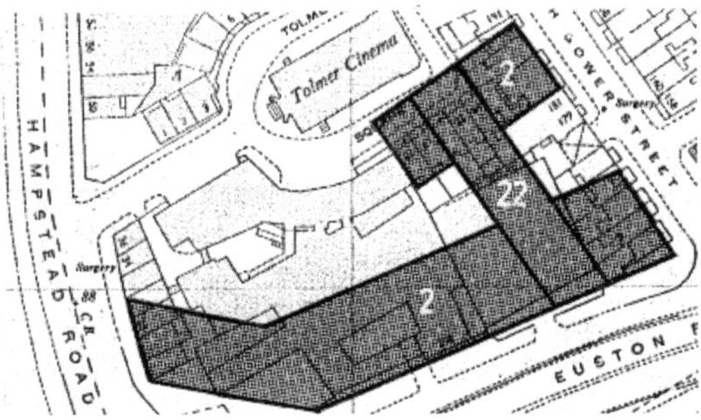

Developer's proposal, August 1959, showing storey heights. (Source: sketch by Ms Zukowski, owner occupier)

Characteristically, the Planning Committee of the Conservative controlled St Pancras Council approved the application, despite the fact that the area was zoned for 'commerce' at that time.

The TSTA acted swiftly and sent a petition to both the St Pancras Council and to the London County Council (LCC), both of whom would have to ratify the decision before it could be implemented.

Their argument was straightforward. If the scheme went ahead, 100 families would lose their homes. Many of these people depended on living in central London for their jobs; railway workers on night work, post office workers, waiters, cleaners and so on. There was already a shortage of cheap housing in the Borough, and over 6,000 people were on the Council's housing waiting list. They also argued that additional office blocks were in any case unnecessary. Within a quarter of a mile radius of Tolmers Square, thirty new office blocks had been erected in the previous three years, almost all requiring the demolition of residential property. Two-thirds of these office blocks were standing empty; a total of 390,000 square feet. To make things worse the LCC was spending vast sums of money on road-widening schemes in order to reduce congestion. These schemes meant the demolition of even more housing. Yet the new proposals for Tolmers Square would increase the congestion still further by causing an extra 2,000 or 3,000 office workers to pour into the centre of London.

The TSTA accepted that the area should be developed, but demanded that the LLC and St Pancras Council should buy up the land and build much needed housing for working-class people. The fact that the developers proposed to build some residential accommodation in their scheme would be of no help to the existing residents. As the Association's secretary remarked to a local paper: 'It is plain these flats will be let at high rents for the greatest profit of the developer, and that the families to be displaced would not be able to afford them . . . We believe there is no other reason for these proposals than greed for rent and profit.' (Rose Gavin, *North London Press*, 6 November 1959).

Following the approval of the development proposal by the Planning Committee, the TSTA took a deputation to the next full Council Meeting. Impressed by the strength of the deputation, the Council vetoed the Planning Committee's decision and the matter was sent back to the Planning Committee for reconsideration.

Even as this was taking place, a planning application was being filed by another developer, for permission to erect 'a modern block comprising residential accommodation, shops, offices and showrooms' on the North side of the Square.

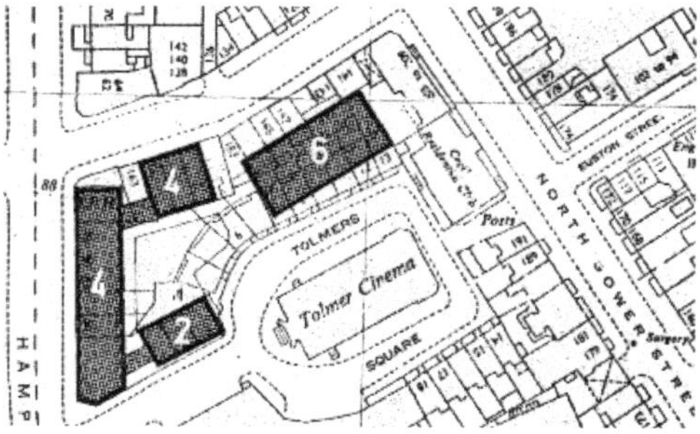

Developer's proposal, November 1959, showing storey heights. (Source: Camden planning records office)

Realising that the pressure was on, the TSTA did not sit back and rely on a change of heart by the Planning Committee, but continued their campaign. Letters were sent to the local MP, councillors, the Chamber of Commerce, and the local press, all of whom were very sympathetic. A letter was also sent to the Minister of Housing and Local Government – Mr Henry Brooke (Conservative MP for Hampstead), who himself had recently made a speech condemning the tendency for offices to crowd central London:

> "In central London 22 million square feet of new office buildings have been completed since the war. And another 9,000,000 square feet or so are in course of erection . . . Office employment in Central London has been continuing to go up, and is very difficult to stop. You can see the direct effects in traffic blocks and crowded rush-hour trains and buses . . . In modern life, with its growing complexity, an increase in office work . . . is natural and inevitable. What is not inevitable – and what I am determined to stop – is that all new office employment should be concentrated in Central London" (*Evening Standard*, 18 November 1959).

The 'determination' of the Minister apart, the tenants themselves were certainly determined, and prepared to use direct action if necessary. 'They were fully united in their opposition and were prepared to barricade the ends of the Square to prevent demolition lorries getting in' (*North London Press*, 25 December 1959).

But three months later, when the opposition was thought to have died down, the St Pancras Council approved the planning application. The application was then passed down to the LCC who had the final say. After pressure from the TSTA, two local councillors took up the case and persuaded the LCC to reject the application, on the grounds that, 'the proposal does not accord with the provisions of the development plan in which the area is zoned for commercial purposes' and 'is contrary to the Council's policy for restraining traffic in Central London . . . and is likely to lead to an increase in commuting and general congestion' (LCC planning records). It was also noted that there was no provision for the replacement of residential accommodation.

The rejection was a major victory for the TSTA. As one of the councillors remarked, 'It is quite clear that had it not been for the action taken by the Tenants Association the application would have gone through. The whole thing is back in the melting pot but with this difference – the application for . . . [office] development has been turned down' (Tom Braddock, *North London Press*, 1 April 1960).

However the victory was soon tempered by the news that yet another planning application had been filed, by a third developer; this time for the erection of a thirteen-storey building for use as shops, offices and showrooms. But a precedent had been established. The application was turned down as were a number of similar applications subsequently. (It is important to emphasise that these early planning applications were made by developers who did not necessarily own any of the site for which they were making their applications.)

However it was one thing to stop planning permissions being granted and another to effect positive action. Many of the tenants were living in appalling conditions, and the TSTA demanded that new housing be built:

> We contend that the whole Tolmers Square site, with some adjoining streets, could be developed for flats – and . . . this would be of real help in remedying the terrible local housing shortage . . . . We contend the area should be redeveloped for housing for the present tenants and for local families - at rents we can afford (*North London Press*, 24 June 1960).

In response to this pressure from the TSTA and local councillors, the LCC declared that it was 'considering' carrying out comprehensive redevelopment of the area. This would involve changing the zoning from 'commerce' to include some residential use, and the Council asked its officers to prepare a report on the subject. It seemed for the moment that the tenant's pressure was really paying off.

The Tolmers Square Tenants association was by now a formidable organisation, with a good track record. Requests for advice and help were coming from all over London, and it broadened out to become Tolmers Square and District Tenants association. Numerous small battles were fought and usually won. A petition obtained a pedestrian crossing over Hampstea-d Road and direct action led to a ban on cars parking in Tolmers Square.

31. Tenants protesting against car parking, 1962.

The TSTA was extremely successful in the late 1950's and early 1960's. They were well-organised, active, had clear demands and knew how and where to apply pressure.

Their greatest asset was Rose Gavin. A mother of seven children, in her fifties, she lived at 12 Tolmers Square, one of the few houses which had been requisitioned during the war and not yet reclaimed by its owner. To earn money Rose did cleaning, but she spent all her spare time campaigning. A local councillor described her as:

> "A dynamic little thin woman with white hair and a habit of getting in everybody's way. She was an annoying little person, and my heart would sink every time the phone would ring, and she would put 6d in, then I knew I was there for half an hour. I don't say this in any disparaging tone because I think this is how people get things done . . . She was very smart and politically she was very left. I doubt really if she should have been a member of the Labour Party . . . She would continue the fight in the Co-op party, and in fact on any other platform. She was a born agitator" (Leila Campbell, Councillor, Interview).

She was in fact once thrown out of the Labour Party and the Communist party in the same week.

As a result of her activity she received several threats. Once she was offered £500 to 'calm it down round there' (Teresa Gavin), by someone assumed to be a developer and on another occasion builders threatened to smash her place up. 'She told me that when she was leading the campaign for the tenants' association, a man came to her who she identified as a developer and said "There's money for you if you shut up". Of course she gave him the brush-off' (Alec Kazantzis, GLC Councillor, Interview)

Rose Gavin's premature death in 1973 was a personal tragedy for her friends and relations. It was also a tragedy for Tolmers Square and the Labour movement in general who lost one of the ablest and most devoted grass-roots campaigners the Borough had known. There is little doubt that without her the battle for Tolmers Square would have been lost in 1959.

32. Rose Gavin and daughters.

(Unfortunately there are few records left from this period. When Rose Gavin died the police took all her possessions and later returned most of them to her daughters. However all the paper work relating to her political activities was lost.)

The Euston Centre

During the early 1960s, the TSTA turned much of its energy to fighting a development, just across the Hampstead Road from Tolmers Square, which is now known as the Euston Centre.

The Euston Centre was the first of the big property bananzas, and it remains one of the largest. It is also one of the most notorious, and has already been written up by others (see Marriot, *The Property Boom*, and Counter information Service, *The Recurrent Crisis of London*). I deal with it here only in that it relates directly to Tolmers Square.

The area of development was originally similar in many respects to the Tolmers area, comprising decaying nineteenth century terraces, industries, warehouses and shops. Additionally there was a thriving street market in Seaton Street. In 1952, a property developer called Joe Levy obtained planning permission to build offices on a one-acre site on the corner of Euston Road and Hampstead Road. Four years later he bought this site, and then discovered that the LCC required most of it for a road-widening scheme. But as he already had planning permission, he was in a good bargaining position, and was able to demand £1 million compensation for loss of development rights. Faced with this massive demand, the LCC made a 'deal' with Levy. If Levy was prepared to give the LCC for nothing a slice of land they needed for their road-widening, the LCC in return would give planning permission for the whole thirteen-acre site, to the same density as if the whole site was to be built over. Levy then started quietly buying up the site. The 'deal' was of course not made public, and so he was able to buy most of the property extremely cheaply, as the many small owners were not aware of its potential value. It was not until the early 1960s that the proposed development became public knowledge, by which time the land had been acquired, and building was ready to start.

The development was undertaken by Balgray Investments Limited, a company owned equally by Stock Conversion & Investment Trust and George Wimpey, the massive construction firm. Demolition started in late 1963, and within a few years the run-down houses and workshops were replaced by 'millions of pounds worth of windswept glass, concrete and steel, full to the brim with office workers'. The development actually contained 500,000 square feet of offices, some showrooms, shops and some luxury flats. At the time of completion, it was estimated to be worth £80 million. As it had cost only £6 million to build, the profits came to a staggering £64 million, much of which accrued to a few men and their families.

34. 1961

35. 1976

As far as the TSTA were concerned, the development was totally unacceptable. The elimination of Seaton Street Market and the surrounding workshops and industries was a serious loss for the working class community in the area, both as a source of cheap food and goods, and as a source of employment. The new scheme was of little use to local people as it failed to provide them with the kinds of jobs they required, or the numerous useful local services and cheap shops that they needed. As for housing, the new development only provided 'luxury flats', some of which rented for as much as £50 per week in 1971; hardly of much use to working-class tenants. In short, the scheme characterised precisely the kind of development that the TSTA had been arguing against in their previous campaigns; the only people to benefit would be the developers.

The TSTA discovered about the development too late to be able to prevent its happening. But they were able to fight for the tenants who were being displaced. In particular they took up the case of the tenants in two tenement blocks, Carisbrooke and Arundel:

> "Over forty tenants rented rooms and flatlets in the dilapidated buildings. These tenants were poor by any standards. Ten were old age pensioners and three were old soldiers who could not work. The rest worked locally, over half on shift-work, in low-paid jobs with catering and office cleaning." (CIS, p.14)

When the LCC made their 'deal' they failed to make any provision for the re-housing of the tenants who already lived in the area, and neither the developers nor St. Pancras Council were at first prepared to take responsibility for them. Consequently those with non-controlled tenancies were given notices to quit, with no alternative provided, and those on controlled tenancies were offered small cash incentives to leave. A local paper reported the following:

> "An 83 year old tenant, protected under the Rent Acts at Carisbrooke House, Drummond Street, alleged this week that an agent for Balgray Investments Ltd, the owners, held her hand as she signed an agreement to leave for the alternative accommodation. She said, 'I don't want to leave. The signature was taken from me by force...I have no idea what I am supposed to have signed. He took the agreement away with him and he didn't give me a copy. But he said they would be coming to take me away on Monday"(*North London Press*, 28 September 1962).

A councillor recalls, 'There was harrassment in a big way, a chap used to go around with a big dog and so on. A lot of the tenants were very frightened' (Leila Campbell, Interview).

The TSTA took up the case of these tenants, organised them, publicised the situation, wrote letters and sent deputations to the LCC. After a long struggle they succeeded in obtaining certain concessions and the displaced tenants certainly received a better deal than they would otherwise have done.

The Euston Centre development was extremely important in providing a tangible and spectacular example of the power of developers over both ordinary people and local authorities. It showed the process by which developers could have developments sewn up before the public knew anything about them, and indicated the need for opposition groups to find out what was going on sooner. Casting a shadow over Tolmers Square even in summer, the Euston Centre became an ever-present reminder of the need for vigilance.

Sadly the TSTA did not learn the lesson. As an active member of the Association said later, 'We were fighting the Euston Tower development without really knowing what we were fighting' (David Goldhill, Interview). The mechanics of how property speculators operated had not yet been exposed and publicised, and few people understood the rules of the game.

If the TSTA had realised what they were fighting, they might have discovered the biggest irony of all. While they were busy struggling for the tenants who were displaced by the Euston Centre, Stock Conversion were meticulously buying up their own houses, in order to carry out almost the same operation in Tolmers Square as they had done with the Euston Centre.

Instead the tenants began to get disheartened. The promised LCC comprehensive redevelopment scheme failed to materialise, and their own houses continued to deteriorate. They gave up hope of being able to achieve anything, and demanded that they themselves be rehoused in decent conditions. After continual pressure, many of the leading activists were rehoused, including Rose Gavin herself who moved into a new block of Council flats a small distance away. Ironically the main reason for her being rehoused was dampness which affected one of her sons who had a lung problem. The Council did not bother to discover the source of the damp, which in fact was merely a broken drain-pipe. After the Gavins left, the house was used by a short-term 'problem family' for one year, and then it was left empty. Eight years later squatters were able to repair the drainpipe in ten minutes.

Rose Gavin and several of the other activists remained active in the Association after they left, but they had become completely disenchanted. Apathy born of cynicism set in, and the TSTA dwindled and finally faded away altogether.

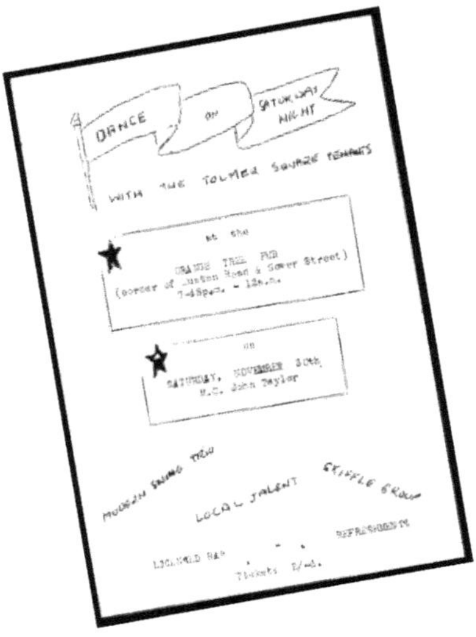

3.

Die slowly, you'll enjoy it more

Anyone who observes a beatific smile playing these days over the features of Mr. Joe Levy of Stock Conversion may be sure that what is occupying his mind is not his recent disappointments over plans to knock down three streets near Piccadilly, but the two magic words 'Tolmers Square' (*Private Eye*, 9 February 1973).

In order to assemble, as you say, this parcel of land, this piece of ground for redevelopment, the first thing these people have to do is to get rid of people – ordinary people and small businesses. And these are the people who are evicted, they are the people who are harassed, they are the people who are allegedly bought out. But they, in fact, are the sufferers because they are pushed out of the area. In fact a community is smashed almost every time, without fail. In an area like this, stress areas in inner London, the main sufferers are the people who have lived here all their lives." (Jock Stallard MP, *Man Alive*, November 1973).

Well they are big people. Their aim is only to pull down this area and make money – as simple as that...That's all, and there is no room for poor people." (J. D. Shah, resident/shopkeeper, *Tolmers Beginning or end?*).

I think that Levy is only out for one thing, he's out for making a profit. I think he doesn't consider the people in the area. When I went and spoke to [someone at] Stock Conversion a few months ago about this, he told me that he felt very sorry for the people in this area. He would not like to live in property like it (Mr Jones, resident, *Tolmers Beginning or end?*).

I don't think that private companies should be able to exploit their position, but so long as the law remains as it is – and it has remained like this for the last thousand years at least – property owners are allowed to exploit their position at the cost of the rest of society. (Frank Dobson, Labour Councillor, *Tolmers Beginning or end?*).

The property system does not look upon property as an asset in a social or environmental sense. (*The Property Machine*, p.58)

36

Stock conversion buy into Tolmers Square

Stock Conversion have received a lot of attention over the past few years. Several of their projects have been particularly spectacular, and have therefore received publicity, and because of this publicity they have become a prime target for anyone wishing to indulge in 'property speculator bashing'. But there have been numerous other companies, operating in much the same manner, which have received little or no publicity. It is important to remember in what follows that Stock Conversion is not unique.

This is borne out by Camden's Chief Valuer, a person who has probably had more contact with them than most people:

> I, quite frankly, have never found anything in all my dealings with them to suggest that they were in any way different from any other reasonable reputable development company...I've never found them to be underhand or anything like that...They are not in business to make losses of course, or to give the Council all their profits, obviously, because they've got shareholders, and no development company would carry on in that way, but they have always looked at the social side, the community side. And what has surprised me throughout this business is that they've been on the receiving end of so much criticism. (Mike Searle, Interview)

The experience of other developers in Tolmers Square had shown that it was not enough for a developer merely to apply for planning permission and rely on a co-operative local authority. The LCC had already turned down three development proposals on Tolmers Square, and there was no way the developers could object. They had no bargaining power. The developer therefore had to get the local authority into a situation where it would be difficult for them to refuse permission. He had to have something which the local authority wanted in order to be able to strike a bargain. In Tolmers Square the authorities were desperately trying to find land to build housing. What better bargaining tool therefore than land.

Stock Conversion started buying up land in Tolmers in 1962, and continued buying for the next thirteen years. The companies used for this operation were Gleniffer Finance Corporation and London

Scottish Properties. In addition, a number of properties were held by Hambros Bank as trustees.

The main objective was to buy up property as cheaply as possible. Secrecy was essential. The owners had to remain unaware of the future potential of the area, otherwise the prices would soar. Run-down properties could then be bought for a mere fraction of the potential land value on which they stood. For instance in 1962 they bought six freehold houses in North Gower Street for £17,000. Ten years later the land on which these houses stand was worth £150,000. In 1969 it is rumoured that five houses in the Square itself were sold for £17,000 when at that time the market value of the land on which they stood was around £70,000.

There was nothing illegal about the way that Stock Conversion bought up land; they were merely persistent, as these extracts from the diary of one owner-occupier show.

> 15 March 1968: received first letter from an agent saying clients interested in acquiring No. 15 Tolmers Square. . . . I made one phone call to agent. . , to say that I cannot do anything until my husband returns from abroad.
> 2 April 1968: second letter from agent asking if I have made a decision (letter ignored).
> 16 May 1968: third letter from agent asking if I am now ready to discuss sale (letter ignored).
> 25 February 1969: agent phoned to ask if any decision forthcoming as clients were going to have a big meeting in the Haymarket office (obvious now that it is J. Levy).
> 28 February 1969: I rang agent who confirmed that J. Levy is their client – they expect to start a development on the triangle of Euston Road/Hampstead Road/ North Gower Street, which includes Tolmers Square, in 2 years time.
> 12 March 1969: first offer received from agent – £3,000 (ignored).
> 27 March 1969: letter received from agent asking for a reply to above offer – clients prepared to increase offer (ignored).
> 15 May 1969: further letter from agent asking 'what are my terms?'
> 21 May 1969: I finally wrote to agent saying not interested as offer does not represent market value of house and not sufficient to buy a comparable house. Told them to come back when plans accepted by competent authority.
> 20 June 1969: agent replies to above saying clients prepared to allow me to remain in the house (at a rental) for a couple of years. What price would I accept? (ignored).
> November 1970: land costs now estimated at £375,000 per acre. At this figure *land* on which my house stands is worth £10,000.
> 3 December 1970: agent rang to say clients now prepared to offer more than previously (£3,000) - would pay in excess of £5,000 if vacant possession given. I told them my position is same as 2 years ago and I'm not interested.
> 17 August 1973: agent wrote to say clients now very anxious to purchase my house and wish to discuss price (letter ignored).
>
> (Ms Zukowski, 15 Tolmers Square)

The Zukowski's were not to be bullied because they simply did not want to move. Many others were not so smart. The Zukowskis' house, being on the south side of the Square, was crucial to Stock Conversion's development, Yet even so, presumably thinking they were dealing with an ordinary individual who would be ignorant of property deals, they persisted in making absurdly low offers. When they thought they were dealing with more sophisticated clients they

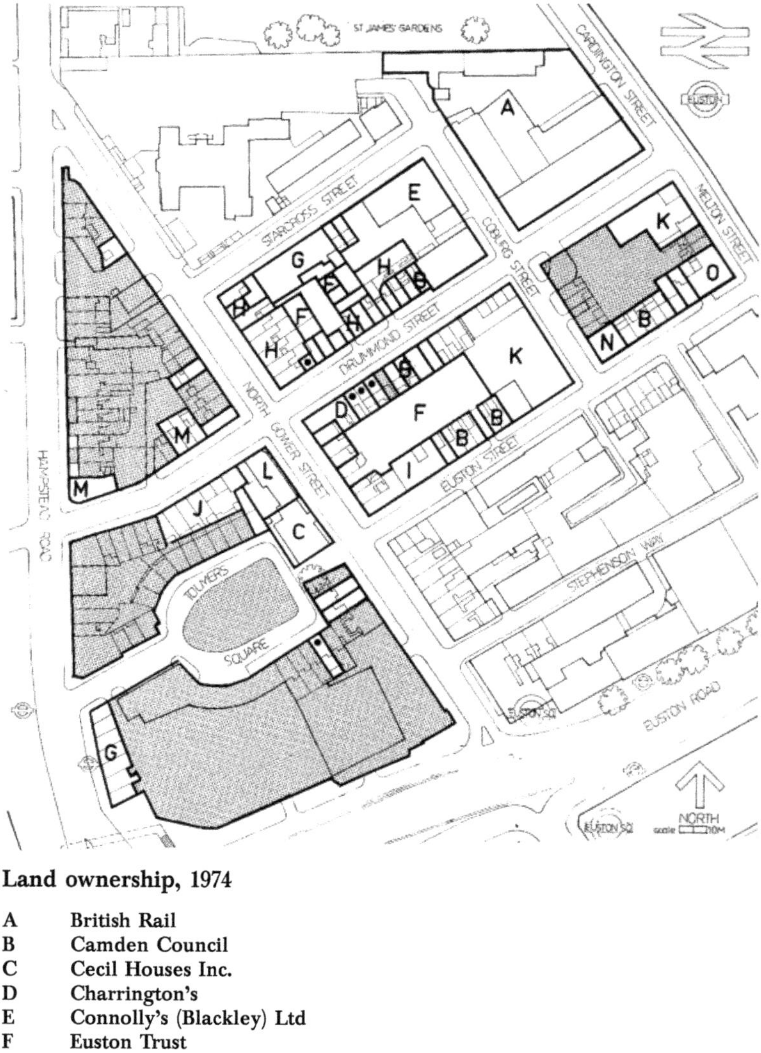

Land ownership, 1974

A British Rail
B Camden Council
C Cecil Houses Inc.
D Charrington's
E Connolly's (Blackley) Ltd
F Euston Trust
G GLC
H Hampstead Investments
I James Mayell Ltd
J London C.H.A.
K London Transport
L TGWU
M Victor Laurence
N Watney's
O Wellcome Foundation
• Owner occupier
☐ unknown (mainly owner occupiers or small landlords)
▒ Stock Conversion and Investment Trust

(Source: Renton Howard Wood and Levin, architects, with corrections) were prepared to pay a lot more. In the same year that they gallantly offered Ms Zukowski 'in excess of £5,000 if vacant possession given', they paid another client £32,000 for two similar properties in North Gower Street, without even getting vacant possession.

Many commercial owners were quite happy to be bought out, Although less than the potential market values, the sums involved were often enough to enable them to move out to a more convenient location and start again, or to retire on the proceeds. Other owners were determined not to go and made pacts amongst themselves not to sell out whatever the price offered (for instance Laurence Corner and the Shah Restaurant). By 1973 Stock Conversion had amassed almost 5 acres in what came to be known as the 'Levy triangle'. The remaining owners were unlikely to sell out.

37

Neglect:

When Stock Conversion obtained ownership of property, the next task was to get rid of the people remaining in it. Having plenty of time, they had no need to resort to strong-arm methods or harassment. Instead they used a more subtle method: they deliberately neglected the property which consequently decayed, leading to the demoralisation of the population who then could not wait to leave. They carried out the minimum possible repairs, and those that were done were generally botched. Many tenants got so fed up that they either rehoused themselves if they were able, or applied pressure on the Council to rehouse them on the grounds that the houses were a danger to their health. The local policeman on the beat recalls one visit:

> I remember being called to a house in Tolmers Square soon after the Cinema was pulled down. Spanish people on the ground floor, and their ceiling had just collapsed. Fortunately no one was in bed at the time. If so it would have killed them. It was just through lack of maintenance, and they could never get hold of the owners of the property - who I take it were the property developers - to do

anything about it. . . I know they'd been complaining about this ceiling for quite a time and they could never get hold of anybody: every time they phoned there was nothing, or there was a promise and it never came about. . . They weren't too upset about it funnily enough. They seemed to have accepted it as the kind of thing that will happen. So I dread to think what must have happened elsewhere in the Square (P. C. Charles Russell, Interview).

And some more testimonies:

The only repairs we ever ask for to be done are essential ones, and we usually have to nag them for about a year or so before anything gets done at all, and anything that does get done, gets done very badly. It just gets sort of patched up and it doesn't last a minute (Betty Norden, tenant for 23 years, *Tolmers Beginning or End?*).

When we came here, this was the most sought-after block of flats in the area. . . . But since Levy bought it everything was left to fall apart (elderly lady, tenant for 30 years, conversation with Dianna Sherston, Camden Housing Liaison Officer).

Ever since the original owner sold the house, it has been bought and sold over and over, and of course they didn't care about the conditions. We could ask and ask for the roof to be fixed till in the end we gave up. It was a waste of breath (elderly lady, tenant for 43 years, conversation, Dianna Sherston).

The following examples are taken from *Tolmers Destroyed*, a pamphlet produced in May 1974 to publicise the situation. (p.148)

Ms E. lives on the top floor. For 3 years her roof leaked so badly that she had to have a dustbin in her room to collect the water. She constantly complained and every few months Levy's builders came around and re-plastered the ceiling; a completely pointless exercise since it came down again the next time it rained. In fact, what was needed was a new gutter. . . .

Mr and Ms C. have lived in North Gower Street for 35 years. They have two rooms on the first floor. They have no bath. They have cracks in the front wall through which you can see daylight. There is damp on the kitchen ceiling. Ms C. used to keep flowers on the balcony but gave it up as she is frightened to walk on the balcony in case it collapses. They have complained to Levy's but the builders say they cannot spend more than £5 or 'the boss would kill me'. . . .

This £5 [upper-limit] for repairs has been mentioned by several other people, and shows an extraordinary mentality on the part of a property company whose net tangible assets in 1973 were over £62 million, and whose total profits for 1972/73 were over £5 million.

Not a penny is spent on painting or maintaining the exteriors. The balconies in Tolmers Square are a symbolic example. These balconies are structurally very strong with steel bars protruding from the front walls of the house. But if they are not painted, the weather penetrates the plaster facing which then cracks and drops off, so giving the balcony the appearance of imminent collapse.

If left in this state for long, the weather erodes the brick pillars until they become unsafe. But at this point instead of re-plastering and painting, Levy's builders merely knock down the balcony altogether, leaving an ugly scar. There is little objection from the residents, as by this time they are terrified that every time they walk in and out of their front door it is going to collapse, and are easily persuaded (wrongly) that the balconies are structurally unsound. The first balcony was taken down in 1969, and now only 8 of the original 15 are left standing.

38. 1960

39. 1976

40. 1903

41. 1976

42. The fate of the Tolmers Square balconies.

> Mr and Ms A live in Hampstead Road with their two children and Ms A's mother. They are Greek and cannot speak English. They live on the first and second floors for which they pay £20 per month. The third floor has been empty since 1960 and is presently occupied by an assortment of buckets and baths to collect the water which comes through the roof and subsequently to their flat. The basement and ground floors have been empty since 1948 and are frequented only by rats. A musty smell emanates from these floors and pervades the whole house. Many of the walls are damp and peeling, and in the toilet it is only several thicknesses of lino which prevent one from falling through the rotten floor. There is no bath.
>
> 'Someone came round from Stock Conversion three months ago, but they said they were not interested in doing repairs because the buildings would be coming down. They didn't say it like that, they used big posh words that we're not used to,' explained Ms A's son-in-law, who was acting as interpreter.
>
> According to a local newspaper report (*Camden Journal*, 7 June 1974), a spokesman from D.E. & J. Levy said. . . 'If you're talking about the top floor, the family doesn't have the top floor as part of their tenancy, so it is no concern to them.'

Leaving property empty

As soon as any property became vacant, it was boarded up and left empty. In May 1974, Stock Conversion owned 67 houses in the area. Of these 14 were completely empty, or occupied by squatters, and 31 were partially empty. Many of these had been empty for up to eight years. Altogether, 242 habitable rooms were empty, which represented 39 per cent of their housing stock in the area.

At that time they also owned approximately 98,000 square feet of commercial space in the area, of which 28,000 square feet were empty, comprising eight shops, a bank, and workshop, storage and office space. Over two-thirds of an acre of their land was vacant or being used for temporary car parking (figures, author's survey).

Stock Conversion were never prepared to re let property, regardless of the social consequences. Here are two more examples:

> The E is an Indian restaurant in Hampstead Road run by Nepalese people. They have obtained a lease from D. E. & J. Levy for the ground floor and basement. As the rest of the house was vacant, the staff of the restaurant moved upstairs, and spent a considerable amount of money in doing it up. When Levy's found out, they asked them to leave immediately. The manager tried to persuade Levy's to [allow him to] rent the upper floors, but without success. He was told that because the roof was in bad condition (although it did not leak) and because the house did not have an inside toilet (like many of the houses in the area, the bathroom and toilet are in the back yard) it was not possible.
>
> The staff now have to commute to Finchley by taxi every night after they close the restaurant at 1 a.m. to get a few hours' sleep before being back at 9am to work. The house upstairs remains empty.
>
> In 1972, Ms. F., unable to find anywhere to live, was staying with a friend in North Gower Street. She noticed that one of the flats in the house was empty so she rang D. E. & J. Levy, the agents of the block, and asked if she could rent the flat. At first they fobbed her off by 'denying the existence of
> 43 the block,' but after further phone calls and persistence, they did admit that

one of the flats was vacant but 'the block is coming down and it's not worth re-letting.'

However, they were kind enough to offer her another flat with a 3 year lease of £2,500 and £25 per week rent. Unfortunately, she had to decline the offer. Two years later, still being without a flat, she decided to occupy without permission and squat (*Tolmers Destroyed*, May 1974).

This policy contributed to the problem of homelessness already extensive in London (see p.160). But homelessness was not the only problem.

As soon as a building is left empty it starts to decay; leaks in the roof go undetected, windows are smashed and left broken, pipes are ripped out for their metal content, and vermin breed.

Several houses have had their roofs deliberately destroyed, the tiles having been taken off and stacked up neatly; probably by lead thieves. With water running constantly through the house, ceilings collapse, rot sets in and decay is guaranteed. This is the inevitable consequence of leaving houses empty. (*Tolmers Destroyed*).

44

45

46

Collapse:

On Saturday 13 October 1973, an occupied house owned by Stock Conversion collapsed with only a few minutes warning. Mr Castro and two friends who were living in the house managed to escape without serious injury, although they lost all their possessions and suffered extreme shock.

The cause of the collapse was never made public despite a call for a public inquiry by the Tolmers Village Association. Camden's District Surveyor felt that there was no need for an inquiry. He commented that 'the building just got tired of standing'. According to the ***Hampstead and Highgate Express*** (19 October 1973), a spokesman for D. E. & J. Levy said they would be holding a thorough investigation into what had happened, but the results of their investigation were never released. The Chairman of Stock Conversion later suggested that 'the life of the building expired' (Minutes of meeting, 4 October 1974).

Various theories were put forward as to why the building collapsed: it may have been the result of heavy traffic in Hampstead Road; or vibration which occurred when piles were sunk for the foundations of the Euston Centre; or possibly a badly designed conversion, which weakened the structure. Some people even believed it was deliberate, as builders hired by Stock Conversion were actually working in the building minutes before the collapse.

While it would be unfair to accuse Stock Conversion of deliberately knocking the building down, this kind of situation was the inevitable consequence of their policies.

This event was very bad for local morale. With the cause of the collapse remaining a mystery, people started to believe that their own houses might collapse any day. It is extraordinary that the Council were not legally obliged to carry out a public investigation, and their unwillingness to do so showed their reluctance to take any action which might antagonise Stock Conversion.

TRUMAN. HANBURY. BUXTON
THE LORD PALMERST

47. 'I heard a crackling rumbling noise and I looked at the building and the whole thing just collapsed before my eyes (Pierre Versluys, *Evening News*, 13 October 1973).

Demolition

Wherever possible Stock Conversion actually demolished buildings, as an empty site was less trouble to maintain and could even bring in revenue by being let out for car parking. For instance, they bought eight houses in North Gower Street in 1969 and after writing to the Council requesting that they re-house the remaining controlled tenants, demolished them. Had these houses not been demolished they would almost certainly have been listed as buildings of historic importance, as were other buildings in the same street a few years later.

48. 49. Housing demolished. . . . . . . for a van park.

The authorities' contribution

It might well be thought that one of the purposes of local authorities and town planners is to prevent this kind of destruction by a private developer. Unfortunately, the authorities merely aggravated the situation.

In 1960, after defeating attempts by several developers to build offices in Tolmers Square, the Secretary of the Tolmers Square Tenants Association made the following observation: 'The position now is that there is every hope that the LCC will develop the area themselves and provide LCC housing for us within that development' (Rose Gavin Speech, 1960). One of the major reasons for the subsequent collapse of the TSTA was the inability of the LCC to fulfil its initial promise to carry out a comprehensive redevelopment,

The first hint that a scheme was in the air was made by a local LCC Councillor in April 1960, at the same time as the first major planning applications for offices were turned down. Ten months later, however, there was no visible progress and a local Councillor asked the Chairman of the Town Planning Committee what was happening. The reply was that 'the Officers are considering whether the Tolmers Square area which is at present zoned for commerce should be re-zoned for other purposes including residential use' (Council Minutes, 14 February 1961). It was hoped that a report would be available soon. Five months later the LCC asked the officers to report on 'the possibility of the Council undertaking a major scheme of housing redevelopment in the area between Euston Station and Hampstead Road' (*North London Press*, 21 July 1961).

But nothing happened. Three and a half years later, when the LCC handed over planning responsibility for the area to the newly formed Camden Council, there was no scheme. Unfortunately there are no records available for this period and one can only speculate on the reasons for this failure. The officers certainly prepared several schemes, though none were accepted by the Council. There were also talks between the LCC and several property owners in the area, including Stock Conversion. As we shall see later, the most likely cause of the breakdown was probably the cost of land, which was already beginning to rise.

Planning blight

Apart from the possibility of declaring the area a Comprehensive Development Area and carrying out their own redevelopment, the other power which the local authorities could exercise over the area was 'development control'; the right to accept or reject planning applications (which have by law to be submitted before any change of building use or new construction).

Under the Initial Development Plan produced in the 1950s the area was zoned completely for 'commerce'. Development would only be permitted if it was for 'warehouses, repositories, and other buildings where the primary use is for storage or wholesale trade. Includes an industrial use carried on in the same premises and which is incidental to the main use.' In 1962 the site bordering on Euston Road was rezoned as 'West End', a new category which allowed development for 'shops, places of assembly, public buildings and certain residential buildings. Also included are warehouses, repositories and light industrial uses which are ancillary to the main functions of the area' (Development Plan Statement, 1962). Offices would also be permitted in certain circumstances. The change in zoning alone considerably raised the value of the land and paved the way for office development.

During the 1960s the local authority planners turned down several development proposals which they considered to be socially undesirable. Most of these were of speculative nature with high density office and commercial building; similar in character to the proposals mentioned in Chapter 1. The planners were also able to prevent the housing stock being taken over for more profitable commercial and office uses. Had the local authorities not had these powers virtually no housing would have remained at all.

But development control also had serious destructive consequences for the area by creating the conditions for sterility and deterioration. Up until the early 1960s the area was in a constant state of evolution. Businesses came into the area, expanded, contracted, often folding up or moving elsewhere, only to be replaced by other enterprises. Buildings were constantly converted and added to, to meet the requirements of the moment; back extensions were constructed and yards covered over. New buildings replaced old in a piecemeal manner. After the LCC decision to carry out a comprehensive redevelopment, this evolutionary process was largely halted by the refusal to grant the relevant planning permissions.

The effect of this kind of policy can be seen by examining the case of Connolly's (Blackley) Ltd, an independently operated subsidiary of British Insulated Calendars Cables Ltd, and one of the world's largest producers of fine-gauge electrical wire. This firm had its headquarters and factory in Manchester but owned a piece of land in the Tolmers area where they had a warehouse for storage and distribution in the London area. Also on their land were eight run-down houses and a vacant site bombed during the war. The existing building was 'inconvenient and uneconomic' and in 1960 they decided to rebuild their premises. They proposed to develop the whole site and erect 30,600 square feet of warehouses with packing, despatch and offices. They were also prepared to include some new housing in the scheme, They submitted a planning application which was turned down by the LCC on the ground that 'the site falls within a larger area to which the Council is giving detailed consideration for comprehensive redevelopment and the company's scheme' would therefore be premature', It was considered that the company's scheme would 'seriously prejudice the proper development of the area as a whole. As an LCC official commented at the appeal inquiry, 'It's all or nothing, This area has got to be either zoned all for commercial use or all for residential use... If this appeal is upheld, the possibility of getting satisfactory development in this area is remote' (*St Pancras Chronicle*, 12 January 1962).

The result was that this company, which incidentally had an important export role, was prevented from expanding, and had to remain in its inadequate premises. Fifteen years later they were still in the same building surrounded by vacant sites.

50

Because of the decision to redevelop comprehensively, planning applications for minor changes of use were normally only granted for a limited period; often only one or two years. This meant that firms and small businessmen were unwilling to invest capital in their premises, with the result that the buildings ceased to be maintained. This also severely affected services to residents.

On one occasion, after requests from residents, a local shopkeeper offered to open a launderette in his basement, The planning department took five months to process the application, and then only gave permission for two years. On such a short-term basis it was not an economic proposition. (There is still no launderette within ten minutes' walk.)

51. Land lost to traffic.

Building an underpass

The authorities also played a more active part in spreading decay. The Euston Road Underpass was planned in the late 1950s as a method for relieving traffic congestion at the junction of Hampstead Road and Tottenham Court Road. It was a natural corollary of the increased traffic congestion which had resulted from the expansion of office accommodation in central London, and was in line with then current philosophy about the car as the future form of transport. It was constructed in the mid-1960s. Whether it did in fact reduce congestion is extremely debatable as traffic merely piled up at the next junction instead. What it certainly did achieve was the destruction of commercial premises and housing, and the creation of a desolate environmental blot. In the Tolmers area alone the frontages of Euston Road and Hampstead Road which were demolished contained pubs, cafes, manufacturers, warehouses, shops and some housing. The underpass also had a more subtle effect on the Tolmers area by cutting it off from the area to the south of Euston Road. Pedestrians could only cross at two points; one a pedestrian subway, and the other by a series of pedestrian crossings at a windswept junction. People no longer wandered into the area and commercial trade declined. One barber in North Gower Street claimed he had to sack his four assistants as a direct result of the underpass construction.

1903 1976

52. Twelve houses in Drummond Street were demolished in 1962 so that bore holes could be sunk for the Victoria underground line.

Clearance

It was in their treatment of housing that the ineptitude of the authorities was shown to its full.

In June 1963 the LCC made a Compulsory Purchase Order on twenty-six houses under Part 3 of the Housing Act 1957, declaring that they were unfit for human habitation . . . or injurious to the health of the inhabitants' and 'that most satisfactory method of dealing with the conditions' was 'demolition' (Council Minutes, 18 June 1963). The Council thought it necessary to make a CPO rather than merely a Clearance Order (which compels owners to knock down the houses without giving up their land) in order to 'prevent piecemeal development'.

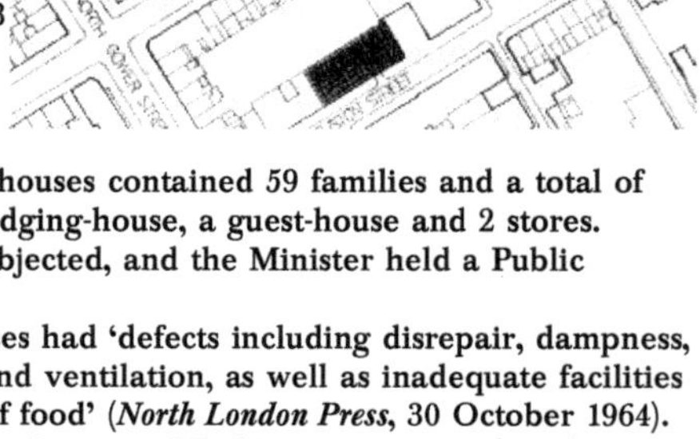

Compulsory Purchase Order, 1963 (Source: Camden Council Minutes, 21 December 1966)

The twenty-six threatened houses contained 59 families and a total of 148 people as well as a shop, a lodging-house, a guest-house and 2 stores. Several inhabitants and owners objected, and the Minister held a Public Inquiry on 27 October 1964.

The LCC claimed the houses had 'defects including disrepair, dampness, and insufficient natural lighting and ventilation, as well as inadequate facilities for the storage and preparation of food' (*North London Press*, 30 October 1964).

The objectors disagreed. For instance, Mr. Livermore owned six house in Euston Street, one of which he lived in himself, and the other five which he let out to students. He claimed that the properties were structurally sound, and that he had recently spent £1,000 repairing them. Being a builder he did the work himself. He claimed they still had 20-30 years useful life, and were serving a useful purpose as there was an urgent need for student accommodation in the area. He was prepared to install any amenities which were lacking.

Despite this opposition the Minister accepted that all but one of the properties needed to be demolished. However, he did not accept that the LCC needed to acquire them and he therefore rejected the CPO and suggested the LCC submit a Clearance Order instead. The LCC did not submit another Order, but instead made various arrangements with the owners. In one case the owners (absentee landlords) sold straight to the council, and on two other sites the owners agreed to demolish provided the council re-housed all the tenants.

But the owners of two terraces in Euston Street refused to accept that the houses should be demolished, and so the council (Camden by this time) decided to reapply for a CPO. The Medical Officer of Health wrote another report, showing that in his view the houses were 'unfit for human habitation' and that they should be demolished. This time the CPO was accepted by the Minister, and in 1969 the houses were emptied and boarded up.

In 1975 they were still standing.

There is no doubt that the twenty-five houses demolished or boarded up in this way were in bad condition, and needed extensive repair or rebuilding. But at a time of housing shortage the effect of the authorities' action was merely to reduce the availability of housing in the area, break up an established community, and disrupt the lives of 140 people, many of whom were perfectly content to remain where they were. As one of the victims remarked, 'No one particularly wanted to go. The Council just moved us' (Kitty, a former tenant from Starcross Street).

54. 'If the houses are acquired by the Council . . . they would be demolished or remain empty for several years' (owner's lawyer at Public Inquiry in 1964). The Council compulsorily acquired the houses in 1969. Photograph taken in 1976.

It can be seen from these few examples that the control exercised by the local authorities merely added to the blight and decay of the area. Far from protecting those people who lived and worked in the area, the authorities actually undermined their very existence. Furthermore, these actions strengthened the bargaining position of Stock Conversion, as the resulting blight merely served to emphasize the urgent need for a redevelopment scheme.

55

MON ★ TUE ★ WED
LEX BARKER
"DIE SLOWLY... YOU'LL ENJOY IT MORE"
The LOOTERS
LONDONS LOWEST PRICES

ER
THUR ★ FRI ★ SAT
KIRK DOUGLAS
CHAMPION
ARTHUR KENNEDY
VICTOR MATURE
VINCENT PRICE
Dangerous Mission

Blight

Perhaps the best symbol of blight in the area was the death of the Tolmer Cinema.

The cinema, a converted nineteenth-century church, stood in the centre of the Square. The building suffered bomb damage during the war, and it was then bought by the Pomson family and restored. They ran it as a 'family type' cinema. There was always a double bill, mostly detective stories and westerns, and the programme was changed three times a week. Few X films were shown even in later years.

At the time that it closed, it was the cheapest cinema in London with seats costing 15p in the stalls and 25p in the circle. It provided a unique facility and attracted all those people who could not afford the West End cinemas – old age pensioners, children, students, dossers and the unemployed. It was extremely popular, with full houses on most nights, and queues of up to 200 for the Sunday afternoon performance.

Despite low prices, the cinema was profitable enough to cover running expenses and minor maintenance charges. But unfortunately the building was old and major improvements were necessary to meet GLC safety requirement. In 1968 the Pomsons made two planning applications to rebuild the cinema, incorporating also hotel or office accommodation to make it profitable. Both planning applications were refused by Camden on the grounds that it would prejudice the redevelopment of the whole site. Before the first application Stock Conversion offered to buy the property but the Pomsons refused the offer. Four years later the Pomsons could hold out no longer; they realized that the cost of the necessary repairs could never be recouped and had to accept Stock Conversion's offer. The cinema was sold in March 1972, and closed immediately.

Aptly the last films ever to be shown were *The Looters* and *Die Slowly, You'll Enjoy it More.*

56

57

58. 'Is this what we call progress?'

The closure was greeted with universal regret but there was little anyone could do about it. One old-age pensioner wrote angrily to a local paper:

> Dear Sir, Again a place of enjoyment . . . is to be closed and pulled down, although it has 1,000 regular patrons. Is this what we call progress? Who decides about this property? Do the 1,000 patrons have a say? Many old-age pensioners will miss it. We were told in 1918 and 1945 this was a land fit for heroes to live in; and take it from me, you need to be a hero to live in it (G. A. Hobbins, *St Pancras Chronicle*, 24 March 1972).

No one answered his questions.

The cinema stood empty for one year. Then, in June 1973, Stock Conversion demolished it, despite a petition from local residents asking that it be left until they were moved. A barbed wire fence was erected around the site and permission requested to use it for a temporary car park. After another petition from local residents objecting to this proposal, the council refused permission, and for over two years the site remained unused.

By the beginning of the 1970s the Tolmers area was suffering advanced planning blight. The combined action of planners and developers had managed to transform a thriving piece of London into little more than a decaying shell. Over fifty houses and a number of commercial buildings had been demolished, while many of those that remained were partially or completely empty and in varying stages of dereliction. Eleven per cent of the land was vacant, numerous businesses had closed down, and the residential population had declined by over a half since 1960. Planning blight is a term frequently thrown around by planners and journalists. The following pages are an attempt to show what it really means.

Population decline in Tolmers Square development area.

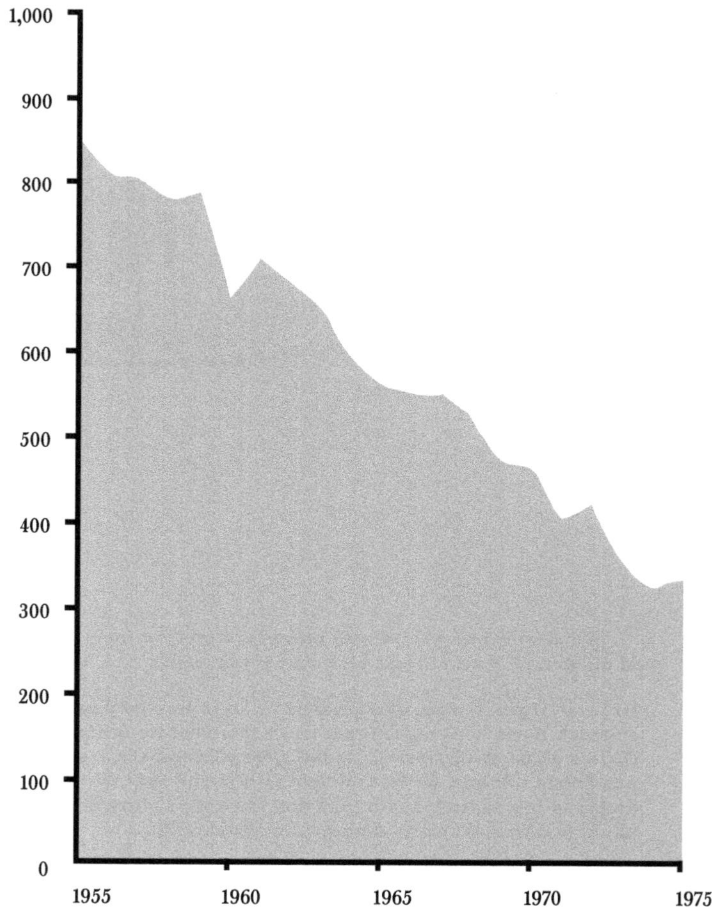

(Source: electoral role. Note: It is likely that the real population levels were as much as 50% higher than shown in the graph owing to low registration level characteristic of such areas.)

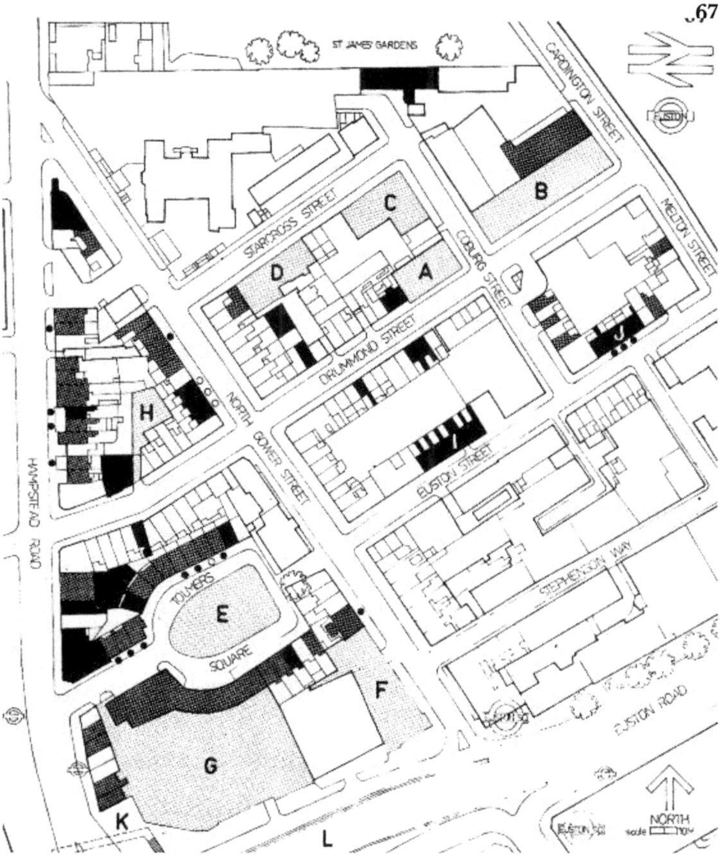

Blight, 1973

■	empty buildings
▒	partially empty-buildings
░	vacant land (including temporary car parks)
•	closing order on basement rooms (1 or more)
o	outstanding abatement notices (section 93 Health Act 1936)
A	6 houses and shops bombed during the war - vacant since
B	12 houses and shops demolished in 1962 to allow bore holes to be sunk for the construction of the Victoria Line - vacant since
C	6 houses demolished in 1968 following a Clearance Order - vacant since
D	7 houses demolished in 1970 following a Clearance Order - vacant since
E	Cinema demolished June 73 - vacant since
F	8 houses demolished in 1969. Site used by Avis
G	Warehouse and factory; demolished in 1970. Used as a car park since
H	Vacant yard: formerly a battery factory and builder's yard
I & J	Houses emptied in 1970 following Clearance Order - left empty since
K	7 houses knocked down in 1962 for road widening - site mostly vacant
L	19 houses and shops demolished in 1964 for Euston Road Underpass and road widening

(Source: author's survey, June 1973, and Camden Council environmental health memo, January 1975)

It was fear that controlled this place . . . apart from war itself, you couldn't have experienced a more war-like experience (Jane French, resident, interview).

Like enemy occupied territory (Gavin Brown, resident, Interview).

Many of the more able people had moved out, leaving a high proportion of pensioners, immigrants and poor people. Those who remained were completely demoralised.

> No one is surprised to see things collapsing any more. Decay and neglect have become 'the way things are'. They are a part of life.
>
> In practice, this means different things for different people. Some people (those that can) give up and move elsewhere. But the majority are not so lucky. . . . These people just sit and wait and watch things falling apart around them. Some are angry, but most are merely disillusioned about everything and everybody and give up all hope of ever being able to do anything constructive. Sometimes there is talk about what a nice place it used to be, but even this is forgotten and gives way to the shame of living in such despicable surroundings (*Tolmers Destroyed*, June 1974).

59

Leaving houses empty and derelict does not merely affect those people who might otherwise have been living in them. It affects the whole community. Empty houses attract vandalism, dossers, damp and rats. Shopkeepers suffer because trade dwindles. Residents suffer if shops have to close down.

In one case, an inhabitated house in Hampstead Road suffers permanent damp because the house next door has had its roof removed. An empty shop in Drummond Street was nick-named 'the pet shop' because people could watch rats playing behind the glass. Eventually the Council came around and white-washed the windows. A symbolic gesture (*Tolmers Destroyed*, June 1974).

60. 'If someone could wave a magic wand and make this place what it was twenty years ago, I'd be the happiest woman alive' (Mrs Dodd, *North London Press*, 13 August 1973).

One of the most frightening things was the uncertainty. No one knew when anything was going to happen. The Council themselves were unable to help as the following notes show. They were compiled from a diary kept by an owner-occupier in No. 15 Tolmers Square.

1959: Notified by LCC of planning application for office development which would mean demolition of house.
1961: Told by LCC architects department that they are considering comprehensive development. Could *take 5 years* before anything happens.
1963: Advised by LCC architects department not to do any expensive decorating or repairs. Redevelopment *in 3 to 5 years.*
1965 (May): Told by GLC valuation department that it will be *at least 5 years* before anything happens.
1965 (November): Camden's planning department say that *demolition may start in 18 months.*
1966: Camden's planning department say that nothing will happen for *5 to 10 years.*
1968 (4 March): Camden's planning department say that CPO will be issued *in 2 years.*
1968 (18 March): Camden's valuation department say that Council now *unable to develop* Tolmers Square.
1969: Levy's agents say that they will be starting a development *in 2 years.*
1973: Receive draft CPO.

61

She was still living in the house in 1975, sixteen years after her first warning. But the house was still threatened by CPO and demolition and she finally gave up and sold to the Council. 'We needn't have gone. We were frightened out of the house . . . I'm very disillusioned with the whole matter' (Ms Zukowski, Interview). Despite the uncertainty, Mr Zukowski painted the outside of the house every 5 years, and not just for money. The last time he painted it was just before he left; *after* a price had been agreed with the Council.

One or two tenants (as opposed to owner-occupiers) also conscientiously maintained their houses in immaculate condition. For example Mr Colson in

Hampstead Road. The houses on either side were empty and derelict and filled with dry rot. Two doors away the house had collapsed completely. The shop on the ground floor was empty and closed, yet he carefully maintained the inside of his own house at the highest standards.

But most people were not so committed, and were reluctant to invest money in maintaining their property which consequently fell further and further into decay.

> Well they're dumps really. There's an outside toilet, you have to go downstairs where it's infested with rats and mice and there's all cracks in the walls and you have to do your own repairs, you can't get anybody else to do them. . . . You can't bring any friends back here. If you do you get the mickey taken out of you at school (Michael Holland, resident aged 15, Interview).

> There were a lot of people round here when I first came. But as the area started running down, people started leaving – to new flats or different areas – they got fed up watching the houses falling down and no one looking after them or doing anything. . . . And I'm still waiting for mine to be pulled down (Maureen Holland, resident, Interview).

> Well, I've lived here eleven years using it as a studio, because I'm a painter. It's always been used by painters, this flat. It's all been running down ever since I've been here. Lots of it has been closed up and allowed to decay – deliberate neglect and malicious neglect too, on the kind of scale where people who wanted to live in better accommodation just couldn't take it any more with their families and just had to move. So the place just died. . . . I'd rather continue to go on living here and working here but the conditions are so unhealthy that I'm going to have to move because it's just fucked me up (Mike Capanaros, *Tolmers: Beginning or End?*).

As a result of years without maintenance and improvement the state of housing was appalling. 'The Director of Housing would say that much of the Tolmers Square housing is among the worst in the Borough' (Council Report, 17 December 1973).

In June 1973 Camden's housing department carried out a survey of almost all the households in the development area (213 in total, comprising 11 owner-occupiers, 102 in unfurnished tenancies, 87 furnished tenancies, and 13 in other tenancies. Hostels were excluded). Of these:

30 per cent had no access to a cooker with an oven.
70 per cent had no access to a sink with hot and cold water.
11 per cent had no access to a sink at all (all of them furnished tenancies).
57 per cent had no access to a bath.

'It is also noteworthy that at least two households did not appear to have access to a W.C.' (Report by Director of Housing to Housing Committee, 11 December 1973).

Where households did have access to facilities they were often shared with other households.

79 per cent shared a WC (many of these were in the back yard).
27 per cent shared a sink, two-thirds of which had only cold water.
30 per cent shared a bath.
Only 9 per cent of the households had exclusive use of a cooker, sink, bath, wash-basin and WC.

There were several cases of overcrowding, especially in the furnished tenancies. 'There were 9 two-person households each occupying only one room, 2 three-person households each living in one room, 1 three-person household living in two rooms, 2 four-person households each living in two rooms and, the most severe case of all, one six-person household living in two rooms' (Report, above). The report concludes – 'the impressions show that a large number of the households in the Tolmers Square area are living in extremely deprived conditions'.

(*Tolmers News*, No. 14)

While the blame for the appalling state of the housing can be attributed primarily to the landlords and developers, who failed to maintain and improve the property, it must be mentioned that the Council did little to remedy the situation. A Housing Liaison Officer working for the Council makes this clear in a report written for the Deputy Director of Housing.

> It was necessary . . . to ask the E. H. I.s [Environmental Health Inspectors] to visit and take out various housing order on the landlord if improvements/repairs were to be done. . . . Visits were made wherever I or a tenant requested but great reluctance was often shown to follow up cases where the landlord failed to
> comply with an order. . . . This has led to an unnecessarily rapid 62
> deterioration of some properties (Report by Dianna Sherston, October 1975).

Perhaps the most surprising thing is that there was no organised opposition from the inhabitants themselves. Although the Tolmers Square Tenants Association was still in existence, despair and cynicism had long since set in. The leading members had mostly got themselves rehoused by the Council and quite naturally did not have the same enthusiasm as when they lived in the area. The Council made no attempt to encourage participation. As Rose Gavin commented, 'They treat us as though we were ignorant and stupid' (*North London Press*, 6 August 1965). It was impossible for the public to find out what was happening, or rather why nothing was happening, and the Council provided no information other than that a development was planned for some time in the future.

In the late 1960s attempts were made by a few tenants to establish an association of some kind, but after a couple of meetings it fizzled out. Neither the established working-class tenants nor the newly arrived immigrants had the degree of political sophistication necessary to break through the almost impenetrable wall put up by the Council bureaucracy or the developers. The only opposition came from a few individuals who were able to get themselves rehoused by making sufficient fuss. To the majority the whole thing just appeared to be 'a story of complete and utter bungling'.

The reasons for the delays, which we will now look into, were
never disclosed. 63

64

4.

Forced into a deal

I would like to stress that it is only by interesting private investment that the Council can hope to redevelop the seven acres which it has earmarked for housing (Letter from Town Clerk to Ministry of Housing and Local Government, 20 October 1967).

A central London housing scheme which was rejected by the Government because it was too expensive may now be built with the help of a private developer (*The Times*, 15 April 1971).

Tolmers Square, just off the Euston Road, is at the centre of one of the crassest property deals in London (*Time Out*, 27 April 1973).

At the end of it all we screwed them for what was a perfectly realistic deal – within the concept that you trade with capitalism to achieve what you want (Peter Best, Labour Councillor, Interview).

Another major scheme is planned at Tolmers Square, NW1, and, subject to receiving full planning consents, is likely to produce a substantial capital surplus which could add some 50p per share to the net asset value (Read, Hurst Brown & Co. (Stockbrokers), Report on Stock Conversion, May 1973).

You can point to any number of schemes in Camden where we've been frustrated. Tolmers Square isn't unique. It's just that it hit the headlines a bit more (Frank Nickson, Deputy Town Clerk, Interview).

That planning blight continued for so long, was not due to lack of effort by the local authorities. But they were constantly thwarted in their attempts to secure a reasonable development by restrictive planning legislation, central Government and above all by the rising costs of land.

The Council tries to plan

In 1965 St Pancras Council ceased to exist. After the reorganisation of London's local Government, Tolmers Square found itself in the newly-formed London Borough of Camden. The LCC was simultaneously replaced by the GLC (Greater London Council). Early in 1965 the GLC proposed that the Tolmers Square area should be designated as a Comprehensive Development Area (CDA) which would give the GLC additional powers to develop the area as a whole. The Town Clerk of Camden objected to this proposal and immediately 'made representations to the Ministry of Housing and Local Government that it should be redeveloped by the Borough of Camden' (Council Minutes, 24 March 1965). The GLC had no real objections to this proposal and it was agreed that Camden should take responsibility for the planning of the area, which became known as the 'Tolmers Square Comprehensive Development Area'. In fact it was never officially designated as a Comprehensive Development Area, and consequently the additional powers for such areas were never available.

Camden's planners enthusiastically started preparing a development scheme. They had to start from scratch as the earlier schemes prepared by the LCC architects' department were never formerly accepted by the Council. The first scheme drawn up by the planners envisaged the following:

600,000 square feet of light industrial/commercial space:
8,000 square feet of office space;
housing for 1,330 people in 1 thirteen-storey 'tower' and 6 seven-storey 'balcony access' blocks;
car-parking space for 500 cars.

The whole site would be redeveloped, apart from one or two newer buildings, with a segregated system of vehicular and pedestrian access. In architectural terms it was an example of the now classic redevelopment schemes of the 1960s; the kind which has subsequently been so heavily criticised for creating desolate and barren environments. But it fulfilled Camden's requirements as seen at that time. There was to be a substantial amount of housing, and the light industrial/commercial space would provide the Borough with a site for locating non-conforming industries from other parts of the Borough. In line with existing central and local government policy there was virtually no office accommodation.

But it was quickly realised that this scheme would not be economically viable. It was estimated that acquisition costs for the land would be in the region of £350,000 per acre on average. As a result there would have to be at least 100,000 square feet of offices to offset the high cost of land, offices being by far the most profitable use.

Central government obstruction

Under legislation introduced by the Labour Government in 1965, specifically to curb office development, it was necessary for councils to apply to the board of Trade for an Office Development Permit (ODP) for any new office buildings of over 3,000 square feet. The Town Clerk therefore wrote to the Board of Trade, but the application was met by a flat refusal to consider any new office building in the area: 'Your proposals are contrary to the spirit of the Government's intention in introducing the Control of Office and Industrial Development Act for dealing in some degree with the problem of congestion in London' (Letter from Board of Trade to Town Clerk, 2 November 1965).

Central Government was also being obstructive on another front. Having decided to carry out a comprehensive development, Camden were naturally keen to acquire any property in the area which came on to the market. One particular property was offered to them in July 1965: Sangers warehouse and factory situated in between Euston Road and Tolmers Square. It consisted of a five-storey building on a site of almost an acre, and the asking price was £400,000; almost £420,000 per acre. Camden wanted to buy it, despite the high cost, and applied to the Ministry of Housing and Local Government for loan sanction (Local Boroughs were not allowed at this time to acquire property without first obtaining permission from the Government to borrow the finance required). The Ministry turned down the request on the grounds that the costs were excessive. (The property was later bought by Stock Conversion, the buildings were demolished, and the vacant site was sold back to Camden ten years later, supposedly cheaply, for £1,000,000 per acre.)

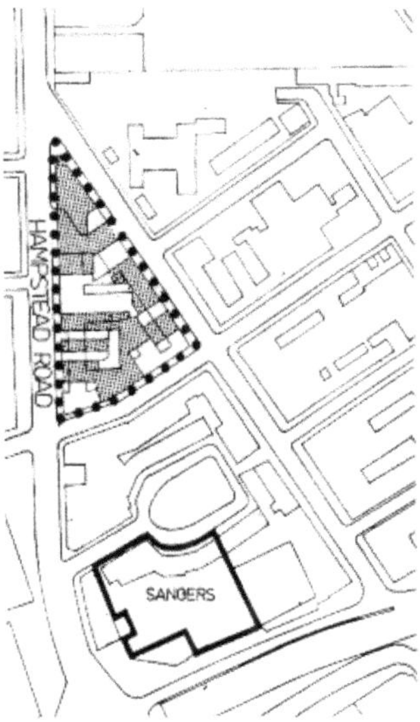

Property owned by Stock Conversion within the 'island site', 1966. (Source: Council records)

A similar thing happened when Camden tried to buy a large part of the 'island site' from Stock Conversion in early 1966. Stock Conversion were perfectly amenable to being bought out, as this letter from Joe Levy (in his role as estate agent for D. E & J. Levy) shows:

> In view of the fact that my clients are so closely connected with your Borough in connection with the development of the Euston Centre and other important properties, nothing would give them greater pleasure than to be able to carry through the sale of this site to you (Letter to Town Clerk, 25 February 1966).

But there was the small question of money. Stock Conversion offered the freehold of all the properties for £330,000 or approximately £460,000 per acre (almost 10 per cent higher than the Sangers price of £420,000 for a less well-sited and broken-up group of properties without complete vacant possession). Once again Camden asked the

Ministry of Housing and Local Government for loan sanction, and once again the Ministry refused saying it was too expensive.

This became a familiar pattern until in November 1966 the Town Clerk was able to write 'the Ministry of Housing and Local Government have informed me that loan sanction will not be forthcoming, at this time, for the purchase of premises in the Tolmers Square Comprehensive Development Area' (Memo to Chief Valuer).

This was a death-blow for the idea of Camden being able to carry out a development on their own. The Labour Government was refusing to allow them to buy property because it was too expensive, and at the same time refusing to allow any offices to be built, the only thing which would enable a scheme to be profitable. The Chairman of the Planning and Development Committee objected strongly.

> I made a personal approach to the Minister at that time saying this was a ludicrous situation. This is some of the worst housing in the Borough and we couldn't redevelop it because of the cost of land. What is supposed to happen? I got a personal letter back, saying, more or less, this is too bad. You really have to reconsider this area for commerce if you can't afford to, or we won't let you, build housing (Roy Shaw, Interview).

The Labour Government was in effect preventing a Labour Council from carrying out a comprehensive scheme to provide badly-needed housing, Sadly, the only protest from the Council was in the form of letters to the Minister, from the Town Clerk and from the Committee chairman, There was no outspoken criticism from the Labour Group and certainly no attempt to organize any political opposition to this regressive Government action. Neither were there any demands that the Government should attack the root causes of the problem.

Escalating land values

The main cause of Camden's problems was of course the very high value of the land over which they had no control. Increasing the 'value' of the land is however a major weapon in the armoury of the developer.

The negotiations over the 'island site' give an insight into the process by which the land values were being forced up. In 1962 Stock Conversion paid £17,000 for six properties with a total site area of 5,300 square feet. This represents a price of £140,000 per acre. Only four years later these same properties (in similar condition) were included in the 'island site' package, for which Stock Conversion were asking Camden to pay £460,000 per acre; an increase in 'value' of over 320 per cent. (The price paid for these six properties was exceptionally low. Nevertheless this example does indicate the principle involved. Information on prices paid for property is not public and therefore it is difficult to build up a complete picture. The information used in this example came from an affidavit presented in court by Stock Conversion during the squatters' court case).

The price being asked represented a 'hope' value; a purely speculative value based on the assumption that an extremely profitable development could be carried out at some time in the future. It bore little relation to the price initially paid for the properties. It was also based on the assumption that the Council would be unable to rezone the area for housing (which would have the effect of bringing the value down) without first obtaining the land. The 'hope' value became self-fulfilling. The high price meant that the Council could not buy the land and rezone it, and furthermore, the high price became accepted as being the 'market value' of the land, so adding to the spiral of soaring land values all over central London.

Stock Conversion could not lose. Either Camden would buy them out, in which case they would make a lot of money, or Camden would make a Compulsory Purchase Order, in which case they would be compensated at the market value which would come to almost the same thing anyway. If neither of these things happened, Stock Conversion would wait until Camden were so desperate that they were forced to consider some form of joint development scheme.

Rise in market land values

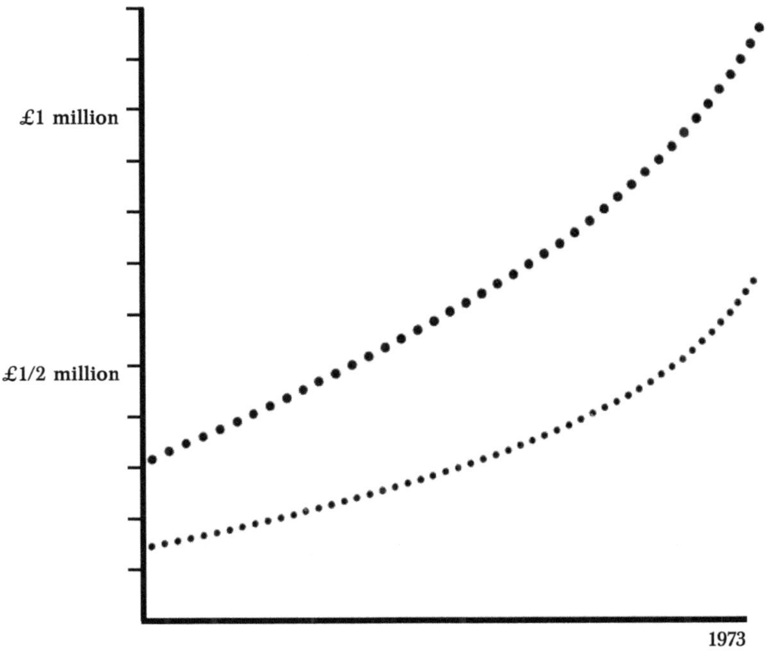

(Source: references in Council reports, details of a few land sales, and discussion with Council valuers. For zoning map see p. 86)

(Significantly, this graph was extremely difficult to compile and the result is a fairly rough approximation. The market value of land can only be assessed by knowing the prices at which land changes hands and this information is not publicly available. Camden's valuation department itself was unable to provide the information.)

Starting a partnership

The Council had reached a dead end as far as their comprehensive scheme was concerned and there appeared to be only one solution. The site would have to be split up. A CPO would be put on certain cheaper sites for housing, while the more expensive sites would be developed in conjunction with private developers. Reluctantly officers gave up the idea of a comprehensive Council redevelopment. A new proposal and planning brief was drawn up and presented to the Planning and Development Committee on 26 June 1967.

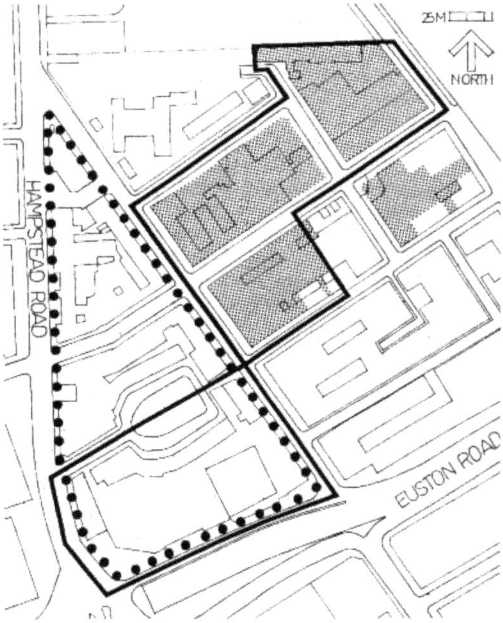

—— boundary of proposed housing area

Council CPO 1968

• • • boundary of 'Levy triangle'

(Source: Council report, April, 1967, and Council Minutes, 14 February 1968)

The housing land would be purchased by compulsory purchase under the Housing Act, and on the remaining sites a joint development would be undertaken with private developers. It should be noted that the areas designated as housing have little to do with planning considerations such as noise and so on, but merely reflect the fact Stock Conversion owned most of the 'island site' (p.77). It is remarkable that the corner site of Euston Road and Hampstead Road could be considered suitable for housing. Nevertheless this policy was adopted and in February 1968 the full Council resolved to make a CPO on a large part of the site to be used for housing. (They did finally leave out the Euston Road and Hampstead Road corner site.)

Meanwhile negotiations were taking place with Levy and other landowners to work out a joint development scheme for what became known as the 'Levy triangle'. The idea of a joint development was first mooted at a meeting between Council officers and Mr Swindon of D. E. & J. Levy in April 1967, and the conflict of interest was soon apparent.

> Mr Swindon thought that the possibility of erecting an hotel should be considered, and possibly some light industrial/warehousing accommodation with perhaps a cinema or an ice rink. He did say, however, that he considered these uses to be secondary to the only use, *offices*, which would make the scheme attractive enough for private development (Notes on Meeting; italics added).

The Council on the other hand wanted to build a 'Health Centre, day nursery, industrial training centre, old people's home, boys hostel and a laundry', as well as a substantial amount of housing (Report, 26 June 1967). Nevertheless they accepted the necessity for offices and wrote again to the Board of Trade urging them to reconsider granting an ODP: 'It is obvious that unless the development includes a reasonable proportion of office development, it will be impossible to consider development for any purpose, including housing' (Letter, 20 October 1967).

This time they asked for a permit for 200,000 instead of the 100,000 square feet asked for previously, as it was considered that nothing short of 200,000 square feet would be enough to show a sufficient return on capital. The irony, of course, was that it was only because the developers were anticipating that they would eventually be able to obtain an ODP that the land prices were so high, The letter also included 'planning' arguments in favour of locating offices on this site despite the fact that Camden obviously did not really believe them. Both Stock Conversion and Camden prepared architectural schemes for the site and several meetings were held between the two parties. Needless to say there was a large discrepancy between the schemes, with Stock Conversion proposing there should be 1.5 times as much floor space on the site as Camden were prepared to accept: a proposal which was way above the zoned plot ratio.

Although primarily interested in the 'Levy triangle', Stock Conversion intimated early in 1968 that they would be interested in participating in a scheme to cover the whole 12.5 acre site between Hampstead Road and Euston Station. It was the first hint of what was to become the 'Levy Deal'.

Conservative rule

In May 1968 the Conservatives gained control of Camden Council. Party politics had played little part in the negotiations to date, as the issue had been handled almost entirely by paid officers. But whereas the Labour Party were hostile to the idea of co-operating with private developers, it was part of Conservative thinking to encourage co-operation with the private sector. Levy lost no time and only weeks after the election wrote to the new Conservative leader proposing a joint scheme for the whole 12.5 acre site. If Camden would consider a joint scheme, Stock Conversion would be prepared to provide a substantial part of the acquisition costs of the land, and would also supply bridging finance to carry out the development. The progressive nature of the idea was pointed out: 'I think you will agree that this would be similar to the various schemes which important property development companies are entering into with local authorities throughout the country in respect of various shopping centres' (Letter, 5 June 1968).

Camden did not take up the offer immediately for two reasons. First they were considering other proposals for the site. There was a possibility that the National Reference Library of Science and Technology could be built there, or a new Town Hall and offices. Second, as already mentioned, they had submitted a CPO on part of the site and were awaiting the outcome of the Minister's decision.

Negotiations continued however for the smaller 'Levy triangle', and in February 1969 Stock Conversion presented new proposals. They suggested the erection of a multi-storey hotel, and European Trade Centre, with accompanying offices. They had raised £30,000,000 to cover the project and wanted to start in a couple of years' time. They admitted that the plot ratio was above that currently allowed, but if the housing site were included, it would average out overall. In any case they thought it would be advisable to 'sterilise' the housing site in case the European Trade Centre needed to expand in the future.

Even the Conservative-controlled Council did not jump at this offer. Alan Greengross, the Chairman of the Planning Committee, considered it was 'socially unacceptable' and went to see the Labour Minister of Land to tell him 'the whole thing was a nonsense'. But he had little success; the Government were intransigent and refused to suggest any alternative solution to Camden's dilemma. Stock Conversion were not prepared to compromise either; they were in no hurry.

Camden's last hopes of being able to carry out even a small development of their own were crushed in August 1970 when the Minister of Housing and Local Government rejected the CPO on the housing land without even holding a public inquiry. The grounds for the rejection were that the land was too expensive; estimated by the District Valuer to be in the region of £375,000 per acre:

> Whilst, therefore. the Minister is most anxious that the Council's house building programme should proceed at the highest possible rate to meet the pressing needs of the area, he does consider that the Council's efforts could be more usefully concentrated on the other sites under consideration by them where major gains would result. In these circumstances he has decided that he should refuse to confirm the Order without hearing the objectors' cases at a public inquiry (Letter, 4 August 1970).

The decision was issued by a Conservative Minister of Housing –Peter Walker, but there is every indication that a similar one was being recommended by Ministry officials to the Labour Minister (Tony Greenwood) before the General Election in June. It is worth recording, though, that there was some opposition to the decision in the upper ranks of the Labour Party. Reg Freeson, later to play an important role in the issue and then Junior Minister to Tony

Greenwood, claims he recommended that the CPO should be granted:

> It was a very finely balanced decision to make, but I think a wrong one was eventually taken. Having recommended in favour of Camden while in Government, I repeated that view when in opposition. But I recognise it was a difficult one (Reg Freeson, Interview).

In Camden the decision united both the Labour and Tory Councillors in protest. The Conservative chairman of the Planning Committee accused the Minister of paying lip-service to the Ministry's own policy of increasing residential accommodation in central London: 'We have been in effect told by the Minister that from a cost point of view this is not suitable land for housing – the implication being there is cheaper land elsewhere. This land is as cheap as we are going to get in Central London' (*Hampstead and Highgate Express*, 25 September 1970). The Labour vice-chairman was also critical: 'It's more than a refusal to understand our problems – it's an inability. I find it incredible that Ministry officials can write bloody stupid letters like this' (Roy Shaw, *Hampstead and Highgate Express*, 25 September 1970).

The implications of this decision for Camden were extremely serious. As the Council spelt out, 'it will now become extremely difficult, if not impossible, to provide further local authority housing in the southern part of the Borough' (Council Minutes, 14 October 1970). Unless, of course, the Council entered into agreements with private developers. There was no other solution. The Council immediately made renewed protests to the Minister, but there was little likelihood of these being listened to. Accordingly Stock Conversion's proposals for a joint development for the whole area were reconsidered, and Alan Greengross, the Chairman of Planning, started negotiations in earnest. Greengross had been arguing all along that the whole area between Hampstead Road and Euston Station should be redeveloped as one site. To consider North Gower Street as a boundary, as was done with the CPO, was completely artificial. Here was an opportunity to solve Camden's dilemma and at the same time obtain the redevelopment of the whole site in a single sweep.

It was just what Stock Conversion had been waiting for, and within a few months tentative terms for a joint development were being placed before the Policy and Resources Committee of the Council. Camden and Stock Conversion as 'partners in this redevelopment will co-operate in the formulation of an appropriate planning application for the area as a whole'. The land would be 'acquired by the two parties working together by such methods as shall prove most appropriate'. Stock Conversion would 'undertake to provide or procure in the first instance all the building finance and finance any land acquisition', although the freehold of all the land would eventually rest with Camden. Camden would be enabled to buy the housing land for £200,000 per acre. In addition there would be a profit sharing scheme for the profits from the commercial development.

The scheme was presented to the Council, and for the first time to the public, as being the only way that Camden would be able to build any housing on the site. The developers were supposedly 'helping' the Council. There was of course no mention of how much office development would be built or any hint of the architectural implications.

The proposed deal with Stock Conversion was claimed by the Conservatives as a significant example of how a progressive council could devise arrangements which were satisfactory both to the community and to private enterprise, while at the same time being socially equitable. In a capitalist society the developer was entitled to a reasonable return on his capital, plus a fee for the skills he brings to bear on the problem. The tax system was there to ensure that he did not make too much. Although not entirely happy with the terms of the agreement, Alan Greengross thought it established an important principle and went so far as to consider it 'a completely new departure in central urban planning. . . . We will now be cut into the equity, the actual take of the company, and not just a share in the profits' (*Hampstead and Highgate Express*, 10 April 1971). 'I thought we'd done a hell of a lot more than any other council in London had ever done' (Interview).

A few months later Labour regained control of the Council.

The beginning of opposition

Until this time, although no one liked it, there was no political opposition within the Council to the deal with Stock Conversion. The negotiations had been carried out in top secret, with only committee chairmen and chief officers aware of what was involved.

The Council had been negotiating with Stock Conversion for five years, over proposals which were likely to affect Camden drastically, and yet this fact was never mentioned once in any non-confidential Council reports. Few councillors knew what was going on, let alone the general public. As for the people who lived and worked in the Tolmers area itself, they only heard rumours. The buildings that they occupied were being demolished or were receiving compulsory purchase orders, and the area was falling apart. Yet they knew nothing about the crucial decisions being made behind the scenes. The TSTA had floundered and the only opposition was from property owners who were fighting the CPOs individually.

But property speculation was starting to become a popular political issue, and several of the new Labour councillors elected in May 1971 were prepared to campaign openly against the property speculators. Brian Loughran, in particular, was publicly opposed to the deal with Levy:

> If commercial [office] development is permitted on housing land in Tolmers Square, then the property speculators will have the green light to buy into any housing development area, force the land prices up, and then 'benevolently' offer a 'new style land deal' in return for planning permission for commercial [office] development. The land available for housing will be continuously eroded (Letter to Hampstead and Highgate Express, 23 April 1971).

In other words Tolmers couldn't merely be regarded as a particular site with a particular problem which affected only the people in the area. Whatever happened here had implications for other areas too.

The view of the majority of the Labour Councillors was much the same as that of the Conservatives; a deal was undesirable but necessary:

> They did not believe there was any way of obtaining Government finance for Council acquisition, and certainly not from a Conservative Government, and therefore the choices were between leaving the place to stagnate and decay, and doing a deal. They were just prisoners in the system, they'd no alternative . . . . No one would have felt they were very keen about doing a deal with Stock Conversion. The gut feeling of the Labour group was that anything that was beneficial to the property developers would be against the interest of the community here. But it was a question of balancing whether the possibility of not doing a deal would be even more damaging (Brian Loughran, Interview).

But a movement grew within the Labour Group of the Council which although not powerful enough to make an open challenge, managed to employ numerous stalling tactics.

> The only foreseeable strategic possibility was to recognise that as long as there was a Conservative Government, we could do nothing, or do a deal with Levy. The only thing to do was to hold on and wait till there was a change of government. And given the kind of noises that nationally the Labour Party was making about the control of development land and so on, to wait for national legislation to change the position.
>
> What was going on was a delaying tactic, combined with attempts to increase opposition to the deal. At that time it was enough to have opposition going on in committee . . . . The major way of stalling was to say that we wanted a comprehensive re-examination of what was involved, and this meant it couldn't be done quickly (Brian Loughran, Interview).

Another attempt was made to persuade the government to change its mind over the issuing of CPOs. The subject was brought up at a meeting (on another issue) between members of the Council and Julian Amery, then Minister of Housing and Construction. Amery promised to look into it but subsequently wrote to the Leader of the Council in a discouraging manner:

> I support your desire to maintain substantial residential communities in areas like Tolmers Square, in the crowded inner reaches of your borough, and since our meeting my officials have met yours to discuss how best to proceed in this particular case. I understand that a possibility has arisen that your Council would acquire the land for housing purposes at much less than its current market value as part of a comprehensive redevelopment of the area in partnership with private developers. Other things being equal, I am sure we would both prefer a solution which would achieve the desired object at less cost to the public purse.
>
> May I therefore leave it that you will consider this possibility, and let me know if it is practicable? If it proves a non-starter, I will then certainly reconsider the question of acquisition under Housing Act powers, although this would have to be done by the submission of a fresh Order, since it is not legally possible to alter the decision on the previous order (Letter, 10 November 1971).

Meanwhile the deal with Stock Conversion was slowly taking shape, although there were a number of technical complications on the planning front: 'It was intended that the Council would seek an ODP and planning permission for the whole of the proposed development (covering some 9.47 acres gross) and use this as the basis for negotiating a partnership arrangement with developers' (Council Notes, 29 October 1971). In order to obtain planning permission for Stock Conversion to build offices, it would be necessary to change the zoning of the area. ('The current zoning inhibits redevelopment on financial grounds', (Report by Director of Planning and Communications to Committee, 24 June 1971). The Director of Planning proposed that the zoning be changed from 'West End' and 'Commerce' to 'Office' and 'Residential'. This would involve a substantial departure from the Initial Development Plan and would therefore have to be referred to the GLC and DOE.

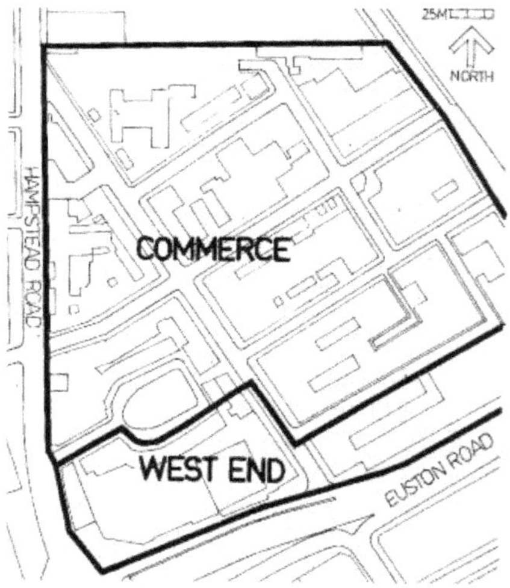

Zoning.
(Source: Administrative County of London Development Plan, 1962)

In planning terms what was envisaged was concentration of offices on the Euston Road frontage, with the remainder of the site developed for housing and ancillary uses. The Director of Planning justified this solution with archaic planning arguments of the 1960s:

> The whole redevelopment could be carried out comprehensively on a basis of modern planning principles, pedestrian segregation, etc . . . The residential element could be designed to achieve a far higher density and standard of environment than would have been possible in a multi-level, mixed use proposal . . . . The end product would be a far better environment which could be designed to link to the areas around (e.g. pedestrian links to Euston Centre across Hampstead Road).

And as for the commercial uses now in the area:

> The Commercial use class is no longer acceptable in this area (Report by Director of Planning and Communications to Committee, 24 June 1971).

Only six years previously the Director of Planning had proposed a development with no offices, and a large amount of commercial and industrial space, The present scheme was a complete reversal. It would appear to be a case of planning merely providing a post-rationalisation for market forces,

The Town Clerk was also negotiating with Stock Conversion in an attempt to get the best terms possible. The main bone of contention was over the precise amount of offices. Stock Conversion were naturally trying to build as much as possible, and originally claimed that 500,000 square feet was necessary for a viable project, whereas the Council was unwilling to allow more than 250,000. Stock Conversion produced detailed costing purporting to show that 325,000 square feet was an absolute minimum, and they threatened to abandon the project if this was not granted. Camden's valuer produced his own costing, and very successfully persuaded Stock Conversion to agree to 250,000.

Because of these protracted discussions and negotiations, coupled with the stalling tactics of Loughran and others, it was September 1972 before the Policy and Resources Committee approved the development in principle. One month later the Planning and Communications Committee approved a detailed scheme 'subject to the Policy and Resources Committee being satisfied as to the financial considerations'. But again the Committee stalled, telling the officers to go back for better terms, and asking for a complete financial appraisal. Finally, in January 1973, the Council approved the Heads of Agreement for a deal with Stock Conversion which subsequently became known as the Levy Deal.

The Levy Deal

> The scheme now put before the Council comprises 250,000 square feet gross of office space and 120,000 sq ft of mixed commercial uses including industry and storage. . . . An area of approximately 8.5 acres gross will be transferred to the Council for housing purposes at a price equivalent to £200,000 per acre gross. . . . this will provide a site for approximately 600 dwellings.

The details were as follows:

> The Council and the developers as joint partners in the development will co-operate in the formulation of the planning application for the whole area in accordance with the Council's overall planning brief.
>
> The land at present not owned by either of the parties to the development to be acquired by the parties working together by such methods as are appropriate in the circumstances. The Council will endeavour to obtain compulsory purchase powers for any properties anywhere in the redevelopment area which it is not possible to acquire by private treaty.
>
> Where owned or acquired by the developers the land to be used for residential development to be transferred to the Council at a price equivalent to £200,000 per acre gross, subject to the overall cost of this land to the

developers not exceeding £650,000 per acre later increased to £680,000). No interest or shortfall charges will be included.

The land to be used for commercial development to be retained by the developers or, if acquired by the Council, sold to the developers at the acquisition cost plus fees etc.

The developers would agree to the development taking place as one or more contracts and if necessary in stages. The residential development to be financed by the Council.

The Council to make or support the application for an Office Development Permit.

The freehold of the housing area will rest in the Council and the Council will have full control of that part of the development.

In addition, the developers are prepared to grant to the Council a share in the profits of the office and commercial development provided the initial yield to the developers exceeds 10 per cent, and we have authorised the officers to pursue the negotiations on this aspect and to report back with an acceptable formula (Council Minutes, 10 January 1973).

The Levy Deal scheme, showing sketch plan of Stock Conversion's proposal for commercial and office development, with store heights.
(Source: drawing by Kaye, Firmin and Partners)

The Levy Deal was in no way unique, but was just one of many so-called 'joint schemes' that local authorities were entering into at that time. More and more schemes in central city areas could only take place with the active co-operation of the local authorities, who provided anything from help with the assembly of the site by compulsory purchase, to major concessions on planning permission – in return for such 'planning gains' as road widening or council flats. And for councils, faced with the stranglehold of developers, soaring land prices and inadequate legislative powers, it was the only way out. As the Council report continued:

> In our opinion the foregoing proposals represent the only way in which the Council will attain the planning objective of a comprehensive development providing a satisfactory housing content in a part of the Borough where it is desperately needed and, at the same time, ensure that the land can be acquired at a cost acceptable to the Department of the Environment for subsidy purposes and considerably below the current market value (Council Minutes, 10 January 1973).

Exposing the issue

Up to this time, details of the negotiations with Stock Conversion were confidential internal Council business. And for the Council, it was merely one small piece of business being dealt with in the normal manner. Although the matter had been discussed a number of times by the whole Labour Group, only a few councillors really understood what was going on, or showed much interest.

But there were a few Labour Councillors who realised that one of the greatest dangers was that the deal might slip through unnoticed, as happened with the LCC deals over Centre Point and the Euston Centre. In mid-1972 they started trying to raise it as a public issue, in order to galvanise wider support.

> Attempts were made during that period to get publicity for the fact that this was going on. What this deal was about. Particularly we asked the Council officers to do calculations on what was in it for Levy. Partly as a stall and partly as a relevant aspect of the thing to see if the Council and the community were being conned or not (Brian Loughran, Interview).

In June 1972 Brian Loughran appeared in a programme entitled 'Who Owns Britain?' in the BBC2 *Money Programme* series. The whole issue of rising land prices was raised and Loughran pointed out how the 'provisional wing of the property speculators' were 'holding the community to ransom and getting their pound of flesh out of the demand for land for housing needs in London'. Loughran had deliberately informed the BBC researchers about the Levy Deal and for the first time pictures of Tolmers Square appeared on television.

As a result of this programme, the Counter Information Service (CIS) picked up the case. They were in the process of compiling 'The Recurrent Crisis of London', an 'Anti-Report on the Property Developers'; a report which attempted to make the public aware of how property companies worked and of the relationship between property speculation and the housing crises. Tolmers Square was cited as a classic example of how rising land values, caused by the developers, were making it impossible for councils to build housing. Brian Loughran gave CIS a confidential report prepared by the Town Clerk in which the Chief Valuer had prepared a financial appraisal of the Levy Deal. According to this report, the sums involved were as follows:

Developer's costs:	
land acquisition	£ 7,000,000
cost of land finance prior to completion of development	£ 1,594,000
demolition and construction costs:	
offices	£ 6,100,000
commercial	£ 1,640,000
bridging finance	£ 774,000
total:	£ 17,108,000
less land sold to Council (8 1/2 acres gross at £200,000 per acre)	£ 1,700,000
total cost to developer:	£ 15,408,000
Income from commercial development (per annum)	
offices: 190,000 square feet (net) (rent at £6 per square foot)	£ 1,140,000
commercial: 108,000 square feet (net) (rent at £1.75 per square foot)	£ 189,000
car spaces: 200 (rent £200)	£ 40,000
total annual income:	**£ 1,369,000**

(Source: Report by Town Clerk, 15 December 1972)

On these figures, assuming an investor would accept a 5 per cent yield (a generally accepted figure), the value of the commercial development when completed would be £27,380,000 (£1,369,000 x 100/5 (p, 25). In other words Stock Conversion would make almost *£12 million profit.* (£27,380,000 - £15,408,000 = £11,972,000). This figure was incredible enough, and yet there were good reasons for believing that even this was an underestimate. It is standard valuation practice to use current market figures for rentals when making estimates of future income from a development. In estimating the annual income from the offices, the Town Clerk used a figure of £6 per square foot per year rental. CIS argued that if office rents continued to rise at the rate then prevailing, by the time the development was completed, £8 per square foot would be more realistic. In which case the profits would not be £12 million but *£20 million.*

Of course not all of these profits would have gone to Stock Conversion, as the financial institutions who put up the capital would have demanded a share too. Nevertheless Stock Conversion would have made a staggering amount of money. The tax system would have had little effect on their profits as at that time property companies enjoyed a double tax immunity. First, by holding on to their buildings rather than selling them, they avoided Capital Gains Tax. Second, they were then able to borrow against the ever-appreciating value of their new assets to finance further borrowings, and could deduct interest on these borrowings for tax purposes.

The publishing of the CIS report in February 1973 sparked off a round of protest against the Levy Deal; the new figures on the profits being made by Levy providing valuable ammunition. The *Hampstead and Highgate Express*, *Time Out* and *Private Eye* took up the story, followed later by the *Sunday Times*. As a result of this publicity, 'Tolmers Square became a kind of microcosm – a particular example of property development that was going on, not just in Camden – but all over Central London. . . . its receiving this publicity gave it an importance compared with other sites in London. It got to a stage where people could refer to Tolmers Square as a code for property speculation in the same way as it was possible to refer to Centre Point' (Brian Loughran, Interview). The delaying tactics within committee had given time for publicity, and criticism was mounting.

But the criticism appeared to have little effect on the Council who were in the last stages of tying up the Deal. In an attempt to stave off the growing opposition, they announced that they had worked out a formula whereby they would have a share in the profits. In the original proposal, prepared by the Conservatives in 1971, Camden was to have a larger share in the profits from the office sector, but when detailed negotiations started the idea was flatly rejected by Stock Conversion on the grounds that there would be an initial loss to the company. However, after pressure from Camden a profit-sharing scheme was devised.

> Camden's share would be calculated as a percentage of the profits made on the first year's rental. Costs and a 3 per cent management charge would be deducted from the gross income to obtain the net income. From the net income, Stock Conversion would then deduct a sum equal to 10 per cent return on the total cost of the non-residential development. The Council would then get' 20 per cent of the sum which represents the return in excess of 10 per cent but not exceeding 12 per cent of the total cost, land) 30 per cent of the sum which represents the return in excess of 12 per cent' (Council Minutes, 16 May 1973). Whatever percentage of the rental the Council got in the first year, they would go on getting for as long as the development stood.

But as a local paper pointed out, the ratepayer was unlikely to benefit much from this arrangement: 'The snag is that if, as is quite possible, profits in the first year are so low that the Council gets nothing at all, it would continue to get nothing for ever' (*Hampstead and Highgate Express*, 25 May 1973).

On 8 May, in a *Today* programme on Thames Television, Brian Loughran made a last-ditch attempt to rock the boat. He compared Camden's problem in dealing with Levy with the problem of deciding whether to pay ransom to a kidnapper or a hijacker, or submitting to blackmail. Levy demanded an apology claiming that he had been libelled, but Loughran refused to apologise as he thought that a court case might force Levy to show his hand. For Levy to have demonstrated that Loughran's remarks were unfair comment, he would have had to reveal quite a bit more about his operations. Unfortunately, rather than become involved in a court case, the Town Clerk disowned Loughran's statement and Thames also apologised.

Levy deal gets the go ahead

This last-ditch attempt appeared to fail, and on 16 May 1973 – two years after the officers had been asked 'as a matter of urgency' to prepare a planning brief – the Council decided 'that an agreement be executed with Stock Conversion and Investment Trust Limited'. The Deal was approved 'with a conspicuous absence of rejoicing' (*Hampstead and Highgate Express*, 25 May 1973). Peter Best, the Labour spokesman, emphasised that they didn't like the deal but that there was no alternative: 'By doing a deal which is against our principles we are making provision for 1,600 people to be housed here. I think we are doing the right thing' (*ibid.*) The Conservatives accused the Labour majority of being in a 'schizophrenic dilemma'; 'Half of them don't want to go on with it; the other half want to go but don't know why' (*ibid.*). They themselves were in favour of a deal but thought that better terms could have been negotiated.

Nevertheless, the Levy Deal was approved. All that remained was a formal signing of contracts.

5.

Claudius to the rescue

The contradictions inherent in late property boom produced the Claudius offer (Christopher Booker, Interview).

My motivation, if you like, has been to take Tolmers Square as an example of the sort of thing which is happening; of the way in which London is being raped. And my view is that if you're going to be raped, you might as well be paid for it. And we felt that we couldn't stop Tolmers Square being raped, but what we might be able to stop, is the profits from Tolmers Square ending up in a few private hands which in any event had enough money already – and that's what we've been doing (Bennie Gray, *Man Alive*, 28 November 1973).

They, Claudius, challenge Levy

THE SUNDAY TIMES, JUNE 3 1973

London property developer gets no-profits challenge

'No-profit' developers make offer to Camden

Profits for the people

Times, 4 June 1973, *Sunday Times*, 3 June 1973,
Hampstead and Highgate Express, 8 June 1973.

The Claudius Offer

On 1 June 1973, only days before the contract between Camden and Stock Conversion was to be irrevocably signed, Camden received an offer which was to make the Tolmers Square development into a national issue. The offer was from Claudius Properties Limited, a £100 company, trading as the Tolmers Square Association. The opening letter read as follows:

Dear Sir,

We enclose an offer, subject to contract, which sets out the basis upon which Tolmers Square Association are prepared to enter into a joint scheme with Camden Council for the Tolmers Square Development.

We understand that your negotiations with another company have reached an advanced stage. Nevertheless many of your councillors have expressed grave reservations about the terms offered, but have accepted the arrangement in the absence of a bona fide and constructive alternative.

We are confident that this new offer, although in many respects similar in outline to that discussed with another company, would bring substantially greater advantages to Camden. Under the terms of the offer, Tolmers Square Association proposes to enter into this development in a non-profit making capacity, and in full co-operation with the Council.

As a result of this we are able to offer very much more advantageous terms to Camden than those offered by the other company. Firstly, Camden will receive their 8.5 acres of housing land for a nominal sum, i.e. £1 per acre, representing a saving to the Council of £1. 7 million. Secondly, all the surplus from the development will be directed towards providing social services, including low-rent housing – any such projects to be undertaken only after full consultation with yourselves. The surplus is expected to be in excess of £5 million.

It is for these reasons that we have no hesitation in asking you to give the most urgent attention to our offer. We are well aware your Council's requirement for housing on this site as soon as possible and we would like to emphasise that we and our professional advisers are well equipped to conduct this matter without delay. We also feel it may be of interest that Gollins, Melvin, Ward have agreed to act as our architects.

We are confident that our reasons for making this offer will be endorsed by the Council, and we would therefore be pleased, at a time to be agreed, to welcome onto the board of Tolmers Square Association a majority representation from the Council or its nominees.

We look forward to having your comments on these proposals and shall hold ourselves available for discussions at such time as is convenient to you.

Yours faithfully, Christopher Booker & Bennie Gray - directors.

The terms of the offer were as follows:

> This offer to Camden Council, hereinafter known as the Council, is made by Claudius Properties Limited trading as Tolmers Square Association, herein after known as Tolmers Square Association. The offer concerns the site shown on the accompanying plan, generally known as the Tolmers Square Development. The plan shows the site divided into two sections, marked respectively 'A' and 'B'. The provisions of the offer, which is subject to contract, planning permission and all other necessary consents being obtained, are as follows;
>
> 1. Camden and Tolmers Square Association as joint partners in the development will co-operate in securing all necessary planning permissions and consents for the whole area, comprising sites 'A' and 'B' (see plan). This is to include 250,000 sq, ft. gross of office space, 120,000 sq, ft. of mixed commercial use and 200 car spaces, which will be constructed on Site 'A' (the 2 acres fronting Euston Road).
>
> 2. The land at present not owned by Camden or Tolmers Square Association will be acquired by the parties working together by such methods as are appropriate in the circumstances. The Council will obtain compulsory purchase powers for any properties which it is not possible to acquire by private treaty.
>
> 3. Where not owned by the Council, Site 'B' (the land to be used for housing) will be transferred to the Council at a sum equivalent to £1 an acre, subject to the overall cost of this land to Tolmers Square Association not, exceeding £680,000 per acre.
>
> 4. Site 'A' (the land to be used for commercial development) is to be acquired by Tolmers Square Association or, if acquired by the Council, using compulsory purchase powers where necessary, sold by them to Tolmers Square Association at the acquisition cost plus fees etc. The overall cost of Site 'A' shall not exceed a sum, which sum shall be disclosed to the Council (having regard to all the circumstances our professional advisers are satisfied that this sum is appropriate).
>
> 5. The Council will make or support the application for an Office Development Permit for 250,000 sq. ft. gross of office space.
>
> 6. The freehold of the housing area, Site' B', will vest in the Council and the Council will have full control of that part of the development.
>
> 7. Tolmers Square Association in consultation with the Council will direct all profits from the development on Site 'A' towards providing social services, and low-rent housing in the Borough of Camden. These profits are expected to be substantially in excess of £5 million.
>
> 8. This offer shall be dependent upon all the above provisions being fulfilled as part of an integrated process.

The letter and terms were accompanied by a letter from merchant bankers Edward Bates and Son, offering to provide the necessary finance, and a letter from chartered surveyors Richard Ellis offering to undertake the project management.

In other words, Claudius was offering to carry out the same physical development as Stock Conversion, only, being a non-profit making company, all the profits (estimated at over £5 million), would be transferred immediately to the Council. In addition Camden Council was offered a majority on the board of Claudius, so giving the Council complete control over the operation.

This proposal represented a potential breakthrough in a stalemate situation. Camden were being offered an alternative to the Levy Deal; an alternative which looked realistic enough to work. Furthermore, if this could work here, it could be applied to any other

situation where Councils were faced with having to make disadvantageous deals with developers. It appeared to be a real breakthrough with national significance.

What, who, how and why?

The Claudius proposal was the brainchild of two journalists, Christopher Booker and Bennie Gray. Christopher Booker, in some ways an old-fashioned liberal, read history at Cambridge, worked for the Liberal Party, was the first editor of *Private Eye* and the resident scriptwriter for *That was the Week That Was*. In 1972 he wrote *Goodbye London* with Candida Lycett Green which firmly established him as a dedicated conservationist. Bennie Gray's credentials were equally eccentric. After obtaining a first class honours degree in Engineering at Cambridge, he became a property tycoon working in house conversions for which purpose he set up over 20 property companies, all with Roman names. In 1964 he launched the Antique Supermarket followed three years later by the Antique Hypermarket in Kensington High Street. In 1969 he started writing articles about property in the Sunday Times and in the Evening Standard. His business ventures made him extremely wealthy, so that at the time of the Claudius offer he lived in a large house in Hampstead, and drove a convertible Mustang. His political sympathies were unclear. One year previous he had been a Trotskyite, running with the then Socialist Labour League, (although never a member), but he had given them up and could perhaps best be described as a liberal cavalier.

65. Christopher Booker and Bennie Gray

Booker and Gray started their partnership as investigative freelance journalists early in 1973, and launched straight into the subject of local authority/developer deals. In doing the research for *Goodbye London*, Booker had unearthed over 400 development schemes within London which were at the planning stage. More developments were being talked about than at any time before or since, and yet the general public was in an extraordinary state of ignorance about what was going on in the planning world. It was still a time of 'planning megalomania', with vast areas being considered for massive redevelopments. The 96 acres of Covent Garden was the largest single proposal, and the 11.5 acres of Tolmers Square came fourth or fifth in the list.

In a series of articles for the *Sunday Times*, Booker and Gray tried to expose the extent to which property companies were getting exemption from tax, and the inequity of current deals being made between Councils and developers. Also, they plugged the fact that local authorities did not need to make these deals, as it was they who held the trump card; the power to give or withhold planning permissions.

They had considerable success. One of their first articles was on Taylor Woodrow's involvement in St Katherine Docks. The article was carefully timed to appear the Sunday before the GLC elections. The following morning 'we were summoned to meet Sir Desmond Plummer and we had a very stormy interview with him in which he said virtually "you've lost me the election", (Christopher Booker, Interview). Of course the Tories were going to lose the election anyway, but St Katharine Docks did become a major issue. One of the first things Reg Goodwin did when he took office was to announce that the whole development would be re-examined.

It was with this previous success behind them, that they wrote an article which appeared in the *Sunday Times* on 22 April 1973, entitled 'Camden's crumbs from £20 million land profit'. The article began: 'A major deal now being concluded by the London Borough of Camden has raised in an acute form the thorny question of whether local authorities, especially in London, get the best possible deal for ratepayers when they undertake joint ventures with property developers'. It went on to castigate Camden for thinking of going ahead with the Levy deal.

But Camden took little notice of their arguments, and three weeks later made the decision to go ahead with the Deal. Booker and Gray then considered whether there was anything they could do to stop it. Of all the schemes they had considered it was the one most obviously unbalanced towards the developers, and closest to home in that they were both residents of Camden. The solution came to them two days later as they were driving up the Finchley Road:

> I think it came up as a joke. Why don't we do the development. And then the joke became slightly less of a joke, and as we thought, it became very clear that the security of the land plus the planning permission would enable anybody who could offer it as title, to raise whatever money was necessary to do the development. So in the space of about four minutes – to be precise – going from Boundary Road to the Odeon Swiss Cottage – what started as a joke turned into a serious proposition; that we would make an offer to buy the site and do the development in precisely the same way that Stock Conversion wanted to do it, with the difference that the profits would go back to Camden in their entirety. So by the time we got half way up Fitzjohn's Avenue, we were absolutely trembling with excitement at the brilliance of this idea (Bennie Gray, Interview).

> The question that occupied us for the second half of Fitzjohn's Avenue was where we were going to get the 30 million quid. . . at which point I confessed that although I am an unworldly soul, living in a rented basement, I had a friend at Cambridge who was a merchant banker . . . so I rang him up that night to put him the proposition: do you think a merchant bank, not necessarily your own, would be prepared to lend money? He listened with unaccustomed eagerness (Christopher Booker, Interview).

The next few days were spent assembling a team of architects, solicitors, and chartered surveyors who were actually capable of carrying out the development. 'What we wanted was a team of advisers that was absolutely unimpeachable; the best in every field' (Bennie Gray, Interview). There was little difficulty. Richard Ellis, one of London's most influential estate agents, agreed to act as agents and also to undertake the project management. Gollins, Melvin, Ward – who designed the P & 0 building, the Commercial Union tower and Castrol House – were enthusiastic about acting as architects. Booker and Gray were already in consultation with a top planning lawyer, David Widdicombe QC, and one of the country's leading valuation experts, Dr Ernest Wood, on the intricate problems of planning and compensation. Claudius itself was a limited £100 company that Gray and his wife had set up a few years earlier, but which had never been used. Booker bought a £1 share and became a director. As for the matter of raising £20 million, merchant bankers Edward Bates were more than willing to lend the money. Within 24 hours of being contacted, two of their directors had agreed in principle to raise the money. 'They finally wrote us the letter of commitment saying that they would provide more than £30 million, to buy the land and do the deal. And we ran out of the office with that piece of paper in a state of total surrealism, I mean it was ludicrous this piece of paper – £30 million' (Bennie Gray, Interview). The offer was delivered to the Town Clerk the same day.

The Claudius offer caused considerable excitement in the press, initiated by an 'exclusive' in the Sunday Times. The following day, major articles appeared in *The Times*, *Financial Times* and *Guardian* and during the ensuing three months, events were covered closely in the local and national press with several major articles in various weeklies.

It was a brilliant liberal reformist solution, enabling social gains to be made without requiring any changes in the rules of the game. Booker and Gray were not revolutionaries. They were not demanding the nationalisation of land, nor were they challenging property speculation *per se*; they merely challenged the excessive sums that speculators were making, and the huge imbalance of advantage between Councils and developers. As Gray said, 'All we are doing in Tolmers Square is to demonstrate that it is Camden and Camden alone which is making these enormous profits possible. And that it is feasible to devise ways of ensuring that these profits go back to Camden' (*Sunday Times*, 3 June 1973), and as they wrote later:

> There can be no question that local authorities seriously under-estimate their power in controlling the many major property developments in which they are directly involved. Even without a change in existing legislation to enable them to conduct commercial developments themselves, they already have power to ensure that every penny of the vast profits generated by planning concessions comes back to the community on whose behalf those concessions are made (*Observer*, 14 October 1973).

The Claudius proposal was able to demonstrate this better than any number of newspaper articles or theoretical propositions.

Camden's reaction

Camden's reaction to the Claudius offer was naturally cautious. They were not accustomed to having young journalists 'appearing like Sir Galahad' to rescue them from their plight. Frank Dobson, the new Leader of the Council, was reported as saying 'I have to look at it with a jaundiced eye, if only because I was not brought up to believe in Father Christmas' (*Hampstead and Highgate Express*, 8 June 1973). But Camden did look at the offer very seriously. The signing of the Deal with Stock Conversion was held up, and for the next three months Camden's officers examined the offer from top to bottom.

One of the early points of dispute was over whether the Claudius offer could stand up financially. The Claudius costings were as follows:

Costs:

Acquisition of 8.5 acres housing land [Not more than £680,000 per acre, as in Levy Deal]	£ 5,780,000
Acquisition of 2 acres commercial land [A maximum figure, unlikely to be approached]	£ 8,000,000
Cost of finance prior to completion [2.5% above current Interbank rate capitalised at 6 month intervals]	£ 5,900,000
Demolition & construction cost including garaging:	
Offices – 250,000 sq ft gross (£24 per sq ft)	£ 6,100,000
Commercial – 120,000 sq ft gross (£13.68 sq ft)	£ 1,640,000
Bridging finance (2.5% above current Interbank rate for a period of 12 months)	£ 920,000
Fees: project management	£ 420,000
letting & disposal	£ 570,000
legal	£ 200,000
Contingencies – say	£ 470,000
	£ 30,000,000

Summary of income from commercial development (per annum):

190,000 sq. ft offices net @ £8 sq ft	£ 1,520,000
108,000 sq ft commercial net @ £3 sq ft	£ 324,000
200 car parking spaces @ £200 per annum	£ 40,000
	£ 1,884,000
Thus, assuming an investment yield of 5% (based on current market conditions) completed commercial development would be worth:	£ 37,700,000

(Source: Claudius costings, 11 June 1973)

So on these figures Camden stood to make a minimum of £7.5 million. In fact, Booker & Gray argued that Camden would make over £10 million, as they allowed an excessive amount for the acquisition of the land. Camden's valuers agreed with Claudius' estimate of costs for the scheme, but were not prepared to accept their figures for the value of the completed development. They challenged the assumptions that offices could be rented at £8 per square foot and commercial for £3 per square foot, claiming that £6.50 and £2 were more realistic for this area. They also argued that the indications of the market at the present time are that a slightly higher yield than 5% will be required for the office development (say 5.5% i.e. 18 years purchase) and an even higher yield for the commercial development' (Council Minutes, 25 June 1973).

Using these figures they obtained a capital value of £26,838,000, which meant that Claudius would make a loss of over £3 million instead of a profit of over £7 million.

190,000 sq ft offices net @ £6.50 p.f.s.	£ 1,235,000
108,000 sq ft commercial/industrial net @ £2 p.f.s.	£ 216,000
Car parking – 200 spaces @ £200 p.a.	£ 40,000
	£ 1,491,000
Years purchase	18
Estimated capital value	£ 26,838,000

(Source: Report by Town Clerk, 22 June 1973)

The variance in the two figures shows the extent to which valuation is far from being an exact science. Both predictions were made by experts. Booker claimed that 'Camden valuers are always three years behind the times', whereas Camden claimed that Booker and Gray were over-optimistic and later cited the ensuing slump in values as proof. Who was right will, of course, never be known In any case as far as Camden were concerned it did not matter who was right, providing that under the proposed deal no liabilities would fall on Camden. After lengthy exchanges between Camden, Edward Bates and Claudius, the Town Clerk was able to report that while he had reservations about the extent of the profits 'there is every indication now that an agreement could be concluded which would ensure that no financial risk would remain with the Council' (Report by Town Clerk, 6 September 1973).

The main stumbling block then became the question of the CPO on Stock Conversion's land. Under the Claudius proposal Camden would have to put a Compulsory Purchase Order on all of Stock Conversion's property; roughly six acres. Stock Conversion would be unlikely to give up easily, and the Council had to try and predict whether the Minister would grant the Compulsory Purchase Order, and whether Stock Conversion would be able to cause delays. The Council had good reason to be concerned about the possibility of a CPO being turned down by the Secretary of State, as a far less controversial CPO on Lissendon Gardens, a privately rented housing estate, had just been turned down without even a public inquiry.

Stock Conversion, had in fact made no public response to the Claudius offer, other than the normal 'no comment' and a reported 'I'm slightly horrified' (*Sunday Times*, 3 June 1973) from a senior executive. However, they were clearly perturbed, and on 19 July wrote to the Town Clerk requesting a meeting.

At the meeting eleven days later, Stock Conversion expressed concern that the Council had not yet signed the contract (an Englishman's word is his bond and so on), and in what appeared to be an attempt to discredit Gray's name, handed over a list of companies owned by him. It seemed evident that if Camden decided to go with Claudius, Stock Conversion would fight all the way.

Compulsory purchase procedure, like much of planning law, is a combination of judicial and political decision-making. In the end the decision at the discretion of the Secretary of State, and in an attempt to anticipate what this might be, the Town Clerk wrote to the DoE requesting an 'off the record discussion' with the Secretary of State or the Minister of Housing and Construction, in order to 'discuss informally the present situation' (Letter, 27 June 1973). This request was turned down:

> The decision of your Council, subject to their being satisfied as to the status of Claudius Properties Ltd, and the financial viability of its proposal, seems likely to be influenced to a considerable extent by their assessment of the respective chances of a Compulsory Purchase Order being confirmed in each case, and that this would be bound to figure in any discussion with Ministers. For this reason it does not appear to us that even an informal discussion such as you suggest would be appropriate, or indeed that it could serve any useful purpose, since Ministers could not express any view (Letter from DoE to Town Clerk, 17 July 1973).

After this positively unhelpful reply from the DoE, Camden sought advice from George Dobry QC, Camden's Legal Counsel, who subsequently obtained notoriety for his review of development control. George Dobry's 'Opinion' was unequivocally clear. Camden should reject the Claudius offer and continue with the Levy Deal. On the main issue of the CPO Dobry states: "In our opinion the Secretary of State would be unlikely in the circumstances of this case to confirm a Compulsory Purchase Order of the land at present owned by Stock Conversion in the face of an objection by Stock Conversion' (Dobry Opinion, 31 August 1973).

He explained that, in the first place, the Secretary of State might not have the legal power to make the Order; and that, in the second place, even if he did have the legal power, he probably would not use it. Dobry continued:

> One holds no particular brief for Stock Conversion but one must recognise that they are well established and experienced developers with considerable economic and building expertise. Normally the Department favours partnership schemes with experienced developers and for many years has commended in its Bulletins and Policy Statements the use by local authorities of commercial experience of major development Companies. If one adds to it the fact that the Camden Council have reached an advanced stage of negotiations with Stock Conversion it would at least expect an equivalent degree of expertise from the new partner. In these circumstances, we frankly think it inconceivable that the Department would view with favour the replacement of Stock Conversion at this late stage by Claudius Properties.

And later on:

> In any event, although we are not qualified to assess the viability of the proposals from the financial point of view, it does seem to us that as at present put forward the Claudius offer is somewhat nebulous. It certainly sounds attractive and interesting and may well be public spirited. It is supported to some extent by the advice of extremely experienced valuers and has some encouragement from one of the leading Merchant Bankers; but at the end of the day one cannot escape the fact that the Council is being asked to commit itself to a partnership with a £100 Company with no track record of any major development scheme. It is not clear that the Company itself can offer anything which it would not be open to the Council to obtain in its own right. This of course is implicitly recognised in the suggestion that members of the Council should form a majority of the Board.

He concludes:

> Having studied the correspondence with Claudius with the utmost care and some sympathy, therefore, we do not see how it can be treated seriously in the context of the present redevelopment scheme. . . . In the hard world of an extremely unstable economic situation and all the difficulties facing the property market the Council would in our opinion be doing far less than their statutory duty in relation to the provision of housing accommodation if they abandoned at this stage the partnership laboriously worked out with Stock Conversion and risked further delay to the provision of some 600 housing units in the Tolmers Square area (Dobry Opinion, 31 August 1973).

Even before reading this Opinion, Booker and Gray felt that Camden was treating them unfairly: 'My impression was that they were probing, not in the spirit of trying to make sure that we could rescue them from their plight, but they were going to crack us if they could, because in fact they resented what we had done' (Bennie Gray, Interview). Dobry's 'unusually vehement' Opinion put the lid on it. By the time Booker and Gray received a copy of Dobry's Opinion there were only four days before the crucial meeting of the Labour Group at which a decision was likely to be made, and the Opinion was likely to carry a lot of weight. There was not time to obtain a written opinion from their own counsel, but they prepared a 'commentary' based on a meeting held with Glover QC and their solicitors, Landau and Landau. This commentary, as well as clarifying the issues at stake, also shows the extent to which even top-class legal advice is not politically neutral. Sadly, few opposition groups can afford the services of a QC.

> Dobry states that 'the Secretary of State would be unlikely . . . to confirm a CPO of the land at present owned by Stock Conversion, in the face of an

objection by Stock Conversion'. He goes on to say that there are two grounds in Law upon which Stock Conversion would be able to challenge such a CPO. First that 'a viable and acceptable scheme' has already been approved by Camden, and second that 'the primary objective of any such CPO would not be to achieve a better planning situation but merely to improve the financial return to the Council'.

This, then, is the nub of Dobry's argument – that a CPO on Stock Conversion's land could be legally challenged on two grounds. In fact, there are substantial reasons not only for doubting the opportunity for a challenge on a point of law would exist, but also for doubting that the two stated grounds could be reasonably established.

Whether or not the entire Tolmers Square site should be the subject of a CPO is indeed a matter of law, but once that principle is established, then in the words of Glover, 'It is a matter of administration, not law, as to whether in the circumstances the Minister should give Camden power to acquire Stock Conversion's holdings on the site against their will'.

Glover goes on to say 'Stock Conversion will no doubt object to the Claudius Properties scheme and they might have a strong case, *but it would not* affect the vires of the Order'.

Apart from this, the grounds for objection are themselves both highly questionable. In describing the Stock Conversion scheme as 'viable and acceptable' Dobry, according to Glover, is merely 'begging the question'. To whom is the Stock Conversion scheme acceptable? Presumably Mr Dobry is not pre-empting the Secretary of State's view. If Camden should choose to proceed with Claudius Properties, then Stock Conversion's scheme would not have been acceptable to Camden. And there is no question that Camden are free to change their mind. Dobry himself confirms that there is no legalcommitment to Stock Conversion. In fact there is no reason to suppose that the Stock Conversion scheme is currently acceptable to anyone except Stock Conversion. . . .

Stock Conversion's second ground for objection, according to Dobry, is that a CPO on their land on behalf of Claudius Properties 'would not achieve a planning gain, but merely improve the financial return to Camden'. . . . In the last few years urban planning has become much more sophisticated. It is no longer concerned primarily with drawing zoning lines on a map and it is certainly no longer possible to isolate planning from the financial resources of the planning authority. According to Glover, 'generally speaking it is right to say that the financial interests of a private individual should not be a factor in planning, but I should have thought that Local Authority finances must be a factor to be taken into account in planning decisions'. . . .

The multimillion pound profits from Tolmers Square could be used in a number of ways which would result in planning gain. First, to improve the quality of the 600 housing units on the site, second to improve the environmental context of the development by the provision of social amenities, and third and perhaps most significantly to purchase further housing land on the open market. Alternatively, the profits from the development presently envisaged could of course be translated into relatively fewer offices and correspondingly more housing in an amended scheme – and this would, even from the most conventional view point represent a planning gain . . . .

Dobry warns that additional delays are more likely to occur if Camden proceeds without Stock Conversion. However, he attempts no specific analysis of these delays. . . . There is no hard evidence to support the argument that a deal with Claudius Properties would result in significantly greater delays than a deal with Stock Conversion. Either way there will be substantial objections, particularly at the public enquiry. . . .

. . . Dobry was invited to express his general views on the Tolmers Square Development, He describes the Claudius Properties offer as 'nebulous', but does not say why. He implies that it is not carefully prepared or thought out, but again does not say why. He is critical of the fact that Claudius Properties is a £100 company, ignoring the immense financial guarantees which have already satisfied Camden. He condemns Claudius Properties for not having what he calls a 'track record', ignoring the fact that Claudius Properties project managers, Richard Ellis, are currently conducting more commercial property development than Stock Conversion.

By contrast he describes Stock Conversion as a 'respected development company' (Claudius 'Commentary', 9 September 1973).

Offer rejected

Faced with conflicting evidence from experts the Labour leadership found itself in a dilemma Eventually, they took the advice of their own officers and opted to reject the Claudius Deal, and to continue with the Levy Deal. The real decision was made at a special meeting of the Labour Group on 10 September. The vote was pro-Levy 18–12 (although significantly 24 members were absent or abstained. Special meetings generally have low attendance because many councillors have pre-arranged commitments.) The Group decision was formalised at the Community Planning and Resources Committee meeting on 12 September at which there was an acrimonious debate, televised by *Man Alive*. A few Labour Councillors even went so far as to vote against the Group decision. Nevertheless the decision was carried; Claudius was out, Levy was in.

66. 67. Councillor Brian Loughran argues against the Levy Deal, but is outvoted.

As reported in a Council press statement:

> The main reason was the Council's desperate need for housing which counter-balanced the possible financial advantages of the Claudius proposals. It was felt to be unlikely that the Secretary of State would confirm the CPO on the Stock Conversion property, in which case the Claudius proposal would fall through leaving the Council with no housing land and in no position to bargain again with Stock Conversion. The Stock Conversion deal, on the other hand, seemed likely (but not certain) to secure the approval of the Secretary of State. With 11,000 people on the Council's housing waiting list, with homelessness increasing, and with a desperate shortage of housing land, it was decided to go for the alternative which seemed most likely to provide homes for about 1500 people (13 September 1973).

In other words the Claudius Offer was too much of a gamble.

The argument that the certainty of housing immediately was more important than anything else was the crux of the Council's justification for their decision. There was also a firm belief that the views and opinions of the Council's own officers and legal Counsel were more reliable than those of Claudius' advisers; despite certain evidence to the contrary, and despite the fact that Council officers inevitably tend to be cautious and reactionary over such issues. One cannot escape the conclusion that other reasons why the Labour Group rejected Claudius were the 'mind boggling unorthodoxy' of the proposal; the fact that it emanated from characters of 'dubious political colour', and the fact that one of the directors of Edward Bates was the Conservative leader of Bromley Council, a council notorious for its failure to provide Council housing.

However the failure of the Labour Group was not in misjudging the technicalities of the case, which could be argued either way, but in failing to recognise that the issue could be used by Camden as part of a political campaign against property speculation. The campaign against property speculation (which everyone supported) was seen as something separate from the decision about Tolmers Square. As one Labour Councillor said at the committee meeting:

> What we should be doing is to get on and build the housing as soon as possible, and then quite separately if we want to campaign about these wicked property developers, by all means let us do so, but the right way to deal with the property developers is a progressive government and I don't for one moment imagine the next Labour government will be in that category because they'll probably be as bad as the last one, but a really progressive go-ahead Labour government might take some action to end the total nonsense of the private ownership of land; let us do something concrete to build the houses now and if we ever get a socialist government they can confiscate every penny that Levy's got and the sooner the better. (Peter Best, *Man Alive*, 28 November 1973).

It was a timid decision, but a safe one – or so it seemed.

Louis Hellman, *Architects' Journal*, 10 October 1973.

6.

The 'stop the levy deal' campaign

There is no doubt that Tolmers Square has now become a symbolic chance for Londoners to take the future of their city out of the hands of the speculators, and back into their own (Booker and Gray, *Evening Standard*, 2 October 1973).

What you had at that stage was a coalition of different interest groups coming together to stop it. No one of them in isolation would have been capable of doing anything (Brian Loughran, Interview).

We feel this is the opportunity to make a stand against developers (Beverley Rowe, Chairman of St Pancras North Labour Party, *Evening Standard*, 21 September 1973).

It was politically too important to avoid having a bash at the people we ought to be having a bash at (Roger Jowell, Labour Councillor, Interview).

At that time you could have won a general election on that issue . . . and others like it . . . all we did was put a match to a keg of gunpowder (Bennie Gray, Interview).

There was a mass hysteria against the concept of whether or not you co-operate at all with capitalism (Peter Best, Labour Councillor, Interview).

Writ against the council

After the decision by the Community Planning and Resources Committee, on 12 September, to reject the Claudius Offer and continue with the Levy Deal, 'all hell was let loose'. The issue took to the streets.

On 14 September Nicholas Tomalin, a journalist friend of Booker and Gray, served a writ on Camden Council.

As a ratepayer of Camden he declared that the proposed deal would be unlawful, 'in that such Agreement would give rise to a loss or deficiency in the accounts of the Defendants which would be surchargeable under Section 228 (1) (d) of the Local Government Act 1933 and/or Section 161 (4) (b) of the Local Government Act 1972'

(Writ of Summons). In other words he was asking for a statutory declaration from the Court that Camden's decision was against the interests of the ratepayers. If the High Court granted the declaration then Camden Councillors could be surcharged by the amount they would be held to have lost, a figure which Claudius estimated to be around £7 million,

The idea of issuing a writ had been established earlier in discussions between Claudius and their legal advisers. It merely had to be wheeled out at the right moment by a well-wishing ratepayer. Gray covered Tomalin against all financial liabilities he might incur.

The writ had to be taken seriously by Camden, although its main value was the publicity it attracted. But it also marked the beginning of overt hostility between those for and against the Deal.

> I don't think it helped at all. What it did do, was to prove to someone like Frank Dobson, that the people who were really opposing him were not the people who lived there, but people that he would call the 'Sunday Times set', who had been a damned sight better educated than he had, who earned a damned sight more money than he did, who could involve themselves in financial deals of all kinds, and then have the cheek to come and tell him he was wrong (Alex Maxwell, Political Activities Officer for Hampstead Labour Party, Interview).

Frank Dobson did in fact issue a press statement the same day:

> I would never wish to prevent anyone in Camden doing what they felt I right, so if any of our ratepayers seek to serve a writ to prevent us going ahead with our housing proposals at Tolmers Square in conjunction with Stock Conversion, it is up to them. However, if they are well off and well-housed I hope they will pause to consider their motives and the consequences of their action on the poor, the homeless and the badly housed. Any delay in building houses in Tolmers Square will be their responsibility (14 September 1973).

The writ was withdrawn after a week to avoid problems of subjudice. Nicholas Tomalin, however, promised to serve it again should the need arise. (Tragically, he was killed a few weeks later reporting in Israel.)

The campaign

At the same time as the writ was being served, the 'Stop the Levy Deal Campaign' (STLDC) was getting under way. The driving force for this campaign came from Booker and Gray, although because of their involvement in Claudius, they had no official connections. The campaign was effectively run from their office, with meetings every few days at Gray's home in Hampstead. The formal, campaign committee consisted of the chairman of a nearby tenants association; the Political Activities Officer for Hampstead Labour Party; a leading activist in the Covent Garden Community Association; the local Shelter representative; a lecturer at the Architectural Association; and a member of the newly formed Tolmer's Village Association. The latter was tremendously important, because a major argument of those in favour of the Deal was that they claimed to be acting in the interests of the inhabitants of the area. It was therefore of enormous psychological and practical value to the opponents of the Deal to have the active involvement of an

Hampstead & Highgate Express, 14, 21 and 28 September 1973, *Financial Times*, 27 September 1973, *Morning Star*, 27 September 1973, *Times*, 27 September 1973, *Guardian*, 27 September 1973, *Camden Journal*, 5 October 1973.

organisation which claimed to represent the interests of the people living there (see next chapter).

The objective of the campaign was to force Camden to reverse their decision to continue with the Levy Deal. There was no intention of persuading them to accept the Claudius Offer, as it was recognised by this time to be politically out of the question; the Claudius offer merely showed that there was a viable alternative. The tactic was to gain support from as many quarters as possible and so form a massive coalition against the deal. Support was obtained from members of tenants associations and community groups; councillors; officials of Shelter, CPAG and NCCL; senior trade union leaders (including Sir Sydney Greene, Ray Buckton and Clive Jenkins); academics (such as Reyner Banham); members of the local Labour Parties; and prominent members of the national Labour Party (including Douglas Jay, Ben Whitaker and Illtyd Harrington who was then Deputy Leader of the GLC). Also of significance was the support of Reg Freeson, then Shadow Spokesman for Housing and Construction.

Freeson's support provided much publicity, and clearly carried considerable political weight. It was a stab in the back for Camden's Labour Group, many of whom were openly critical of his action, especially as he publicly supported the campaign without first contacting Camden's Labour leadership, or for that matter the local Labour MP, Lena Jeger. He gave his reasons for this unusual behaviour in a letter to Frank Dobson:

> I have been asked to support the Stop the Levy Deal campaign. Only in exceptional circumstances would I agree to lend my name to any campaign involving essentially a local issue. After serious thought I have done so in this case because it represents a fundamental national issue. . . . Given the present

> background it seems to me that the Tolmers Square-type situation (and there are many other situations throughout the country) provides the chance to Labour authorities, particularly during the run-up to the General Election in which land ownership will be a big issue, to prepare the way for radical changes in national policy and the (Labour) Government's method of applying such policy. . . In the light of all the points raised I believe that Camden would be more than justified in not proceeding with the Stock Conversion scheme. There arc other alternatives, of which Claudius is one, which could be considered. I believe that what happens at Tolmers Square will be of great importance nationally as well as locally and that Labour in Camden could provide an important sign-post for local authorities up and down the country (Letter, 25 September 1973).

Freeson himself had misgivings about giving support but clearly saw it as a step in a campaign towards land nationalization, a policy which he had advocated for many years.

> Often in politics you go a bit rough on the edges in order to get some central point raised in the public mind, and in the opinion leaders' minds. . . . And you forgo the deeper things in order to get that dramatic situation. I'm not prone to do that too easily because I tend to be a bit more painstaking in my political work in this field. But there are times when you've got to do that. . . . Pressure of events and time compelled one to act in a certain way, and basically I don't regret it. It was the right thing to have done at that time (Reg Freeson, Interview).

Having gathered this broad spectrum of support the campaign committee published a typeset, well produced leaflet-cum-petition and launched the whole campaign at a press conference held symbolically in one of Stock Conversion's empty houses in Tolmers Square which had just been squatted. Both Reg Freeson and Illtyd Harrington made short speeches, Paddy O'Conner (Camden and GLC Councillor and GLC Whip) threatened to resign if the Deal went ahead, and the press loved it. Camden were forced to hold a hastily prepared press conference the same afternoon in order to defend their position.

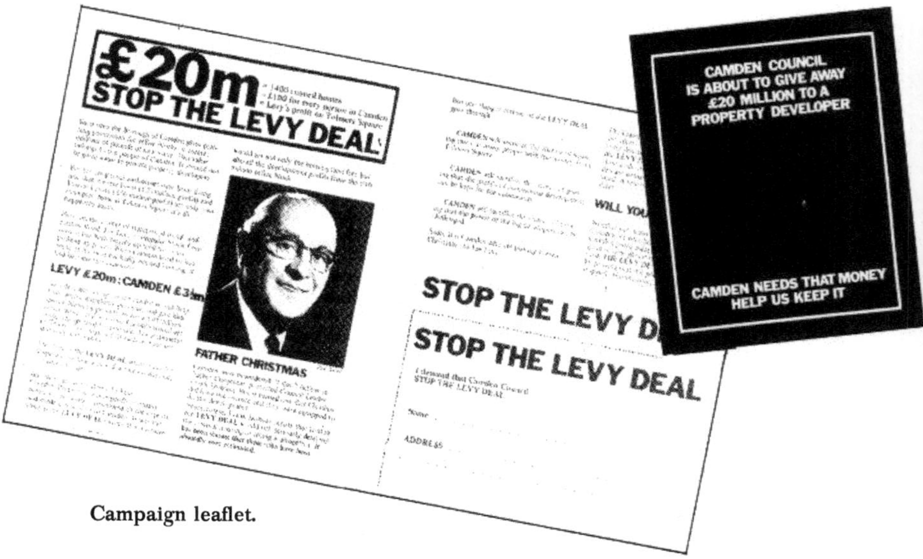

Campaign leaflet.

The media played an important role in the whole campaign. Booker and Gray naturally had a number of contacts and also knew how to stage things so that they would appeal to the media mind. *The Times*, *Financial Times*, *Telegraph*, *Guardian* and *Evening Standard* all followed the campaign closely. For the local papers it was front page news, and the *Hampstead and Highgate Express* in particular printed lengthy exchanges of correspondence and several leaders. Some technical journals like the *Architects' Journal* printed substantial articles.

Television also played a part. A freelance journalist who lived in Camden had got a commission from the BBC to make a *Man Alive* programme on property speculation. He picked on Tolmers Square as a case study, and filmed much of the campaign, including the two crucial Council meetings, so giving the issue an even greater air of importance.

The Left press also continued to publicise the issue.

In the summer, *Time Out* had carried a four-page article entitled 'Speculation by Stealth may cost Joe Levy £20 million', in which they showed how Stock Conversion and other speculators were in the process of carrying out similar operations in Camden High Street.

At the beginning of the campaign they produced another article entitled 'Levy's Golden Mile', in which it was disclosed that Stock Conversion were buying up property around Kings Cross, where there were plans to build the main terminal for Maplin. It was also shown that Stock Conversion had interests in Peachey Property Company which was developing the site in front of Euston Station for 405,000 square feet of offices. 'A few years ago the area around Euston Road might have been described as a varied, if run-down, working-class community. In the future it may be better known as Levy's Golden Mile' (*Time Out*, 14 September 1973).

In an attempt to combat the speculation in Camden High Street a 'Speculators Investigation Centre' was established there by a group of activists who were totally committed to opposing 'the unremitting encroachment of property speculators into working-class communities' (Letter to Councillor). They, along with the Camden Federation of Tenants and Residents Associations, campaigned actively against the Deal and highlighted the effect that property speculators were having in Camden as a whole. Levy became the symbol of their campaign.

An important aspect of the campaign was the use of expert opinions. Every argument put forward by the pro-Levy side was meticulously answered, and in every case the authorities used carried as much weight in terms of professional expertise as those of the opposition. Lengthy correspondence appeared in the local papers and in the *Evening Standard*.

Towards the end of the campaign the main argument of those in favour of the Levy Deal was the question of the housing which would be lost if the Deal was dropped. This argument was torpedoed by Booker and Gray in a full-page article in the *Evening Standard*, in which they released two crucial pieces of information. Dick Hobin, a lecturer at the Architectural Association, estimated that in 1965 the number of rooms in the Tolmers Square development area was no less than 1,499, 31 more than Camden were hoping to achieve in their new development. In other words after ten years of planning blight the result would be a net loss in housing. Furthermore, a survey carried out by five students at University College London, showed that there were around 700 people still living in the area, as opposed to the 200 or 300 assumed by Camden. There were also many people employed in almost 100 small businesses.

> This is dynamite. For what it means is that when these 700 people have been re-housed there will only be new accommodation for a mere 500 people, little more than 100 families. In other words Camden Leader Frank Dobson will only be helping a tiny handful of his waiting list – in exchange for disrupting the lives of another 700 people, destroying what remains of the community and losing several hundred jobs. It is for this that Camden is proposing to allow a property speculator to make profits of £20 million – equivalent to nearly £200,000 for every family rehoused, or £100 for every man, woman and child in the borough. We believe these new figures to be so startling that Camden must be forced to rethink their whole approach to Tolmers Square (Booker and Gray, *Evening Standard*, 2 October 1973)

The figures used in this article were disputed by Camden, and in fact were slightly (although only slightly) inaccurate. But the significant thing was that the campaign had free access to a 54 column-inch article in the *Evening Standard*, with photographs, whereas Camden's reply the following day was limited to 15.5 column-inches with no photographs.

Campaign timetable

10 Sept: Camden Labour Group vote pro-Levy Deal (18 – 12, 24 absent).

12 Sept: Community Planning and Resources Committee vote pro-Levy Deal.

13 Sept: Holborn and St Pancras South Labour Party Executive Committee meeting – no mention of Tolmers Square.

14 Sept: Hampstead Labour Party General Management Committee vote anti-Levy Deal
Nicholas Tomalin issues Writ.

18 Sept: St Pancras North Labour Party Executive Committee vote anti-Levy Deal (6 – 0)
STLDC first meeting.

20 Sept: Holborn and St Pancras South Labour Party General Management Committee vote for reconsideration (nem con).

25 Sept: St Pancras North Labour Party General Management Committee vote anti-levy Deal (13 – 2).
Reg Freeson supports STLDC.

26 Sept: STLDC Press Conference to launch campaign.
Local Government Committee vote pro-Levy Deal (12 – 7).

8 Oct: Camden Labour Group vote anti-Levy Deal.

10 Oct: Full Council vote anti-Levy Deal.

Party split

In terms of shifting the Council it was the Labour Party revolt which was decisive. The media campaign on its own I don't think would have shifted the Council. But the party revolt would not have been conceivable without the media coverage (Anon).

The sole purpose of the campaign was to force the Council to reverse their decision to carry on with Levy. The campaign would have been completely ineffective had it not succeeded in persuading the Councillors to change their minds. Alongside the Stop the Levy Deal Campaign, a parallel campaign was being waged within the various Labour organisations in Camden.

The following diagram shows the power structure within Camden at the time of the campaign. When the Labour Party is in power, the Labour Group is the real decision-making body, made up of all the Labour Councillors. They in turn are selected by the Ward parties of the three constituency Labour Parties within Camden; Hampstead, St Pancreas North, and Holborn and St Pancreas South. The General Management Committee of the constituencies are made up of delegates from each Ward plus some Trade Union delegates and can be extremely influential, especially in candidate selection.

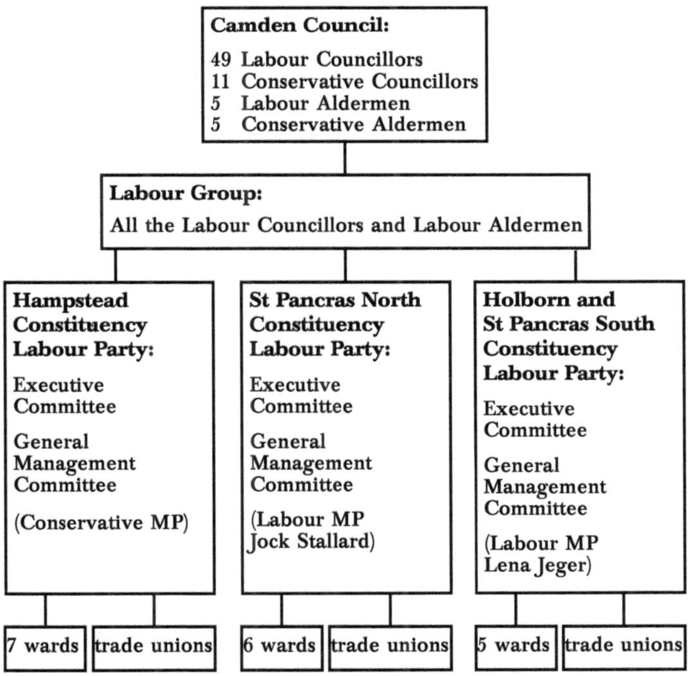

Political power structure in Camden Council, September 1973

Because of the cycle of meetings it was Hampstead which lead the attack. Way back in July, Hampstead Town Ward Labour Party had invited Gray to speak to them about Claudius and hence they knew something about the issue. Although not normally particularly concerned with Inner London housing they took up the Tolmers issue. The Political Activities Officer of the Party suggested that 'Hampstead were only interested in Tolmers Square because there were some big names around' (Alix Maxwell, Interview). Whether or not this cynical view is true, the party 'voted overwhelmingly' to call for the reversal of Camden's decision and for a publicity campaign to show that 'in the event of the necessary CPO's being disallowed by the Tory Government, such a decision would be fully understood to be a political one and not in the interests of a fair and just society' (*Hampstead and Highgate Express*, 21 September 1973).

Several days later the Executive Committee of the St Pancras, North Party passed a similar resolution. 'The Executive Committee takes an exceptionally grave view of the likely political consequences of the proposed deal with Stock Conversion and urges the Labour Group to reverse its decision' (Minutes, 18 September). This was endorsed by the General Management Committee (21 to 1) the following week. It was also agreed to organise a petition among members of the party, and to send a personal letter to all members of the Labour Group. (The St Pancras North party also prepared a chart comparing the likely outcomes of different decisions, concluding that there was 'an 80% chance of being financially, politically and in housing (both here and throughout the country) far, far better off.' (letter, 29 September 1973).

But the third party, Holborn and St Pancras South, was not prepared to turn against the leadership. Interestingly it was the consistency which actually contained Tolmers Square, and was also the Leader of the Council's home constituency. The Leader was well known to be anti-developer generally, and if he was in favour of the Levy Deal, the Party were prepared to back him. They resented the other two parties' outspoken and much publicised resolutions, and passed the following emergency resolution nem con: 'This GMC asks the Group on Camden Council to hold further discussions on the Tolmers Square issue with the three constituency labour parties. It further asks the other two Camden parties to abstain from public controversy within the Camden Labour Party until these discussions have taken place' (GMC Minutes, 20 September 1973).

In effect there was a party revolt, with two out of the three constituency parties voting against the party line as laid down by the Labour Group. At the beginning of the campaign the Labour Group was split as follows: opposed to the Levy Deal, there were a handful of principled left-wingers who opposed capitalism and hence deals with developers on whatever terms; there were also a few moderates who saw the Claudius deal as a good idea. In favour of the deal was what might loosely be called the leadership group, plus the right wing of the Labour Group. Generally supporting the line put forward by the Leader, this group included most of those who had been involved in the Tolmers development the longest; they felt they had tried everything else and that the Levy Deal, although not in any way desirable, was the best practicable possibility. Interestingly enough, this group contained several left-wingers, who considered that the Levy Deal was the only way to get housing under capitalism. They associated an anti- Levy position with a pro-Claudius one, and they considered the Claudius Offer to be an unprincipled, non-socialist, market solution, proposed by two unreliable right-wingers. They were therefore in favour of the Levy Deal.

To begin with, the majority of the Labour Group were prepared to go along with the leadership view as normal. But as the campaign gathered momentum, an increasing number of people started to take what might be called a tactical left position. By stalling, the Council might be able to hold out until a Labour Government pledged to land nationalization, gained power. The Council should therefore reject both the Levy Deal, and the Claudius Offer, and take an active part in the general campaign against property speculation. The time had come to make a stand, and Tolmers Square was as good as anywhere to take that stand. The issue was no longer over how to get the best immediate solution to the development of Tolmers Square. It had become primarily a political campaign.

Other people joined the opposition lobby as it became increasingly clear that many of the arguments used by the leadership could be challenged with authority. And of course, as the pro-Levy Deal arguments were based on the likelihood of a political decision by the Secretary of State regarding the CPO, then as the campaign gathered momentum, these arguments became increasingly questionable. Additionally, the constituency parties were initiating the candidate selection procedure for the next year's Council elections, and councillors were unwilling to offend grass roots party opinion, for fear of losing their seats. Finally, for the weak-minded, there was no doubt which was becoming the 'side of the angels'.

There was also a considerable amount of lobbying going on at a higher level, within the Party: at the Blackpool Conference, in the House of Commons and in the GLC. The GLC was influential in that they owned a small crucial piece of land on the Hampstead Road which Camden would have to acquire in order to carry out the Levy Deal. The GLC leaders vowed that they would not sell the land and would resist any CPOs if Camden went ahead with the Deal.

By this time the whole campaign was beginning to get rather nasty. It had become extremely personalized, there was a lot of mud slinging and character-assassination (especially of Bennie Gray and Frank Dobson), and tempers were roused. There were inevitable accusations of corruption, and of deliberate attempts by both sides to mislead the public. These diversions naturally hit the headlines, but achieved little, except to cloud the real issues and render the public even more confused.

But time was running out, and the Council would have to make a decision. As the wave of protest grew, the Labour leadership group became increasingly isolated. They were being attacked on all flanks; by the Camden public, the press, the local community, trade unionists, tenants' associations, the Labour GLC, senior members of their own party and, most important of all, their own constituency Labour Parties. The leadership had unwisely entrenched themselves in a pro-Levy position, and they would have to perform somersaults to get out of it.

In a last-ditch attempt to stem the tide, a hastily called (some even suggested rigged) meeting of the Local Government Committee threw out a motion calling on the Council to reject the Levy Deal. It helped to save face but had no constitutional power.

The vital decision would be made at the Labour Group meeting on 10 October. Realising that if it came to a vote they could easily lose, and horrified by the prospects of a widening party split, the leadership decided to climb down. They did it as gracefully as they could. At the Labour Group Meeting, Council Leader Frank Dobson recommended that both the Levy Deal and Claudius Offer be dropped; his recommendation was accepted without a vote.

Victory

Two days later at the full Council Meeting, amidst television cameras and reporters, the Tolmers Village Association read out a petition, and presented over 8,000 signatures opposing the Levy Deal. The Labour Group was able to present a united front against the Deal, in asking for a withdrawal of the report of the Community Planning and Resources Committee of 12 September. Neither the Levy Deal nor the Claudius Offer would be accepted. Instead the Council would carry out a review of alternative approaches to the problem of the Tolmers Square Redevelopment Area.

68. 69. 70. The Tolmers Village Association present their deputation, the Council Leader withdraws the report, and the Labour members vote unanimously to reject the Levy Deal.

The Leader of the Council announced:

> In withdrawing this report we may lead to some delay in the provision of adequate housing on the Tolmers Square site. That may be the case, we take the responsibility for it, but I believe the delay will be justified (*Hampstead and Highgate Express*, 12 October 1973).

He continued:

> Last night I had preliminary discussion with Sir Reg Goodwin, the Leader of the GLC. I've also been in touch with a number of other central London boroughs who are faced with problems similar to our own, and I've been in touch with the chairman of the London Boroughs Association, and I am hopeful that we can, as the elected representatives of the beleaguered population of central London do something in the way of a concerted and sustained effort to get the Secretary of State to acknowledge that he must do something to redress the balance between the developers and ourselves (Frank Dobson, *Man Alive*, 28 November 1973).

It was later announced that on the one hand representations would be made to the Secretary of State by local MPs Lena Jeger and Jock Stallard, and on the other, a conference would be called with other Inner London Boroughs to discuss the whole relationship between developers and local authorities. The Leader ended his speech with a rallying cry which united the Labour ranks: 'My final word is this: there is no long-term solution to this problem which does not involve the public ownership of the land on which such developments have been taking place and may take place in the future' (Script, *Man Alive*, 28 November 1973).

The campaign had succeeded.

Tolmers Square row: residents win

Victory in Euston offices battle

Inside Politics

The tide turns against the developers

EXPRESS

Tolmers somersault

DELEGATION BILL PRESS

RIPPON TO GRANT CPOs

ello little Joe
sittin on yer pile
gribby grabby little Joe
you'll ave to wait a while

(*Tolmers News*, No. 1)

Evening Standard, 9 October 1973, *Inside London*, 11 October 1973, *Hampstead & Highgate Express*, 12 October 1973

An assessment

The Levy Deal was called off because of the opposition to the Council from a number of different groups. Of primary importance were certain Labour Councillors, the local Labour Parties in Camden, the press and media, the general public in Camden, senior Parliamentary and GLC Labour Party spokesmen, and the Tolmers Village Association. Without the coalition of all these groups, it is unlikely that the Council could have been prevented from doing the deal. It would be invidious to isolate anyone group as being the key factor, but it is interesting to notice the roles played by certain groups.

The role of Booker and Gray was of particular significance, as they acted as catalysts and stage managers. They used all the traditional vehicles of British middle-class protest: the press, television, and influential contacts. They harnessed and co-ordinated a multitude of individuals and groups to form a seemingly united and massive opposition, which they then directed at the enemy. The whole campaign was handled more like a sales drive for a new product than a political protest. They were able to play this unique role because they possessed tools normally only available to the establishment. They had the intimate knowledge of property mechanics, the contacts, and the finance to put Claudius into operation. And they had access to the means for influencing public opinion, necessary in order to sustain a powerful and effective publicity campaign. Sadly none of these attributes arc normally found among community activists, which is why radical community protest is often not very successful. The 'Stop the Levy Deal Campaign' was the exception which proved the rule.

For the Left generally, the Tolmers Square campaign was secondary to the campaign against the Government's Housing Finance legislation. While the Conservative Government's Housing Finance Act was in force, no low-rent housing provision on Tolmers Square would be possible. Property speculation was intimately related to the Housing Finance issue, and a facet of the housing campaign was the national campaign against property speculation. This national campaign created a climate for the Tolmers Square issue, and indeed Tolmers Square became one of the foci of the national campaign. In general the Left helped to create the right political climate for a change in Council policy on Tolmers Square. The strategy was to delay decision, and to publicise the issue so as to prevent a deal being pushed through the Council quickly and secretly. In this they were totally successful. Later, at the crunch point, vital contributions were made by left-wing councillors, MPs and members of the constituency Labour Parties, all of whom were co-ordinated by informal contacts rather than by any formal organisation.

The role of the Labour Party is also interesting. It is often assumed by radicals that the Labour Party is a joke at Council level, and that it is impossible to achieve anything useful by working with it. Yet the grass roots of the party was decisive in creating the Party revolt which forced the Council to back down. The campaign showed clearly that it is possible for grass-roots members of the Party to play a significant role in affecting Council decisions. Although rejecting the Levy Deal was not exactly a revolutionary decision on the part of the Council, it was a great deal more radical than accepting the Levy Deal, because by doing so, the Council were making demands on the system which could not be met without a change in the system. As we will see, subsequent events show that the decision did in fact have certain radical repercussions.

But it is equally clear that this kind of issue cannot be left entirely to the Labour Party to sort out. Despite making frequent assertions, both locally and nationally, about ending property speculation, the Labour Party on its own was impotent. It required a vast tide of opposition to the Deal so that in the end the leadership could no longer continue with a 'King Canute act' and had to give way.

Too few people realise how limited Governments and Councils are on their own. Once they have been elected to power, it is assumed that they can and will carry out their programmes as outlined in their manifestos, and that nothing needs to be done until the next election.

In fact, especially if elected on a radical platform, they need constant back-up in order to achieve any significant change, and to carry out their pledges.

The Labour Party has often been criticised for not taking a more radical line over Tolmers Square. It was after all a Labour Council which first started negotiations with developers. It was a Labour Government which refused to allow the Council to buy land to undertake its own development, and a Labour Council initially approved the Levy Deal.

But the failure of the Labour Party was not that it made these decisions at particular historical moments, because the alternatives were usually worse. It is pointless for Labour Councils to refuse to do deals with developers if the alternative is that large areas of city decay, and opportunity for creating jobs and homes is lost. The failure of the Labour Group Leadership was that it did not actively seek to gain support from wider sections of the community. It did not attempt to mobilise a potentially active opposition, and use this strength to pressurise the Government to take the correct course of action. Instead, the Labour Council carried on secret negotiations with developers, wrote the occasional confidential letter of protest to the Government, and then paternalistically presented the public with fait accomplis. When a minority of Left Labour Councillors did attempt to galvanise public support, they were extremely successful, sparking off a major wave of opposition which then enabled the Council to take a more radical stance against the government.

Labour Governments are of course in much the same position as Councils. With money in short supply, allocations naturally go to those who shout loudest. They are unlikely to spend a lot of money on buying expensive land for public use, unless they consider it is likely to gain them some votes in the next election. It is therefore imperative for the public as well as local councils to put pressure on them. It is a major failing of Labour councils that they do not realise the potential for mobilising public support against the Government. Too often they are reluctant to attack the Government openly, especially when it is of their own party.

Cover of Tolmers Village Association constitution.

-7.

Don't let them do it to us

Student intervention

At the same time as the Claudius attack on the Levy Deal, another movement of protest was growing, which was also to become of key importance to the area. This movement was initiated by students from University College London (UCL), part of London University situated a few hundred yards south of Tolmers across the Euston Road.

In May 1973, while Booker and Gray were preparing the Claudius proposal, five undergraduates embarked on a five-week planning project. Disenchanted with the remoteness of much theoretical academic work these students wanted to be involved in 'reality'. They wanted to break down the gulf that exists between the universities training professionals, and the people whose lives those professionals would be affecting. Their tutor had read about the conflict over Tolmers Square, and it being only a few hundred yards from the University it seemed a suitable place for a project on the operation of the planning system.

It did not take the students long to discover that although everyone in the Tolmers area knew that some kind of redevelopment was going to take place, no one seemed to know what, when or where. Even more extraordinary, few people considered that it was their *right* to know, or felt that they could or should do anything about it.

It has to be realised that although the Council and the developers had been discussing the redevelopment of the area for over twelve years, very little information had been available to the public. There had been no participation of any kind, the only source of information for inhabitants being Council Minutes, and the occasional report in a local newspaper. For many people their first news of the development was receiving notification of a CPO or Clearance Order.

This in itself, although depressing, was not unusual. But what was surprising was that the Council appeared to know little about the area, or the people who lived and worked in it. They had no survey information at all, and no studies to suggest what would happen to these people following redevelopment. For them Tolmers was merely a site of a certain acreage with a certain value; the people who lived and worked there were not even statistics.

Horrified by this inhumanity, the students carried out a survey to find out what the area was really like: who lived there, what they thought, and what would happen to them if it was redeveloped. They then produced a report criticising the Council: 'The decision-makers fail to understand the nature of the area as it is at present, and are unwilling to recognise its value in today's urban complex. The [comprehensive] redevelopment of Tolmers Square would replace exciting variety with a drab uniformity' (UCL Survey). They also condemned the Council for failing to find out what the people who lived and worked in the area wanted, and for not encouraging local people to participate in making decisions about the future of the area.

Instead of comprehensive redevelopment, the students proposed that development should take place in a sensitive piecemeal way, with the emphasis on catering for people already there. As many buildings as possible should be rehabilitated, and new development should be phased over a long period, buildings being pulled down and replaced as and when they came to the end of their useful life. There will then be no need to disrupt the life of the community unduly as people could be moved *within* the area. No one would have to leave against their will. They concluded:

> In attempting to improve an area as complex and diverse as Tolmers Square, planners need to have a far better understanding of the functioning of cities than they appear to have at present. Unless Camden's planners can show that the redevelopment of Tolmers Square will have advantages for the people who live and work there at present, as well as those who might live there in the future, they should reconsider their plans. Merely satisfying property speculators is not good enough (UCL Survey).

The case against comprehensive redevelopment

It was the first time that anyone had suggested that Tolmers Square be comprehensively redeveloped. For fifteen years it had been assumed that comprehensive redevelopment was the only solution. The arguments had been over who should do it, and what should be built.

Camden's official justification for comprehensive redevelopment contained in a report by the Director of Planning:

> The residential accommodation in the area is in poor condition and is in a close proximity to undesirable uses.
> There is a conflict between commercial vehicles and pedestrians.
> There is no off-street parking.
> If development is not undertaken comprehensively the full density will not be achieved.
> (Report to Committee, 24 June 1971)

These were meant to be arguments in favour of comprehensive redevelopment but if examined more carefully they prove to be nothing of the kind.

No one disputed that the property was in poor condition, but this did not mean that the buildings had to be pulled down. Structurally they were in fair condition, as the Council's consultant architects later confirmed:

> . . . The houses have stood for over a hundred years and are capable of a useful future life. . . . The case for retention should not be based on the extent of structural work required. Virtually all of the buildings in the area will have a further 30 year life if certain localised repairs are carried out (Renton Howard Wood, Report No.2, March 1974).

Many of the buildings were of architectural or historical importance, and indeed have since been listed by the Department of the Environment. In addition, many of the buildings could have been converted and modernised to provide homes of an equally high (and in many cases higher) standard to that possible by rebuilding, which is restricted by rigid space standards and government cost yard-sticks.

Another argument used in favour of comprehensive redevelopment was that the mixture of commercial and residential uses was undesirable. The Council never provided any reasons for why they considered it undesirable, and it appeared to the students that far from being undesirable, the diversity was actually an asset. Commerce certainly did not suffer, and, provided the industries and commercial interests did not create undue noise or smell, they were a positive advantage to residents. They ensured that the area was constantly alive and stimulating. The streets were never empty, which reduced vandalism and crime, and services were provided which would not have been otherwise: for instance, small sandwich bars, grocery stores, restaurants and pubs, which served workers during the day and residents in the evenings. It also meant that it was possible for residents to obtain work nearby, and several people lived and worked in the same building. Fifty per cent of the residents were able to walk to work, so saving money and time; an exceptionally high statistic compared with London as a whole.

As for the 'conflict between commercial vehicles and pedestrians', this malady exists in all our cities. The Council wanted to solve the conflict by 'the provision of segregated systems of vehicular traffic and pedestrian circulation to serve the area' (Report to Committee, 24 June 1971). In other words they wanted to build pedestrian underpasses and bridges which past experience showed would almost certainly have led to a barren environment for pedestrians. According to the student survey (based on a 24 hour traffic count), 70 per cent of the vehicles entering the Tolmers area were private cars, and 13 per cent were taxis. Much of this traffic was passing straight through, merely using the back streets as short cuts to avoid the congestion on the main roads. The conflict was between pedestrians and private vehicles rather than commercial vehicles, and could largely be remedied by the strategic use of road closures to prevent through traffic.

As for using 'no off-street parking' as a justification for a comprehensive redevelopment scheme, this was clearly absurd. The Tolmers area was better served by London Transport than almost anywhere in London, being on four tube lines and numerous bus routes. If the declared policy of limiting private transport in central London meant anything at all then it should have meant that off-street parking was not provided in areas like Tolmers.

The final argument that 'if development is not undertaken comprehensively the full density will not be achieved' was quite simply wrong. The student report showed that by merely reoccupying empty buildings (admittedly at existing densities) and using vacant sites, the population could be jacked up to the same level as that planned under comprehensive development. By strategic infilling and rebuilding (no one was ever arguing that the whole area should be preserved) the density could be increased even further.

Apart from all these general 'planning' arguments there was the fundamental political issue of the effect that redevelopment would have on the people already there; the 700 remaining residents and the 600 employed in businesses. No one had ever asked them if they wanted redevelopment, let alone explain any of its implications.

The Council had as yet made no commitment to re-house those people living on the site, although it is likely that they would have done so eventually. Most residents could probably have been accommodated in modern flats relatively nearby, but the rents, although moderated by rebates and subsidies, would have been much increased. Also, many people preferred to live in traditional housing rather than modern flats with all their much publicised problems. Many residents, for purely emotional reasons, simply did not want to move from Tolmers which in some cases had been their home for over fifty years. Despite the appalling state of the houses, only 50 per cent of residents interviewed by the students positively wanted to leave their present homes.

Comprehensive redevelopment would also have been disastrous for many of the businesses:

71

I think it [redevelopment] would mean the total extinction of our business, because there is just not another place within a reasonable area of Euston which would be available at an economic rent. We have made several enquiries about buildings. . . and the rent was so astronomical that it would just not be on at all, which would mean most of the staff would be redundant (Ralph Cooper, Manager of Simmonds, *Tolmers: beginning or end?*).

72

If we had to move we would be finished. We could not carry on with the business any more, it's too expensive for a small shop . . . . Once we are pulled up by the roots, like a plant we die (John Vine, a small shopkeeper, *Tolmers: Beginning or End?*).

Average rents for commercial space at the time were around £1 per square foot per annum. After comprehensive redevelopment they would probably have been around £1. 7 5 per square foot or even higher. This would have squeezed many firms out of business, especially the small craftsmen, light industries, second-hand stores and small shops. Of course rents were artificially low because of the uncertainty, and would have risen even if a rehabilitation scheme had been decided on. But in this case they would not have risen so high, nor so fast.

Shops which sell everyday consumer goods (food shops, newsagents, tobacconists) tend to disappear in high-rent areas as they arc unable to compete with supermarkets. This is particularly disadvantageous to the elderly, the car-less, and people who depend on being able to shop after work. In Camden the number of shops in this sector defined by a quarter between 1966 and 1971 (*Camden Scene* p.77).

Perhaps more important to existing tenants than increasing rents would be the loss of capital invested in the properties and in the location. Many of the buildings had been designed specially or adapted to fit the needs of the business.

73

Location is crucial to trade, and moving only a small distance can be destructive, as the manager of Simmonds writes: 'We know the effects of a CPO from past experience. Although it only meant moving our business a mere 150 yards (from 242 Euston Road) it took us 7 years to rebuild trade to its previous level' (Ralph Cooper, *Tolmers News*, No. 1).

Laurence Corner, nationally known for their range of army surplus gear, also make this point in a letter to the Town Clerk:

> The particular corner site of our main store is a very well known land mark. . . . Large sums of money have been spent by this company in promoting and advertising its present site and therefore disturbance costs would be very considerable (17 May 1973).

74

For the Asian community too, comprehensive redevelopment would have been disastrous. It had taken fifteen years to build Drummond Street up as one of the main Asian shopping areas in London, and it could not just be transplanted overnight. There was little chance that any redevelopment scheme would make provision for the special needs of the Asians.

> It's going to mean a lot of hard work down the drain, and then we have to start all over again (Mr Patak, Asian shopkeeper, *Tolmers: Beginning End?*).

Many Asians had already suffered as a result of redevelopment schemes. In 1958 one businessman started a grocers shop at 32 Hampstead Road which flourished to such an extent that queues sometimes extended for 30 yards along the street. It did not last long. In 1962 the LCC decided that the shop had to be knocked down to allow for road widening in Euston Road. He then took shops in Drummond Street, Whitfield Street and Grafton Way, but could not regain his custom. His factory in Kentish Town also had to close down for lack of a market. Finally he managed to build up Bhavneeta Novelties, a sari shop in the Hampstead Road. If this shop is pulled down, he says, 'We are finished'.

And not only businesses would suffer. The Countrywide Holidays Association (CHA) had been based in Drummond Street since 1925, with their own freehold, providing facilities for a large number of groups and societies.

> If a CPO is made and confirmed and alternative premises are not provided before the present building ceases to be available, a Club which is 72 years old and has been a feature of the neighbourhood for 48 years providing social, recreational and cultural amenities not available elsewhere in the vicinity, would cease to exist. Similarly, the Clubs who use these premises, because they are centrally situated and are available at a very reasonable rent, would also cease to exist since they would be unable to afford the rents asked for similar accommodation in Central London. Thus about 1,400 people would cease to be able to enjoy their particular interests and hobbies (*Tolmers News*, No.3).

The final arguments against comprehensive redevelopment were the unquantifiable psychological ones. Some apparently insignificant places and buildings may have special meaning to local inhabitants because they add to the identity of the area, act as landmarks, and satisfy their need for a secure and familiar local environment, in contrast to the vast scale of the metropolis. The importance of these aspects could only be appreciated by the planners if they had an intimate knowledge of the area and of the people in it.

The arguments against redevelopment put forward by the students were not original. They were in fact the standard arguments against comprehensive redevelopment being freely banded around in the late 1960s and early 1970s. But it is one thing for new ideas to be floating around in the media and in the universities, and another for them to have any practical effect. The students' invaluable contribution was to apply the arguments to Tolmers specifically, and to carry out the necessary research to be able to back up the arguments with statistics. Equally important was to ensure that the information was given to people who could use it; reports by themselves are useless. At the end of their five-week project, the students invited three local inhabitants to the examiners' review at the university. The inhabitants were alarmed by the students' presentation, and the discussion soon turned to what they could do about the situation. It was suggested that some form of community organisation was needed and that another meeting should be held in the area in a couple of days to get something off the ground.

Two days later a meeting was held in an office in North Gower Street. In addition to the students and their tutor, there were nine local inhabitants present: a couple who ran a geological information service and lived in a flat above, two shopkeepers, and five tenants (four of them young). One local Councillor was invited, and the students' tutor brought along a town planner who was involved with community projects in other parts of the country. After agreeing that there was a need for some form of local opposition to the Council's proposals, the nine local inhabitants formed themselves into an ad hoc committee and decided to start a community association. .

The students then left for their summer holidays, their role as catalysts completed.

The birth of the Tolmers Village Association

> It's what this area has needed for a long, long, time. Someone to stand up and fight (Maureen Holland, resident, *Tolmers: Beginning or End?*).
>
> Only that organization could help the people who arc really concerned. . . . Nobody else cares, neither the Council nor any big developers (Mr. Shah, resident/shopkeeper, *Tolmers: Beginning or End?*).
>
> One of these local associations which set themselves up as do-gooders (spokesman from D. E. & J. Levy, *Camden Journal*, 7 June 1974).

To launch the association the ad hoc committee decided to prepare a petition objecting to the proposed use of the Tolmer Cinema site for a car park; an issue that everybody would almost certainly agree with. The petition stated:

> Our immediate concern is the use proposed for the Tolmer Cinema site. The rumour is that it is to be used as a car park. If this is true we object. This space should be used for children's play and open space. In the absence of assurances from the Borough we intend to occupy and convert the site for the community's use (Petition).

Over 300 signatures were sent to the Town Clerk, and the planning application for the car park was refused. The application might have been refused anyway but it was a good morale booster. 'The main benefit was not so much stopping the car park, but actually we all went round the street, knocking on people's doors and got to know who lived here' (Gavin Brown, resident, Interview).

The ad hoc committee then drew up a draft constitution in preparation for the first public meeting, arranged for 2 August 1973.

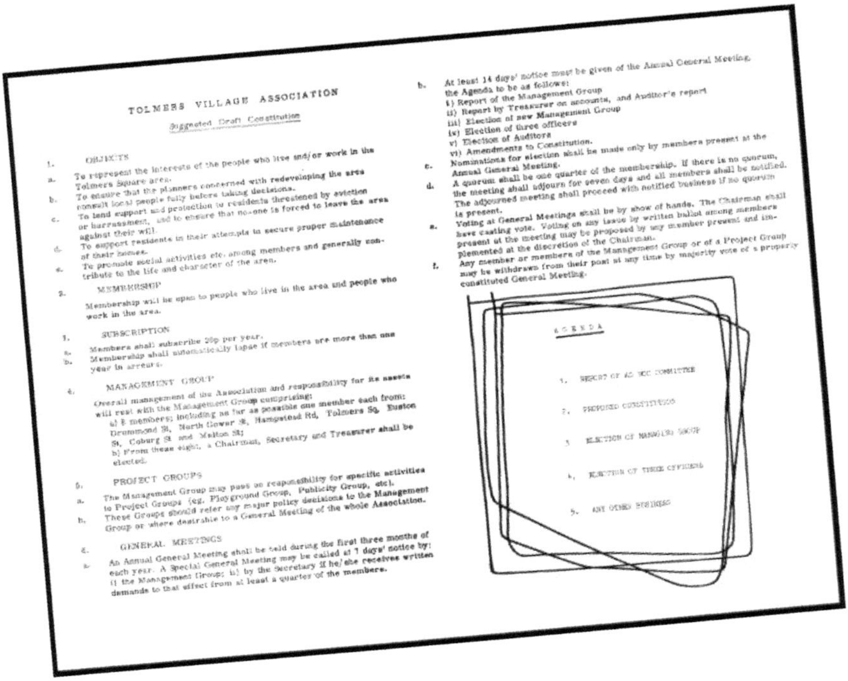

TOLMERS VILLAGE ASSOCIATION

Suggested Draft Constitution

1. OBJECTS

a. To represent the interests of the people who live and/or work in the Tolmers Square area.

b. To ensure that the planners concerned with redeveloping the area consult local people fully before taking decisions.

c. To lend support and protection to residents threatened by eviction or harrassment, and to ensure that no-one is forced to leave the area against their will.

d. To support residents in their attempts to secure proper maintenance of their homes.

e. To promote social activities etc. among members and generally contribute to the life and character of the area.

2. MEMBERSHIP

Membership will be open to people who live in the area and people who work in the area.

3. SUBSCRIPTION

a. Members shall subscribe 20p per year.

b. Membership shall automatically lapse if members are more than one year in arrears.

4. MANAGEMENT GROUP

Overall management of the Association and responsibility for its assets will rest with the Management Group comprising:

a) 8 members; including as far as possible one member each from: Drummond St, North Gower St, Hampstead Rd, Tolmers Sq, Euston St, Coburg St and Melton St;

b) From these eight, a Chairman, Secretary and Treasurer shall be elected.

5. PROJECT GROUPS

a. The Management Group may pass on responsibility for specific activities to Project Groups (eg. Playground Group, Publicity Group, etc).

b. These Groups should refer any major policy decisions to the Management Group or where desirable to a General Meeting of the whole Association.

6. GENERAL MEETINGS

a. An Annual General Meeting shall be held during the first three months of each year. A Special General Meeting may be called at 7 days' notice by: i) the Management Group; ii) by the Secretary if he/she receives written demands to that effect from at least a quarter of the members.

b. At least 14 days' notice must be given of the Annual General Meeting, the Agenda to be as follows:
i) Report of the Management Group
ii) Report by Treasurer on accounts, and Auditor's report
iii) Election of new Management Group
iv) Election of three officers
v) Election of Auditors
vi) Amendments to Constitution.

c. Nominations for election shall be made only by members present at the Annual General Meeting.

d. A quorum shall be one quarter of the membership. If there is no quorum, the meeting shall adjourn for seven days and all members shall be notified. The adjourned meeting shall proceed with notified business if no quorum is present.

e. Voting at General Meetings shall be by show of hands. The Chairman shall have casting vote. Voting on any issue by written ballot among members present at the meeting may be proposed by any member present and implemented at the discretion of the Chairman.

f. Any member or members of the Management Group or of a Project Group may be withdrawn from their post at any time by majority vote of a properly constituted General Meeting.

AGENDA

1. REPORT OF AD HOC COMMITTEE

2. PROPOSED CONSTITUTION

3. ELECTION OF MANAGING GROUP

4. ELECTION OF THREE OFFICERS

5. ANY OTHER BUSINESS

The inaugural meeting was not a tremendous success. Roughly fifty people were present, two-thirds of them residents and one-third from businesses. Conflicts of interests were immediately apparent. The ad hoc committee had taken their cue from the student report and their aims were stated clearly on the leaflet advertising the meeting under a section entitled 'What we want':

To keep the village atmosphere of houses, shops and streets
To preserve the buildings that are worth keeping
To restore buildings that have become run down
To pull down buildings that are derelict and a health hazard
To preserve the variety of the local community
To maintain low rentals
To CLEAN UP the area and to IMPROVE SOCIAL and SHOPPING FACILITIES

The ad hoc committee also declared themselves opposed to the Levy Deal.

Several people, generally those who had lived in the areathe longest, were clearly opposed to these aims as the following extracts from the minutes show:

> A questioner from the floor [said] . . . he believed that 75 per cent of tenants were not interested in the Levy scheme but just wanted to get a new roof over their heads, with running hot and cold water, instead of sharing a sink on a landing . . . he could see no point in forming an association which would delay a plan the Council ought to have implemented years ago . . . Another speaker gave as his opinion that nothing can be done to improve many properties, and new housing would be much better (Minutes of meeting, 2 August 1973).

A few people actually left the meeting after stating that they thought there was no need for an association.

But despite this opposition the constitution was adopted without amendment, a management group and officers were elected, and the Tolmers Village Association (henceforth TVA) came into existence. At this stage it consisted of an uneasy coalition between small business interests, middle-class residents, and a few young working-class tenants. From the start, the long-standing working-class community played little active part.

Constitutionally the TVA was a democratic non-political organisation representing the interests of the majority of the inhabitants (residents and workers) within the Tolmers Square area who became members. Policy would be made at public meetings of all members, and would be carried out by the management committee and paid employees.

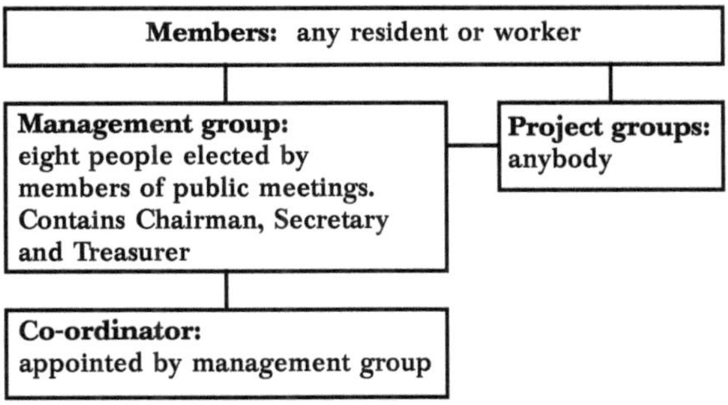

Tolmers Village Association organisation structure

As in most community organisations the practice was somewhat different from the theory. Most policy decisions were made by the management group. Throughout the two years in which the TVA was active, the management group was made up of a few young, often idealistic, residents (including squatters), some older middle-class residents, and a number of business owners (including Asians). Policy decisions were then executed by members of the management group, or by the paid employees of the Association, or by anyone else who was willing. In practice much of the work was done by a few activists who consequently also had considerable influence over policy.

These activists (including myself) were largely middle-class interventionists; students and professionals who had recently moved into the area (usually by squatting), occasionally with the primary aim of being politically active. Their political philosophy was fairly typical of community activists at that time. Basically they were socialists with a particular concern for the physical environment, for the way that people have so little control over the localities where they live and work, and the way that those places are exploited by external financial and bureaucratic forces. In order to combat this, power had to be taken away from the capitalists, the landowners and the bureaucrats, and given to people who actually live or work in any particular neighbourhood. The activists hoped that this could be done by creating grass-roots organisations, which could begin to take control of various functions like housing maintenance and management, street services and certain land-use allocations. These functions could be controlled better in the neighbourhoods than in the Town Hall. The objective was therefore to involve as many people as possible in community organisations, and build up a power base. As these organisations grew in strength, they could begin to demand power, if necessary taking it through direct action. It was recognised that the whole process would require a radical change in attitudes and would be a slow educational process. But eventually by being involved in the process of trying to make decisions, people would gain a greater understanding of the forces which controlled their environment, and begin to realise the need for radical socialist change.

The activities of the TVA have to be seen both in relation to the aspirations and motives of these activists, as well as in relation to the needs and aspirations of the various classes of residents and businesses within the area.

Initial demands

Following the first public meeting, the TVA sent the following 'requests' to Camden Council:

> 1. No decision be taken [on the Levy Deal] until Tolmers Village Association have submitted their proposals for the area on behalf of residents and workers.
> 2. Set up liaison with Tolmers Village Association with monthly meetings; first meeting: end August.
> 3. To let us know all that is happening concerning the area and to set up a notice board to keep us up to date.
> 4. Do not undertake wholesale redevelopment of the area but bring pressure to bear on landlords to recondition buildings.

(TVA 'plans', 2 August 1973) (Notice that three out of the four were requests for involvement.)
At the same time as making these requests the TVA decided to obtain statistics on whether people wanted to stay or go, and to canvass for membership.

Community newspaper

An immediate need, as all community groups have discovered, was an effective means of communication within the neighbourhood. A group of students (including two of those who had carried out the original survey) started a community newspaper, the *Tolmers News*. Its aims were 'First, to keep local people informed about the latest development of plans affecting our area, and second, to provide people who live or work in the area with a means to express their views about what is happening' (*Tolmers News*, No.1). The *Tolmers News* was produced with varying irregularity for a year and a half, by which time it had reached issue No. 20. It was edited by different people each time with consequent variety in style and content. Although production was often inefficient, it provided a useful source of information, as well as a great deal of amusement, especially for those producing it. Unfortunately it only provided a voice for a literate few, owing to the inability or reluctance of the majority to write.

The Association expanded fast. Membership reached 200 within a few months, increasing to 450 after 1.5 years. Initially meetings were held and information gathered in a private office in North Gower Street. Then in October 1973, the Association took over a shop in Drummond Street which became an office, meeting place and information centre. A local restaurant owner collected £40 from the Asian community for a telephone, and a local furniture store provided filing cabinets and furniture. An artist designed headed notepaper, a rubber stamp, and painted a geranium on the window, and the TVA became physically established; it was no longer just a name.

All that was then needed was a full-time worker to run the office and carry out the enormous number of tasks which the TVA was setting itself. An application was made to the Rowntrees Trust, who much to everyone's surprise offered £750 with no strings. The TVA management group offered me the job, and in January 1974, I started to work full-time for the Association as its 'co-ordinator'. After six months, a local resident, Rachel Syers, took over the job, which then became funded by Camden Council.

Formulating a community plan

The Stop the Levy Deal Campaign took place two months after the inauguration of the TVA, but it was not until the end of the campaign that the TVA played a significant role (see p. 114). This role was mainly to be a showpiece. The decision to support the campaign was made only by the management group, without any attempt to obtain a consensus view. It is quite likely that many of the residential tenants in particular would have been opposed to the decision as it could only serve to delay even further their being re-housed. Despite this, the TVA publicly supported the campaign, and the management group took advantage of being thrust into the limelight to put forward its own case for alternative approaches to development. A letter was sent to all Councillors and a deputation was taken to the Council meeting on 10 October 1973.

> Our area has urgent needs:
> 1. Immediate, short-term improvements in homes and the general environment for those living and working in the area.
> 2. A long-term plan which can emerge more slowly, making sure that everyone concerned is brought into the planning process.
> Towards this end we therefore urge the Council to:
> Reject the deal with Stock Conversion, casting it out once and for all,
> Investigate alternatives, such as rehabilitation and infill, and put these alternatives to the people of Tolmers area, who can say what they want on a long-term basis.
> *Meanwhile*, bring the full pressure of the law on landlords who are not keeping up their property adequately.
> *Meanwhile*, open up all empty property on the site.
> *Meanwhile*, make temporary use of spaces for gardens and playgrounds.
> *Meanwhile*, increase rubbish collections in the area.
> *Meanwhile*, hold a meeting as soon as possible between the Stop the Levy Deal Campaign committee, the Tolmers Village Association and the Council in order to pool information from all the surveys each of these parties has done (Deputation).

The TVA also made a bold announcement that, in conjunction with the Stop the Levy Deal Campaign they would 'embark immediately upon all the necessary research, planning, professional consultation and study of the economic feasibilities which will enable them within three months to present to Camden a fully worked out alternative scheme' (Deputation). The scheme would be based on the following principles:

> 1. That the existing community in the area should remain.
> 2. That most of the houses now on the site will be retained and rehabilitated.
> 3. That most of the 900 or more people who now work in the area need not lose their jobs and places of work, as has seemed likely under previous proposals.
> 4. That the scheme will be economically viable without the necessity of giving permission for a 250,000 square feet office block (Deputation).

It was a rash pronouncement but the TVA tried hard to make it work. Additional survey material was collected with help from students, and a number of sketch proposals were drawn up. The proposals generally assumed the setting up of some kind of non-profit-making development company, similar to the Claudius Offer except that much less office space was proposed. Also the office content was spread around the site, enabling more of the existing buildings to be preserved.

An exhibition

Although the first draft schemes were sketched out by a small group of planning students from UCL, an important part of the activists' ideology was that the new plans should be worked out by local people so that they truly reflected local needs. If they were worked out by an elite they might be no better than the Council's plans.

In an attempt to put this ideology into practice, the TVA held an exhibition in February 1974 entitled 'What do we want to do with our area?' There were three main aims: first, to inform local people about the development situation and to explain the position of the Council and the developers; second, to test some alternative development proposals prepared by students and members of the TVA; and third, to obtain ideas, suggestions and criticism from people in the area, so that a truly grass-roots development proposal could be drawn up. On top of this it was also an opportunity to increase membership and support, make new contacts, and generate publicity.

76

The exhibition, scheduled to last for one week, was extended for a further two, and parts of it remained on the walls for months. For the activists, the exhibition was largely disappointment, and led them to question many of their original aspirations. It cost £250 to prepare (a large proportion of the Rowntrees grant) and yet only 350 people attended, only 150 of whom were local. The activists had naively assumed that all the people who lived and worked in the area would be only too eager to come. It was well publicised, easy to get to, free, open all day and in the evenings.

The low turn-out reflected the degree to which the activists had failed to involve the majority of the inhabitants. It also emphasised the way that years of social conditioning have made ordinary people think that the forces that control

The village people

77

Whose space?

78

What do people like about
the area?
Why do they live here

79

How it could be

80

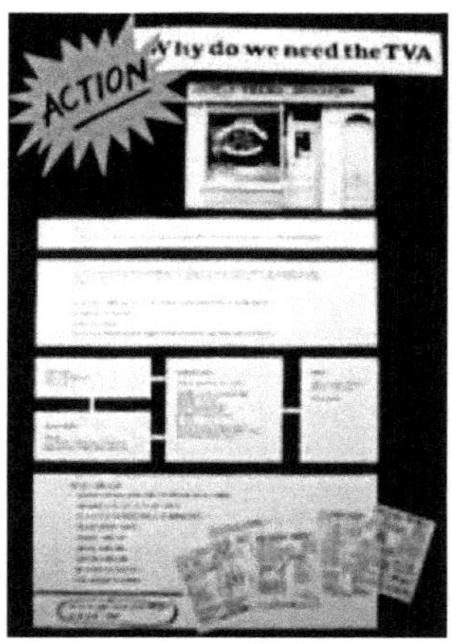
ACTION
Why do we need the TVA

81

their environment are incomprehensible, and consequently beyond their control. The TVA exhibition, like those held by the Council, was seen by people as irrelevant because the TVA had no visible power. Their attendance would achieve nothing.

A radical change in people's understanding of the environment is essential if participation and tenant control are to become a reality, and this requires education. The exhibition was one small step in the educational process of raising people's awareness of the urban system and the forces controlling it. But it was only a very small step.

However the exhibition secured a number of immediate benefits. Many members were enrolled, and new links established within the community. Contacts were also made with other tenants' and community associations, councillors, political groups of various kinds and the local MP. The exhibition enabled the TVA to find an identity. 'Its most remarkable and astonishing feat was to change the very reputation of the TVA from that of apathetic dryness to bright togetherness' (*International Times*, May 1974).

A change in tactics

But the TVA was still unable to present its promised proposal to the Council. Although numerous physical planning proposals were now in embryonic form, the financial and political aspects had changed. First, the property boom had ended and the Government had issued a ban on Office Development Permits. There was little or no market for office blocks, and land prices were falling, which meant that it became increasingly difficult to work out how many offices would be necessary to finance any scheme. Second, at the end of February 1974 the Tories were kicked out of office by a general election and replaced by Labour. This altered the situation drastically. The Labour Party was pledged to ending property speculation and nationalising development land and if they lived up to their promises they would have to allow Camden to compulsory purchase Tolmers Square.

As a result of these national changes, the TVA altered its tactics. Instead of attempting to produce its own viable alternative development scheme, the TVA would concentrate its energy on pressurising the Council to make a CPO as quickly as possible, and then to carry out a development acceptable to the community. To achieve this, the TVA embarked on a number of activities which for the sake of clarity, can be categorised as follows:

1. Liaison with Council architects.
2. Maintaining and enhancing the community.
3. Continual publicity.
4. Direct action.
5. Building a strong representative body.

I will deal with each of these separately.

Tolmers News, no. 14

Talking to architects

During this period (February 1974), the TVA finally manage to establish links with the firm of architects (Renton, Howard, Wood & Levin) who were acting as consultants to Camden Council for the Tolmcrs Scheme.

Liaison between architects and planners, and the people they design for is rare, particularly when those people are a heterogeneous, poor neighbourhood. There are several barriers, among the most important being restrictive professional structures, misconceptions as to who the clients really are, and class differences. Basically it boils down to 'who pays the piper calls the tune.' A major aim of the TVA was to 'demystify' these professionals, and to ensure that they worked *with* and *for* the community.

The architects had already produced a development proposal for the area which had been exhibited at the Town Hall in September 1973. But in the preparation of this proposal the architects had made no effort to contact the TVA or anyone else in the area. Their scheme was based entirely on the little information supplied by the Council, plus observation from wandering around on foot. Consequently the scheme lacked any clear understanding of the place, or the people in it. Although the architects asserted that it was essential to 'maintain the character and identity of the existing community' (Letter, 26 October 1973), their plans did not bear this out. There was no analysis of the effect they would have on individual businesses or tenants, or of the disruption that would be caused by the development. (What would happen to the Asian community? What would happen to Denny's butcher shop? Where would Fenn's engineering workshop go? How many existing residents would be able to remain?)

In January 1974 the architects were commissioned by the Council to prepare another, more detailed scheme, with a greater proportion of rehabilitation. This time, after constant pressure from the TVA, the Leader of the Council instructed the architects to contact the TVA, and at least listen to them. So in February the TVA management group met face to face with the architects for the first time. The architects were shown the schemes which had been worked out by students and the proposals being put forward by the TVA. They were also given a considerable amount of survey information which they were surprised to find was better than that of the Council. (They had produced their first scheme without even a current land-use plan.) The TVA was also able to provide the architects with information about specific businesses: whether they wanted to move or not; the effect of their being moved; how much space they needed; and so on. For instance, there were some firms, which had no particular reason to be in the area and were quite happy to be moved out. On the other hand there were others which would be totally destroyed by such a move.

Simmonds Second-Hand Furniture Store is a good example. This business had been established for 80 years and dealt in every conceivable class and condition of household, shop, and office furniture, carpets, curtains, linens, household goods, pictures, bric-a-brac, china and glass. It supplied the needs both of the local Euston area, and of a wider public with exports representing 10 per cent of the turnover. Because the firm owned the building (through a trust), it did not have heavy rents to pay. In 1962, their main premises in Euston Road were bought by Compulsory Purchase Order, to allow for an office development coupled with the widening of Euston Road and the building of an underpass. Consequently they put all their resources into their building in North Gower Street and spent £48,000 converting it to suit their needs. Although the move was only 150 yards it took the business 7 years to regain its former trade.

So what did the architects want to do with this firm? Simmonds was situated in a warehouse in the centre of a block of houses. The architects' attitude was to say that the houses surrounding the warehouse needed gardens. The warehouse would therefore have to be knocked down to make way for green open space.

The TVA questioned this approach for a number of reasons: first, if Simmonds had to move again it would be disastrous for them. Even if they could find a building of comparable size (30,000 square feet) in the vicinity, the rents would be too high for them to afford. If they moved out of the area, their identity would be lost and it would be years before they could build up their clientele and reputation again. Either way, the twenty-five staff would almost certainly lose their jobs. Second, it would be a social and economic loss to the community, for the people who depended on them for second-hand goods. And third, the houses surrounding the warehouse did not greatly need gardens or green open space. Most of these buildings were occupied by shops, restaurants, and hostels on the ground floor, with some offices and flats above. The people who lived in the flats at the time of the students' survey had very little desire for gardens. Certainly the need for gardens was not sufficient to justify the demolition of Simmonds.

Another example was Vines' grocery store, a small family business which had been in Drummond Street for 40 years. The building they occupied was structurally dangerous and would have had to be completely rebuilt. But it was essential for the Vines, and important for the people who depended on them for supplies, that they remained in the same street, and that there should not be a long suspension of business. The TVA argued that the architects should renovate another building in the same street, which the Vines could then move into before their own building was demolished.

In both these cases the TVA was successful.

The relationship between the TVA and the architects was far from ideal. For one thing the architects were inclined to communicate only with members of the TVA who had some architectural training (of whom there were several). They were reluctant to communicate with ordinary members of the community. Furthermore, they were not accountable to the TVA, and in effect the TVA was merely providing them with a cheap source of survey information. Nevertheless, the architects were perceptive enough to realise that TVA opinions carried a certain amount of weight within the Council. Their subsequent proposals incorporated many of the TVA's suggestions and, although by no means perfect, were a substantial improvement on their earlier schemes.

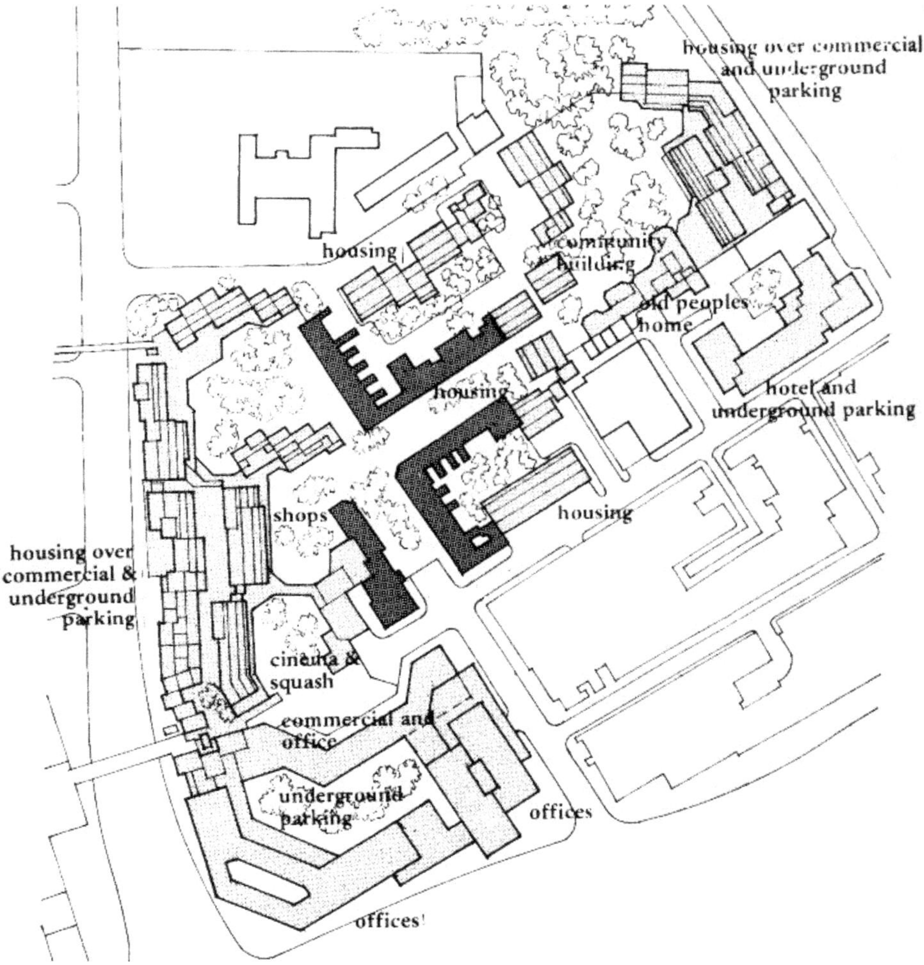

Architects' proposals, August 1973 (rejected by the Council following the 'Stop the Levy Deal' campaign).

retained buildings (existing use maintained)

new buildings

Architects' proposal September 1973

Housing: 1492 bedspaces, plus old persons' home for 40.
Commercial: 75,000 square feet.
Office: 250,000 square feet.
Shopping and recreation: 36,000 square feet.
Hotel: 67,000 square feet.

(Source: *Tolmers Square redevelopment proposals,* report 1, Renton Howard Wood Partnership.)

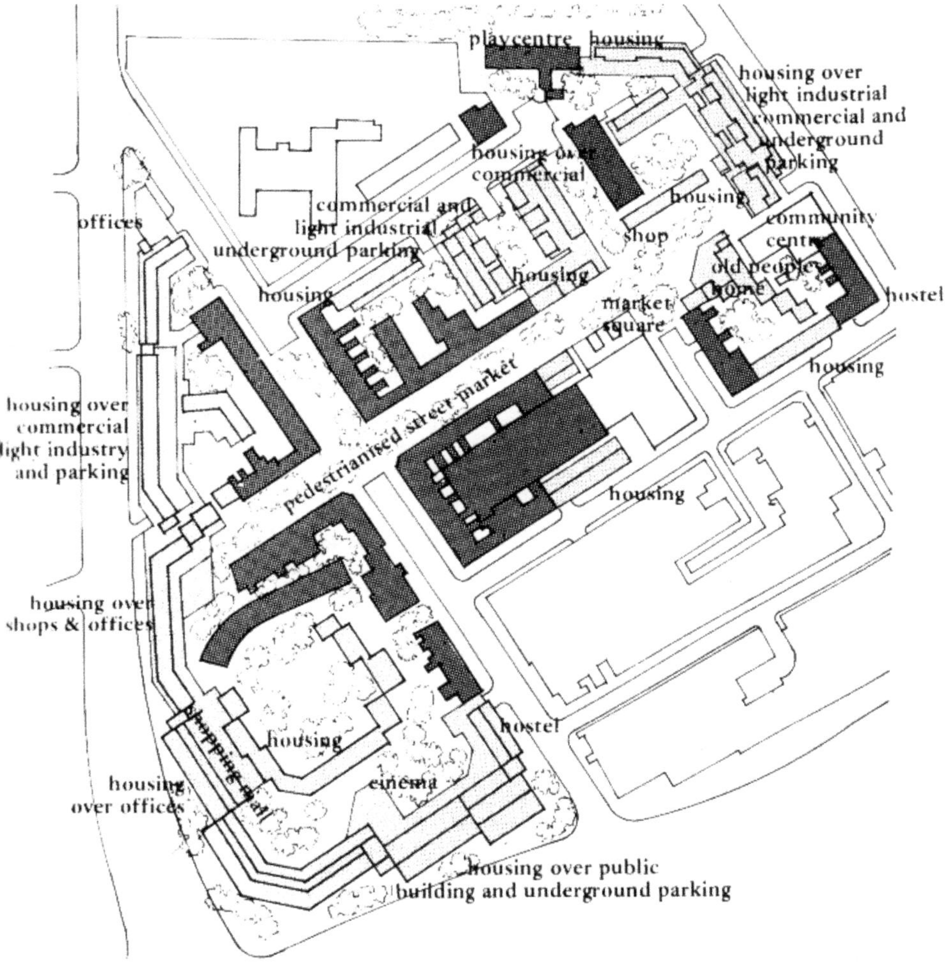

Architects' proposals, September 1974 (accepted by the Council).

retained buildings (existing use maintained unless shown)

new buildings

Architects' proposal September 1974.

Housing: 1707 bedspaces, plus old persons' home for 40, and hostel for 85.
Commercial: 82,250 square feet.
Office: 85,000 square feet.
Restaurants and shops: 27,500 square feet.
Public buildings: 57,500 square feet.
Light industry: 7,000 square feet.
Miscellaneous community facilities: 14,000 square feet.

(Source: *Tolmers Square redevelopment proposals*, report 3, Renton Howard Wood Levin Partnership)

Maintaining and enhancing the community

One of the main worries of the TVA was that by the time the Council finally got round to redeveloping, the 'community' would have disappeared altogether. It was vital to halt and if possible reverse, the spiral of decay.

Preventing physical decay

The TVA had initially demanded that the Council should pressurise landlords into doing repairs on the houses, but the Council were unwilling or unable to do this, and Stock Conversion were clearly unlikely to do anything unless forced to. The TVA considered taking legal action themselves under the 1936 Public Health Act, but came to the conclusion that it would be too difficult and time-consuming, and in any case might not have the desired effect. Instead the TVA wrote the occasional letter to Stock Conversion about specific cases, and resorted to publicity. A number of small repairs were carried out by volunteers, but this only had a marginal impact on the overall situation.

The only effective way of preventing the physical fabric from deteriorating proved to be by squatting the empty buildings. The TVA actively encouraged squatting by providing an information service for people wanting to squat in the area. The influx of squatters brought a number of other benefits as well as some problems, as we will see in the next chapter.

Information and advice

Another function of the TVA was to help local inhabitants by providing them with information and advice about a number of day-to-day matters – social security, parking permits, rebates, rubbish collections, and so on. One of the most successful services was a weekly legal advice evening when lawyers came in and gave free legal consultation to anyone who wanted it.

The main problem, however, was that the TVA became swamped with casework, and the co-ordinator had no time for anything else. It became like a mini welfare agency and attracted people from all over London. In many ways it was extremely successful at this activity, being able to respond to individual problems without the restrictions found in official welfare bureaucracies. Many people were helped with homes, job and welfare benefits to which they were entitled. But not surprisingly, many of the long-standing residents were critical of the amount of time and energy spent helping mainly 'outsiders' rather than themselves.

Building a 'community'

A major aim of TVA strategy was to regenerate the idea of Tolmers as a 'community'. The name 'Tolmers Village Association' was carefully chosen, and at the time was extremely pretentious. But after one year the aspiration become a reality; Tolmers was like a village.

To achieve this aim considerable effort was put into organising community events.

Social and cultural activities are of fundamental importance to any political group; community associations are no exception. They provide a valuable means of bringing people who have little political motivation into the ranks by building up a network of formal and informal contacts. Several attempts were made to establish a community centre. For a short time, the basement of the Diwana restaurant was turned into a club with regular discos. Later on, a derelict ex-National Westminster Bank was squatted and cleaned up. Toilets and lighting were installed, and it became used for meetings, parties, jumble sales, yoga and dance classes and discos. Sadly lack of maintenance and organisation led to its decline and return to a derelict state.

At one point, the TVA tried to persuade Stock Conversion to give a licence for the bank, so that funds could be obtained from the Council to convert it into a more usable centre. Rachel Syers and John Stansfield (TVA co-ordinator and Chairman) actually had a meeting with two of the directors of Stock Conversion to discuss this possibility, but their efforts carne to nothing. (Incidentally this was the only formal meeting ever held between the TVA and Stock Conversion.)

community events

83

84

85

86

87

88

89

90

92

93

94

The first carnival, in 1973, grew up around a show performed by an alternative theatre group. Seven actors spent the three preceding weeks in the area, writing and rehearsing a series of sketches, songs and poems about property speculation in Tolmers Village. The show was performed on a stage erected on the empty site of the former Tolmer Cinema, in the centre of the Square.

> 'It wasn't a question of how many people we could attract or the number of side shows we could put on. It was our main concern to show how well the inhabitants of Tolmers work and live together' (Ian Cooper, Carnival organiser, Carnival Report, 1974).

95

96

97 98

99 100

Direct action

There were many situations in which the only way the TVA could achieve their immediate objectives was by taking direct action. Direct action was also seen by many of the activists as being an important experience in itself as it provided an opportunity for those people involved to gain a greater understanding of the forces at work in the system, and to gain confidence in their own ability to change things through collective action.

Obtaining an office

The first direct action taken by the TVA was obtaining its own premises in October 1973 (p. 129). Up until this time the TVA had no base. There was a desperate need for an office which could be open to everyone, where meetings could be held and information displayed. Several shops in Drummond Street were vacant and approaches were made to their owners to assess the possibility of renting. All these approaches proved negative. Eventually one of these shops was occupied by squatters who offered the ground floor to the TVA.

The building was formerly a dairy but when the owners retired it changed hands several times without ever being let, presumably for speculative reasons. The current owners – London and County Houses Ltd – soon contacted the TVA threatening court action if the building was not vacated immediately. They claimed that they were in the process of negotiating a sale to the Council in anticipation of a CPO. The TVA then wrote to the Council asking them to buy the building and make it available to the TVA on a short-term basis. This in fact happened and the TVA remained in occupation for over two years. Squatting empty property was in fact the major form of direct action, and will be dealt with in more detail in the next chapter.

A bonfire site

When the TVA wanted to hold a bonfire on 5 November 1973, approaches were made to all the owners of the vacant plots of land in the area, to ask permission to use one of them for the evening. Despite the fact that the TVA arranged insurance cover of £100,000, all the owners refused for basically bureaucratic reasons: fire risk, planning permission, damage to the fence and so on. There was no option but direct action. A large site owned by British Rail was chosen and a bonfire secretly built. British Rail only discovered what was happening when the fire was already lit, by which time they were too late to do anything about it.

Taking a garden

In Tolmers Village there was nowhere for kids to play, nowhere for old people to sit, no trees, no gardens and nowhere to hold community events.

'Mongst flowers and bushes, grass and seats
So much better than sitting on the streets
The sun beams down and our eyes are greet
by colour and softness instead of concrete
The great blue dome of the sky smiles down
on our garden - so good - in the midst of the town.

'Mongst glass and grit and rubbish and shit
We'll make a garden out of it
Some say no, but we'll have a go
Though it won't look like Hyde Park for a bit.

(*Tolmers News*, No.9)

At the same time one tenth of the land was vacant, either being used for temporary car-parks or boarded up and left unused.

Right next to the dairy was an empty site which had been empty since the war when the original houses were bombed. In November 1973 the TVA asked the owners (Connollys (Blackley) Ltd, an electrical wire manufacturing firm based in Manchester) if they could use the site for the bonfire but permission was refused. In early March 1974 the TVA wrote again to ask if they could use the site for 'a temporary garden and children's play space until such a time as it is needed for redevelopment' (letter, 11 March 1974). As before they offered to cover Connollys against losses. There was no reply but at the beginning of April a strong gale knocked over some of the timber fencing surrounding the site.

One of the workmen sent to clear up the old fencing reported that a new chain fence had been ordered and was being sent down from Manchester in one week's time. It did not appear that the Company were going to be co-operative.

So the TVA decided to take it over without permission. The legal position over squatting vacant land (as opposed to buildings) was not clear. There seemed to be no recent precedents in this country. In theory the occupiers would be committing a civil offence of trespass, but the police could do nothing unless any vandalism or nuisance occurred. The TVA's lawyers thought it unlikely that the owners would take any action, especially if public opinion could be galvanised. To that end, the day before the planned occupation was spent preparing press releases and leaflets.

At 2 p.m. one Saturday about 20 of the younger and more energetic members of the community moved onto the site. Rubble and metal were collected and carried off, earthed areas were swept and raked off and rubbish was burnt. Old bits of wood were sawn up and nailed together to construct an inoffensive but significant picket fence, which was then painted white. A large slogan was painted on the wall to declare the occupation. People came from everywhere to help or watch and one old man was so impressed that he took the whole work force for a drink. Surprisingly, the police took no action apart from reprimanding an over-enthusiastic youth for painting a traffic pole red. They merely cruised past in their vans several times and then went away. Work went on until after dark.

The first thing that the owners knew about the occupation was when the company secretary read about it in Monday's *Guardian*. The company owned three adjacent sites in Tolmers Village, two of which were empty, the third containing a warehouse used for storage. The company secretary rang the manager of the warehouse who sent a workman round to the TVA to find out what was happening. He said that the firm were going to put up another fence during the week so that the occupiers would have to leave. He was told that if they did put another fence up, the TVA would take it down again, so that it would be a waste of their effort. He went to report and an hour later I (being the TVA co-ordinator) was invited round to see the warehouse manager, who said that although he agreed with our motives, the situation was out of his control and he would report to his boss in Manchester.

A week later, the company secretary came to London. Apparently the directors took a dim view of the publicity they had received. They particularly objected to the TVA press release which implied it was their fault that the land was empty. They considered that it was the Council's fault for refusing to give them planning permission to build anything (see p. 58). The company secretary told the TVA that they would have to leave the site, but he soon backed down when it was made clear to him that the TVA had no intention of leaving without a fight. He then said that there would have to be a compromise and offered to rent the site to the TVA for £1 per year. He even offered to make a small donation towards plants. All the TVA had to do was agree to the terms of the lease which would be drawn up by Connollys' lawyer, and 'it would be nice' if they could paint out the slogan.

A complete victory for direct action. Faced with a fait accompli the company had little choice. They either had to give in, or face considerable adverse publicity and an expensive court case. The rent was only necessary to cover them against liability and to prevent us obtaining squatters' rights after twelve years.

The site was used for a variety of activities. Kids built structures out of old timber, adjacent walls were painted and jumble sales organised. Later Rank Xerox, whose headquarters were nearby, donated £1,000, which enabled the concrete foundations to be broken up, and a lawn and flower beds to be laid out.

The garden occupation was a good example of what direct action can achieve. The inadequacy of the planning system was clearly manifested in its inability to use this piece of land which had lain empty and derelict for twenty-six years. At the same time there was a lack of play space and gardens in the area. The community was unable to rectify the situation by negotiation, and they therefore took direct action of a semi-legal nature. By doing so they were able to alter the balance of power sufficiently to enable them to do what they wanted with the site, without going so far as to warrant repressive action against them by the company or the state. It would be naive to suggest that this action in itself was revolutionary. There was no change in land ownership, and no significant change in the balance of power. In concrete terms all that happened was that TVA managed to rent a piece of land for a very small fee. Neither the Council nor the company lost anything. (The company actually gained, as their donation was less than the cost of a new fence.) But what the action did achieve was to give those involved a greater confidence in their ability to do things for themselves, and to take on the authorities. Through involvement, people gained a clearer idea of the forces which control the environment, and an experience of collective action.

101

102

103

104

105

106

107

Camden Journal, 15 February, 24 May, 7 and 28 June 1974, and 28 February 1975, *Morning Star,* 21 June 1974, *Hampstead & Highgate Express,* 17 May 1974.

Publicity

The effectiveness of community groups in exerting political leverage, largely depends on their ability to build up and maintain a high level of public interest. The Stop the Levy Deal Campaign generated considerable interest, but there was a danger that the issue would be forgotten, and that after a number of years a new deal would slip through unnoticed. A primary concern of the TVA was that this should not happen and much effort was spent ensuring that Tolmers Square remained a live issue. In addition it was felt the lessons learnt in Tolmers should be disseminated to other groups involved in similar struggles. Every opportunity was therefore taken to use the press, radio and television to advantage.

Much of this publicity was frivolous and missed the real issues but it served a purpose in keeping Tolmers in the news. However, the TVA did not rely solely on existing media organs and published its own material.

Pamphlet

The community newspaper *Tolmers News* has already been mentioned. In addition, in June 1974, the TVA published *Tolmers Destroyed* a sixteen page 'report on the activities of property speculators Stock Conversion and Investment Trust in Tolmers Square and their effect on the community'. It was well produced (typeset and illustrated with photographs) and was sold for 15p. It was published at a time when the Council had not yet made any public decisions on how to proceed with the development of the land owned by Stock Conversion and it included the demand that Tolmers Square be brought into public ownership immediately. The TVA hoped that it would stimulate the Council into action, but it also had wider aims: 'We hope that *Tolmers Destroyed* will lend weight to those seeking to bring about legislative change to bring property speculation to an end, (press release). The report was well received and sold over 1,000 copies. Orders were received from as far away as Wales, Holland and even Canada.

Making a film

The single most effective piece of publicity was *Tolmers: Beginning or End?*, a 30-minute documentary film shot in the summer of 1974. It was made by an independent film-maker who worked in an advertising agency in Euston Street. A member of the TVA management group who also worked in the agency, suggested that he make a film about what was going on around him and he started straight away. I wrote the narration and arranged the interviews and he started filming.

The main problem was of course lack of money. The BBC would probably have spent £8,000 on making a similar film, but by doing most of the filming, editing, research and scriptwriting with volunteer helpers, and by scrounging cheap materials and editing rooms, it was done for £1,600. But this was still a lot of money. An appeal was made to local businessmen and a few other benefactors which raised a few hundred pounds, and the remainder was borrowed.

There were many production disasters, but the end result succeeded in showing the effect of Stock Conversion on the lives of local people, the failure of the Council to intervene, and the growth of the TVA. The message of the film was that local organisations could be partially successful in combating speculators, but that in the end, government support and legislative changes are essential so that control of development is with the people concerned. The film was screened at the Gate Cinema in Notting Hill and was subsequently shown to various small audiences at universities and community centres. It was also taken abroad to Holland and the USA where it was shown on TV.

The main goal was to get it shown on British television, where it would have an audience of at least one million, and where it might actually have some impact. The BBC at first rejected it on the grounds that there might be legal difficulties with libel, but after several months, *Open Door*, a BBC 2 'access' programme, offered to show it. The reaction was excellent. After the programme was over the TVA phone was jammed with calls of support (and a few of abuse) from all over the country. Letters followed with more encouragement and some money. The following letter was received from Matthew Finlay Nicholson of Glasgow:

> Dear Sirs, I saw your excellent film on T.V. last night. It filled me with a slow burning wrath against the faceless Mr Levy, and the dilatory Camden Council. But more than this, was the courage and dignity portrayed by the people. I felt pride and kinship watching them. 'And they shall build houses and inhabit them; and they shall plant vineyards, and eat the fruit of them. They shall not build and another inhabit; they shall not plant and another

eat; for as the days of a tree are the days of my people, and mine elect shall long enjoy the work of their hands.' (Isaiah 65 : 22. B. C. 550)
I enclose £1 for your fighting fund and wish you continued success
'Wha does the best he can will whiles dae mair'.
I am yours sincerely (20 May 1975)

The critics were also enthusiastic. The *Sunday Times* described it as a 'committed documentary . . . professional enough to be a "Man Alive", which it much resembles' (18 May 1975), and the *Sunday Observer* said, 'It was a telling, angry, "World in Action" type ploy . . . the programme . . . did credit to the concerned and imaginative involvement with common life which is the best vestige of the now super-annuated Youth Culture' (25 May 1975).

But perhaps the most valuable result was the effect it had on the people in Tolmers itself. Most people had not bothered to see the film at the cinema or even when shown in a hall locally. But it was more difficult to miss it on TV, especially as the TVA circulated a leaflet reminding everyone (and ITV happened to be on strike). No one in the area really liked it. Some complained that there was too much on squatters, others thought there was not enough, some thought it too radical, others thought it was not radical enough. There was too much about the Indians or about the dossers. 'Why was my shop not in it?' and so on. But the important thing was that almost everyone was forced to spend half an hour watching it, and much of the following day talking about it. As all the advertising people know, half an hour on TV is worth any number of posters, leaflets, pamphlets or even books.

Trying to be a strong representative body

'The only way our individual wishes are going to be heard and considered as an important party in any deal affecting our area is to form a powerful and representative association' (*Tolmers News*, No.1).

Politically it was of vital importance that the TVA be a democratic organisation, and that it be as representative as possible. For one thing its effectiveness as a pressure group largely depended on its views being seen to emanate from the community as a whole. Then there was also the economic fact that the Council would only continue to provide a grant if they thought the organisation was representative and democratic. Finally, democratisation of decision-making was a fundamental objective of the activists, who provided much of the leadership.

Management group meetings, open to everyone were held every week during periods of activity, and in addition special meetings were held for separate groups, for instance small business owners or tenants. There were also a number of general public meetings to discuss specific issues such as a new Council scheme or the rehousing of tenants.

A fundamental problem was the different class interests within the area. In reality there was no 'community interest'. Tenants,

108

owner-occupiers, squatters, business owners, workers and the Asian community all had different interests. Initially, virtually the whole community was united against the developers. Stock Conversion were a common enemy, and if they had their way almost everyone would lose out, residents and businesses alike. But when it came to discussing alternatives, conflicts became apparent.

For example, the tenants had everything to gain from Council ownership, whereas the small businesses were almost unanimously opposed to it as there was little evidence that the Council was particularly enlightened about the need for small businesses. In particular, the Asian community was afraid that it would be dispersed, as had happened elsewhere. The TVA attempted to resolve this conflict by sending a resolution to the Council demanding a guarantee that none of the existing businesses should be 'displaced against their will when the property comes into Council ownership. Unless this guarantee is made formally in writing, the Tolmers Village Association will not support the compulsory purchase order' (Resolution, 3 May 1974). Unfortunately the Council refused to give any formal guarantees although they did say 'the Council will endeavour to ensure that existing residential and business occupiers are given the option to return after their premises have been rehabilitated or redeveloped' (Council Minutes, 17 July 1974). On the strength of this, the TVA was prepared to support Council ownership; indeed it became a major demand that the Council should make CPOs on all the property immediately. But in making this demand, the TVA lost many former supporters among the small businesses and Asians who were not prepared to put so much trust in the Council.

The TVA also could not count on the support of all the long-standing elderly tenants. Most of them were passive towards the Association, but there were a few who actively objected to its very existence. They had been living in appalling conditions for many years and not surprisingly just wanted to get out as fast as possible. The activities of the TVA were seen as likely to add to delay, and therefore they were not prepared to support it. For them the politics and the long-term future were unimportant, as Camden's Housing Liaison Officer observed:

> Whether what is on the planners' boards is wholesale redevelopment or rehabilitation, profit or non-profit, or other academic points of contention, is irrelevant to the everyday stresses of leaking roofs etc. What is of concern is today, this week, not 1999 when it's all going to happen (Dianna Sherston, letter, December 1975).

This opposition emanated from a real conflict of interest, but the TVA also had to cope with a considerable amount of paranoia and prejudice in the long-standing community, against squatters, Asians, intellectuals, long hair and so on. Many of the activities of the TVA antagonised one or more sections of the community, and received criticism accordingly.

The TVA leadership attempted to smooth over these differences and present a united front against both the developers and the Council. For a short crucial period of almost two years they were successful, but eventually these underlying and unresolved conflicts led to the increasing impotence and eventual disintegration of the Association as an effective political force.

Successes and failures

By forcefully reiterating the demand that the Council should make a stand against Stock Conversion, the TVA forced the Council to make public assurances that despite their lack of overt activity they did intend eventually to put a CPO on Stock Conversion's land, and that they were not thinking about doing another deal. There was little chance that another deal could slip through unnoticed.

It is difficult to estimate how much credit the TVA can take for the fact that Camden finally bought out Stock Conversion in 1975. As we will see in Chapter 9 there were a number of factors involved. But there is no doubt that the constant pressure applied by the TVA would have made it extremely difficult for the Council not to have taken the chance when it did arise.

It would seem that the TVA did have quite an impact within the corridors of power in the Council. The Deputy Town Clerk remarked, 'I think they've made quite a good contribution to the Council's thinking about what should be done in the area' (Interview), and Camden's Housing Liaison Officer confirmed that the TVA was considered 'a force to be reckoned with' by the Council Officers.

It is difficult to isolate particular decisions taken by the Council as a direct result of pressure from the TVA. It can always be argued that they would have made the same decisions anyway, but it is likely that a number of successes can be attributed to the TVA. First, indisputably, was obtaining a grant for running the Association from the Council, even if not as much as asked for. At a time of cash shortage, councils are reluctant to spend money on community groups unless there is a lot of pressure. With this money the TVA was able to operate more effectively as a pressure group, and was also able to provide help for a large number of people in need.

Second, the TVA was partly instrumental in achieving the rehousing of the worst-off households in new Council flats; the TVA constantly asserted that those people living in appalling conditions who wanted to leave should be rehoused by the Council immediately, even though the Council did not own the property. One public meeting in particular, at which the Chairman of the Housing Committee was present, was primarily concerned with this issue. Shortly afterwards, fifty households were offered new flats across the Hampstead Road.

Third, as already mentioned, the TVA was able to persuade the Council to undertake a far more sensitive development scheme. The architects' later proposals were fairly acceptable to the TVA and included a higher degree of rehabilitation, and a phasing programme so that disturbance would be minimal. There is even a possibility that the Council will set up a neighbourhood office with Council architects, surveyors, housing officials and so on when the development really gets under way. This could go some way to ease the inevitable disruption.

Apart from specific gains within the community itself, the publicity produced by the TVA, particularly about the effects of property speculation on local communities, has been useful to other groups all over the country who have been faced with similar problems.

As a pressure group then the TVA was extremely effective. But as an agent for long-term structural change it was largely a failure. The TVA never became a *truly* grass-roots organisation, playing a major role in the decisions affecting the area and it failed to seize any significant power from the Council as many of the activists had hoped. After just over two years in existence, the TVA ceased to be operational; with no meetings, action, money or employee.

It would be easy to attribute this failure to a number of factors internal to the organisation of the Association: a lack of adequate leadership; a failure to find a consistently reliable chairman, secretary or treasurer; a failure to sustain pressure on the appropriate sections of the Council; a failure to make and maintain external links with other groups and labour organisations; and a lack of office organisation and executive back-up. Alternatively, it could perhaps be attributed to the small size of the population and the high proportion of old, inactive people.

But while these factors may be significant, the main causes of the failure are to be found outside the area itself. The internal shortcomings largely reflect external factors which severely limit the potential of community action. Two of these which are worth expanding on are, the lack of information available to community groups, and the reluctance of councils to involve these groups in decision-making or give them any real power.

Lack of information

Without up-to-date information about what is going on, community groups are impotent.

Needless to say Stock Conversion were not prepared to provide any information about their activities and almost nothing of any value could be gleaned from their Annual Reports or from Companies House.

Sadly, the local authorities did not provide much information either. Camden Council (and possibly the LCC before them) were negotiating with Stock Conversion for five years before this fact appeared in any publicly available document. To this day, they publicly declare that negotiations started in 1970, when in fact they started in 1965, as shown in chapter 4. The public did not know that Stock Conversion was buying up property in the area until 1971 (nine years after they had started), by which time they had become 'the major landowner'. Even at that time, the public was not allowed to know which parts of the area they owned or how much. In fact information about land ownership was never made publicly available.

It is ludicrous that the public does not have the right to know who owns what land and how much they paid for it. It makes nonsense of any pretence of democratic planning, and national legislation is needed to rectify the situation.

Negotiations about developments usually occur in meetings between officials and developers. Occasionally one or two councillors may be present, but in any case the meetings are confidential. Much of the crucial information is contained in letters or telephone conversations, records of which are only to be found in a file kept by the Town Clerk. The public has no access to this file, even assuming they know of its existence. Despite repeated protest from the TVA, and a resolution from the St Pancras North Labour Party calling on the Council to 'open all its correspondence with Levy to inspection by the Labour Movement' (GMC, May 1975) the Council's files on Tolmers Square remained closed. (I was fortunate in finally obtaining access to these files relating to Tolmers Square, after three months of asking, and after they had been vetted by the Leader of the Council. Even then, I was advised not to use certain information, despite it being ten years out of date.)

Even elected Councillors may not have access to such information as it is at the discretion of the Town Clerk whether to allow it to be seen. If a Councillor objects to a decision by the Town Clerk to refuse him access, he may take the matter to court, in which case the judgement will be made on whether or not it is necessary for him to see the information in order to do his job as an elected representative. Few Councillors can afford to go to such lengths.

The TVA was even denied access to any statistical information about the area itself and had to compile all its information by time-consuming surveys.

The reticence of councils on the subject of property development can perhaps best be illustrated by Camden's planning department, who seem reluctant to acknowledge that property speculation even exists, let alone that it is creating havoc in the Borough. In the autumn of 1975 they republished Camden Scene, a planning survey of Camden containing 114 pages of dense text accompanied by figures and maps on population, housing, employment, traffic and so on. It contained a wealth of information on everything from 'Migration and socio-economic group' to 'Criteria for Zebra and Pelican Crossing', yet there was no mention, let alone discussion, of property speculation, or of the extent of the land ownership of developers, or of the effect that developers were having on the Borough. This seems all the more extraordinary when it is realised that that *Camden Scene* was 'conceived above all as part of the process of producing a new Borough Plan'. Its function was supposedly 'to provide information which can be used by everyone to discuss problems and needs and to evaluate the worth of the various policies which the Plan might contain' (*Camden Scene: A Planning Survey*). Its stated aim was participation: '*Camden Scene* tries to put forward the facts and asks the reader to make the choices'. Yet how could the public make choices without information on property speculation? It would appear from the Tolmers Square case that property speculation can have a more than negligible impact on the life of the Borough, and that any attempt to make 'Plans' without taking it into account would be folly. A more useful 'Camden Scene' might contain information on land ownership, land values, development companies, office rents, legislation in existence, and community groups.

The purpose of mentioning these examples is not in any way to discredit any officers or elected members of Camden Council. It is, I think, generally accepted that Camden Councillors are among the most sophisticated in the country, and I have found nothing to suggest that Camden's officers are anything but extremely honest and competent.

The fact is that while there is a free market in property, development decisions will inevitably remain secret. It is in the interests of both developers and Councils that information remain secret, because the deals being worked out are likely to be against the interest of a large number of people, for reasons already explained. If people know what is happening they are very likely to object, which will cause delays, as indeed happened at Tolmers Square. Yet there is no good reason why the public should not be told about these deals. It is after all *their* community that the property developer is getting his money from, and quite probably at the cost of their *homes* and jobs.

A fundamental duty of all Councillors should be to ensure that the negotiations being conducted are made public.

Faced with this dearth of information, opposition groups start with a disadvantage. They are unlikely to find out what is happening until it is too late. Even then it is extremely difficult, and it is a full-time job for skilled researchers to piece the picture together in order to know exactly what they are up against.

In one or two cities in Europe, community groups have overcome this problem. In Amsterdam, for instance, they have developed a city-wide organisation, have contacts inside most major departments of the authorities, and have computerised a large amount of information about land ownership and details of developers (including many British ones). This information is available to all action groups in the city, and activists have been known to boast that they have better information than the Burgomaster of Amsterdam himself. As a result they have been much more successful.

Lack of involvement

The second barrier, linked to the lack of information, was the Council's unwillingness to allow the TVA to become involved in making any decisions, despite its reputation as a progressive Labour Council, and despite repeated utterances from Councillors about the importance of participation.

The TVA made persistent demands for greater involvement. In August 1973, they asked for regular monthly meetings with the Council. In October, they asked for a meeting to pool information. Neither happened. In January 1974 a specific meeting was requested with members and officers who were involved in the area. The only result was a meeting between the TV A co-ordinator and the Leader of the Council. In June 1974, the TVA took another deputation to the Council.

> Despite the efforts of the TV A, there is still a lack of communication between those people making decisions about the area, and local people. As a start to overcoming this, we propose that a meeting is held within the next couple of weeks, to which Council members, Council officers, Council consultants, members of the TVA and other local people should be invited . . . . No plans for the future of the Tolmers Square area will be successful unless they . . . give people who live and work in the area, participation and responsibility in the planning and management of their area, and do not treat them as captive victims of the planning machinery (Deputation, 24 June 1974),

No meeting took place.

There were a few meetings with the architects as already mentioned and one specific meeting in 1975 to discuss re-housing. In addition, a housing liaison officer was able to communicate with the TVA after January 1975. But apart from this, there was no liaison between the TV A and Council officers. During the whole two-year period, no member of the TVA ever met any officials from Camden's Planning Department. (Bruno Schlaffenberg - the Director of Planning – even declined to meet me to discuss this book, a book surely with some relevance to planning in Camden!) Ironically the Planning Department was too busy embarking on a 'public participation exercise', with the usual charade of video films, glossy leaflets, and public meetings where the planners explain why they are unable to do anything that the people want. The planners had no time to meet members of the TVA.

Another blow to any hope of community involvement in planning was dealt in June 1974 when the Council turned down the TVA's application to employ a community planner in the area. The idea was that 'the TVA be given a major role in the redevelopment processes that are likely to be taking place over the next ten years'. In order to do this the TVA proposed to continue employing a community worker to act as co-ordinator, and in addition to employ a professionally trained planner whose job would be to:

> Generate participation within the community by organising public meetings, questionnaires and so on;
> Communicate with Camden's planners, architects and other officers concerned with the development;
> Formulate proposals for development;
> Handle day-to-day enquiries about the development from local residents, businesses and landowners.
> (TVA application for grant aid, April 1974).

It was a real attempt to break through the barrier posed by lack of expertise and information, a barrier faced by all community groups. Planning could be done in and by the community, instead of in the Town Hall by bureaucrats. Unfortunately Camden would not accept it because it might have threatened the status quo.

In the final analysis the TVA did little to alter existing balances of power and control. This experience is mirrored by other community groups up and down the country and must force community activists to reassess their strategy. In the early 1970s the aspirations of the community action movement were high, and it was hoped that the rapid increase in such activity could lead to major structural change. But it now seems that community action has seldom achieved

significant structural change. What it has achieved, apart from numerous short-term reforms, is to emphasise the need for such change. It has for short periods, given some people greater control over certain aspects of their environment, and therefore enabled them to gain a greater understanding of the forces at work, both in the community, and in the system as a whole. When the experience from a number of groups all over the country is pieced together, it adds up to a growing critique of the system which the system will not be able to ignore.

The ineffectiveness of the tenants and community movement in this country has been largely due to the failure to organise on more than a parochial level; a few acres or at most a borough. Unfortunately developers and finance capital do not recognise these physical boundaries, and will move to those areas where the greatest profits are to be made. If Tolmers Square is difficult they will try somewhere else in Camden, or perhaps another borough, or even Bristol or Amsterdam. To be effective, the opposition must cover the same areas. It has long been accepted in the field of employment that trade unions have to be organised nationally or even internationally in order to prevent capital being switched from one area to another. Workers in one factory can achieve little on their own. The community action movement only has real potential for radical change as part of a wider movement. It remains to be seen whether this potential will be realised.

109. Wall painted in 1974.

Eloquent,
Wealthy,
Intelligent too,
Playing around with me
And with you.

Living with the other half,
But just for a while,
They are given away by their insincere smile.

They're here for our benefit,
Improving our homes,
But our cause is only a stepping stone.
Tomorrow, Town Planning and back to the wealth,
And Madame Andre will be left by herself.

It's trendy to squat,
To save beautiful houses,
To be seen helping others,
And doing their bit.
Like self-righteous missionaries, they can afford
Self-denial for a while, it's good for the record.

But the system is our problem, it seems to me,
And these people are tools of the bourgeoisie,
For we are led to believe that they are 'left-wing'
And I think this is the most dangerous thing,
Because when they return to good jobs and the wealth,
And their politics are put to rest on the shelf,
The people then laugh at socialist talk,
And believe even more in 'each man for himself'.

Your problem is housing, they say to us all,
But really the problem is not nearly so small,
The system's at fault, yet so well in control,
Because it works the country as a very clever whole.
No change will be forced without public unrest,
And with associations like ours, they are doing their best,
To get immediate improvements, and I ask them why?
Because all it can do is to pacify
Those who should really stand up and rebel
Against all who manipulate their lives so well!

So I ask you to look closely at our TVA
And maybe you too will be filled with pessimism
Because there's a socialist cloak that's hiding away
What is really radical PROGRESSIVISM. . . . .

(Anonymous contributor to *Tolmers News*, No. 10)

8.

Squatting

> The real question is not whether one should pay rent or not, but why is it the rents are so high, and why is it that there are homeless, and why is it that in order to find somewhere to live one actually has to take over houses that are standing empty . . . . (Jackie Gray, squatter, interview).

To Mr. J. L.

> To Squat or not to Squat
> That is the question.
> Whether 'tis nobler in the mind to suffer
> The slings and arrows of outrageous speculation
> Or taking courage 'gainst a sea of troubles, end them;
> To sleep perchance to dream
> Of plans existent and plans yet to come
> Conversions dream'd of to improve our Stock
> And contracts social which with conscience limned
> Shall bring us peace that we may have a home

From J. S. with apologies to W. S. (*Tolmers News*, No.15)

> Squatting should be the movement of ordinary people to challenge the authorities on the whole issue. It must become the living demonstration that ordinary people will no longer accept the intolerable housing shortage. It must become the threat that will compel government, national and local, to change its priorities (Ron Bailey, *The Squatters*, p.34).

Alongside the growth of the TVA, another protest movement grew which was also to have considerable political importance: squatting - the taking over of empty buildings.

By this time, the squatting movement in London, though disorganised, was well established and expanding rapidly.

The current movement was born in 1968, and by 1973, around 10,000 people had taken direct action to house themselves, the number rising to an estimated 30,000 by 1975. It was a direct response to the housing crisis – to the fact that in Greater London 12,000 people were living in temporary hostel accommodation and over 200,000 were on council waiting lists, while at the same time 100,000 houses were lying empty. In Camden alone, 4,890 dwellings (18,558 habitable rooms representing 6.5 per cent of the housing stock) were empty in 1971; an increase of 142 per cent on the 1961 figure of 2,017.

The precise size of the homelessness problem in Camden is difficult to assess. In 1974, there were over 13,000 people on the housing waiting list, many of whom had been waiting for over a decade. In February 1973, there were 2,400 people in hostel accommodation for the homeless and in October 1972, 252 people were counted sleeping rough. In assessing the pressure for housing one must also consider the 'hidden homeless', those people living in grossly inadequate accommodation or staying with relatives or friends. In addition, there were many thousands of people, especially students and young single people, who would have liked to have lived in Camden to be near the University or their work, but instead were forced into expensive bedsits in the outer boroughs, with consequent costly and time-wasting commuting (figures, *Camden Scene*).

Squatting is politically significant, for several reasons. First, a large number of people are housed. Second, it exposes the ineffectiveness of existing planning and management of housing. Third, it can have a politicising effect on the squatters themselves, and fourth, squatters can experiment with alternative forms of lifestyle in a way that owner-occupiers and tenants find more difficult.

In Tolmers Village the squatters played another key role, which was to keep the community and the whole development issue alive. By 1973, the population had dwindled, the remaining residents had lost the will to fight, and the buildings were decaying. The squatters brought new energy. They halted the decay of the buildings, provided custom for the shops, and injected new enthusiasm into the battle.

The invasion

The first people to use the empty houses were 'winos': the alcoholics who hang around all the main London terminals. They were surreptitious, creeping in through a broken window at night and moving from house to house to avoid being caught by the police. They made no effort to clean up the houses, rather the reverse as in many cases they chopped up doors and floorboards for firewood to keep themselves warm.

The first 'proper' squatters were three architectural students who moved into a Council-owned house in February 1973. Over the next two years, 49 houses were occupied involving over 180 people (personal survey, June 1975).

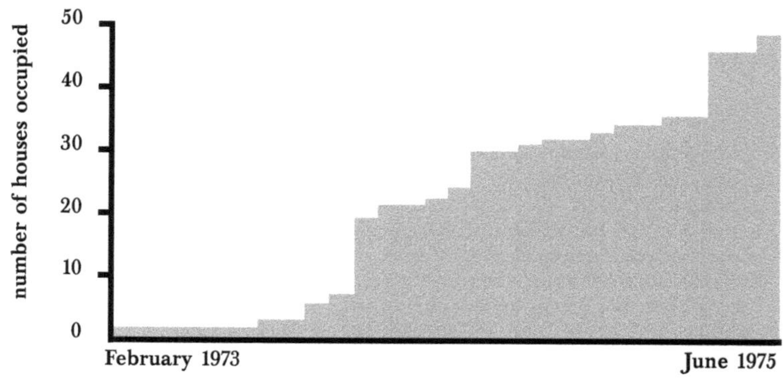

The invasion was gradual for two main reasons. The first was that the growth of squatting was closely linked with the growth of the TVA. Many of the early squatters provided the leadership and workforce for the TVA, and this was resented by some long-term residents who viewed it as a threat. Many of these residents were already prejudiced against squatters generally, because of the adverse coverage squatting received in the media, and because it went against their entrenched attitudes about private property and 'paying your way'. Squatting was a potentially explosive issue, and could have led to a complete breakdown of community relations, which would have been disastrous for the campaign against Stock Conversion. Such breakdowns had already occurred in other areas of London. Therefore, while the TVA supported, and indeed encouraged squatting, it was determined that the intrusion be as gentle as possible to allow the long-standing community to adjust to the new situation. At times as many as five people per day were arriving at the TVA office asking for a place to squat. Other people went directly to houses already squatted. Whether they ended up squatting or not depended on how helpful other squatters or the co-ordinator of the TVA were in pointing out suitable houses, and in giving encouragement. There was in effect an informal screening system.

The second reason for the slow rate of squatting was the derelict condition of the houses. Most of the houses had been left empty for a long time, up to eight years in some cases, and were extremely dilapidated. It required a great deal of energy to make them habitable, and many people felt it was not worthwhile, especially as they might be thrown out at any time. Only people who were determined, politically motivated, or absolutely desperate were prepared to take on the task.

The following extract describes an extreme, although by no means unique, example. It is taken from an affidavit presented in the High Court by John Wood.

> I moved into 213 North Gower Street in May 1974 . . . at which time the house was totally uninhabitable and full of rubbish and excrement. . . . On our arrival we discovered that all the lavatories, soil pipes, cisterns and hand basins had been systematically torn from their moorings and smashed. The floorboards in the back rooms all the way up the house had been torn up and thrown in the yard outside. The slates had been removed from the back

110 111

> slope of the roof so that the rain poured right through the house from the roof to the cellar where it had collected in a stinking quagmire. Ferns and huge fungi fed by the downpour sprouted from the walls. The ceilings on the stairs and in many of the rooms had collapsed forming damp mounds of plaster and rubble. Broken glass and splintered woodwork were strewn everywhere together with thousands of empty bottles of assorted spirits left by derelicts and alcoholics who at some time or another had sheltered in the house.
>
> It took me three to four months to complete the cleaning and repair of the house. Floorboards were replaced, ceilings repaired, plumbing installed and all the rooms, stairs and corridors repainted?. The wiring in the house was replaced and connected to the mains by the London Electricity Board after examination of our wiring.
>
> The exterior facade . . . was in an appalling state upon our arrival. This was a result of neglect and the running damp arising from the state of the roof. In view of the fact that this house is one of a terrace of five Georgian houses, it was particularly sad that the front of the house should have decayed and been allowed to fall into such a state. After two months of our occupation I undertook the restoration and the repainting of the facade of the house. . . . This house has recently been listed by the Department of the Environment as of architectural and historic interest. (John Wood, affidavit)

During the first weeks of occupation, water had to be carried from nearby taps in buckets, lighting was provided by paraffin and candles. And open fires were the only form of heating. Euston Station 'superloos', the university, or neighbouring houses provided lavatories and baths.

Some households never progressed beyond a type of urban camping arrangement, while others painstakingly built their own facilities. Gas, water and electricity supplies could be obtained if you had the money for deposits and the know-how to wire up internally. Roofs were repaired, walls plastered and painted, windows unbricked and mended. A local furniture store generously provided free or cheap second-hand furniture and within months, derelict houses became homes.

New Energy

Of the 186 squatters in Tolmers Village in June 1975, there were 40 students, 16 white-collar workers, 16 workers in service industries, 13 artists and musicians, 12 manual labourers, 12 skilled labourers, 11 children, 10 professionals, 8 teachers, 8 'housewives', 4 bakers, 3 resting travellers, 2 pensioners, 25 registered unemployed (including a number of people in unclassifiable community activities), and 6 unknown (author's survey).

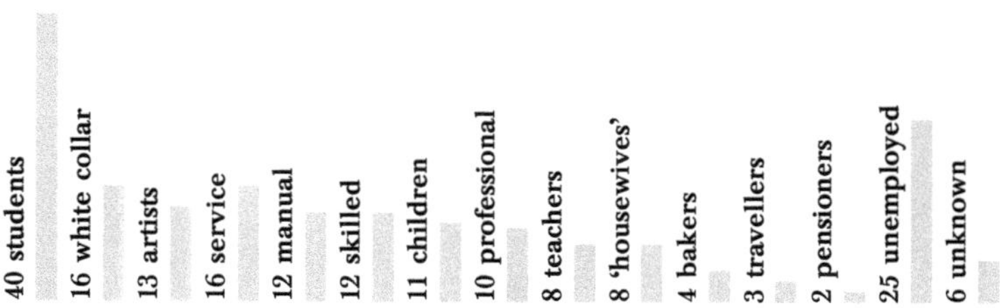

The only thing which the squatters had in common was that they all needed somewhere to live in central London and were unable to find it in the traditional housing market. Otherwise they constituted a diverse range of people of differing social status, age, wealth and attitude. The most effective way of describing the squatters is to give some examples:

> **217 North Gower Street**
> I now share the house with seven friends whose occupations are as follows: one medical student, three local authority social workers (one senior), one housing surveyor, one medical research assistant and one student of music at the Royal Academy of Music. . . .
>
> I moved into this house because I had been asked to leave a squatted house in Stepney by Stepney Council so that they could begin work on that house. . . . My income consists of my student grant of £480 per annum and it is impossible for me to afford rent out of this income. I believe the average rent for a room in London is £8 per week.
>
> I have squatted in empty property over the last two years because as well as needing cheap accommodation I wish to involve myself directly in the appalling housing situation in London. . . . Homelessness in London is of appalling proportions and paralleled by an increasing number of empty properties resulting from property speculation and delays in Council developments. I felt that by occupying such a property I could understand better these problems, and show the needlessness for properties to remain empty, when they can provide accommodation in the short term for many people. This fine Georgian house has provided accommodation for eight people for the last nine months at no inconvenience to the landlords. . . . We now pay rates of £148 per annum to the London Borough of Camden Rates Department. Before our occupation of this house the dwelling had been rated at nil value (Margaret Fitzpatrick, affidavit).

This building is now listed (Grade 2) as being of historic importance.

112. 1974

113. 1976

> **213 North Gower Street**
> Some of the people who have moved recently into the area, most of them squatters, have a high consciousness of the need to create a community which will stand against the generalised alienation of London, and a firm commitment to alterative ways of living (*Peace News*, 13 June 1975).

One middle-aged couple completely renovated another Georgian house, thought previously to be beyond repair, and called it 'Community House'. In one room they built a workshop which any local resident was free to use, and in another room they built a grain store and ran a wholefood shop selling muesli, nutbutter, honey, grains and dried fruits. In the basement they started a bakery, which produced 30 loaves of bread every day made with hand-ground wholemeal flour, as well as small pies and cakes. They also constructed a store room for plaster, cement, sand, recycled timber, nails and other building materials for use on repairing houses. The whole enterprise was non-profit making and everyone was encouraged to be involved so as to break down alienation between producers and consumers; almost a return to a rural peasant economy, where craftsmanship and barter replace mechanisation and money. Squatting was the only way that enough space could be obtained to experiment with alternative lifestyles.

114

115

116

117

118

119

120

121

To get a house like this any other way we would need to pay an enormous rent, or have a lot of money, or raise funds. Money is poison, it diverts you from the real thing. As soon as you come to believe that you can do things only with money you are lost. In the end you will become fit for nothing but rattling the begging bowl. . . . People need bread and need to relate to the person who bakes it. Shop bread is alienating. There is no contact between the farmer, miller, baker, supermarket, and customer. People want to see the bread being made through the window, smell it as they walk down the street, talk to the baker (John Wood, quoted in *The Times*, 14 February 1975).

They see themselves as much in struggle against the council as against Levy and feel that their own approach to a community centre is more relevant to people's needs than the £1/4 million concrete community centre the council will probably build 'where you can see the Vicar in Room 340 at four o'clock on Thursdays' (*Peace News*, 13 June 1975).

8 Square

I live at 8 Tolmers Square . . . with my husband Giorgio and my son Nimo aged 4.5. I am 40 years old and my husband is 46 years old. I am a housewife and my husband is currently employed . . . as an assistant cook. He earns £30 per week.

I was born in Italy and lived in Italy until 1964 when I came to England . . .

We moved into 8 Tolmers Square on the 21st December 1974. Before that we had been living for 4.5 years at 1 Westland Place. . . . On the ground floor my husband ran a cafe for four years. . . . Unfortunately, because of the rising price of the rent, rates, and food, we were unable to make ends meet and over the last year we were making a considerable loss. In October 1974, we decided to sell.

At this point we had to find somewhere else to live. We had been on the housing list of Hackney for 18 months, but received no offer of accommodation from them. . . . We went to see many flats in the North London area but every time we were refused mainly because of our son. Eventually in December 1974 we were forced to move. My husband had . . . noticed that 8 Tolmers Square was empty on the ground floor. In desperation we decided to move in. . . .

If we are evicted from this flat we shall have nowhere to live. We have a lot of furniture in this house and we have no money. We would like to move to a Council flat but none has been offered to date. . . . If we are evicted my husband and I will be put on to the streets with our baby son and the furniture (Franca Monachino, affidavit).

12 Tolmers Square

When my friends and I occupied 12 Tolmers Square in September 1973, we were strongly motivated by a desire to involve ourselves in the community by living within it and building up the work of the Tolmers Village Association (Barry Shaw, affidavit).

Squatting in No. 12 Tolmers Square offered me the first real opportunity since coming to London to determine my lifestyle, in terms of the people I lived with and the physical aspects of my environment (Caroline Lwin).

122. 1973

123. 1975

19-25 Tolmers Square

These seven houses had been converted for commercial use, by the removal of party walls. Squatters reconverted some of the space for living in, and other parts were used for a variety of activities.

124. A poster workshop established by a group of radical artists.
125. A general workshop mainly used for repair work on the houses.
126. A motorbike repair shop.

102 Drummond Street

Harry left the army in 1950 and started wheeling a barrow round the streets buying and selling odds and ends. He rented a room in Camden Town until the landlord wanted it for a bathroom. He then dossed in an old derelict building until it was boarded up and he was forced to live in a dumped van. Finally, bronchitic and at the age of 62, he was befriended by two young people who gave him a room in their squat.

Pam, aged 57, worked in a hostel in North Gower Street, making beds and so on. Then she discovered that she had a serious spine disease and had to give up work. Of course she had to give up her room too, and so she also came to live at No.102.

For a long time this house was the only squat with a bath, so became the community bath-house.

118 and 129 Drummond Street

> The prime function of Gorilla Welfare is to provide for families and those single people who are incapable of squatting without assistance. . . . We seek also to be as active as possible in general political spheres and more specifically where individual and collective rights are threatened by legislative or other, more direct, force. . . . Gorilla Books was opened in order to make information on this subject easily available to the general public in the Euston area, and to go some way towards meeting the running costs of Gorilla Welfare. (Leaflet)

Gorilla consisted of a small group of militants who felt that the TVA was too passive and reformist. They first occupied a sweet shop owned by a local publican, which had been empty for over a year. After a few months they wereevicted, and they then moved across the road to an empty shop owned by Stock Conversion.

Gorilla initiated many squats outside Tolmers Village, including the Crown Commissioners' property in Regents' Park, Cornwall Terrace.

127

128   129

117-119 Drummond Street

A fruit and vegetable co-operative was set up in the basement. Every week, someone drove to the Covent Garden market and bought fruit and vegetables in bulk. Anyone who joined (by paying £1) could then weigh out their own vegetables and pay for them at about two-thirds of shop prices.

142 Drummond Street

130. Space for community events and parties.
131. An artist's studio in the basement.

132

58-66 Euston Street

[The houses have] outlived their useful life. Most of the basements are in dilapidated condition. . . . There is settlement of the staircase, and springy sloping floors. There is defective wall and ceiling plaster. Some houses have defective and ill-fitting windows and doors and worn stairtreads. There is bulged, fractured and perished brickwork. There are leaking roofs. . . . There is rising and penetrating dampness. . . . [The houses are] unfit for human habitation [because of] disrepair, dampness, insufficient natural lighting, unsatisfactory ventilation, unsatisfactory sanitary amenities, inadequate facilities for the preparation of food and disposal of waste water and for the storage of food (Report by Camden Medical Officer of Health, 19 June 1967).

Five adjacent houses were occupied; three were used for living in, and two for workshops and storage. A second-hand store was set up in one of the houses with a shop frontage. There was no mains water supply, and water was collected from the roofs or carried in buckets from neighbouring houses. A wind generator was built on the roof in an attempt to generate electricity.

133

134. Improvising windows.

135. Dividing walls between backyards were knocked down, and beds laid out for vegetables and flowers. An old wash-house was converted into a sauna bath.

When our latter-day Shakers decide to bug out of modern civilisation they do it by . . . rejecting the world of the unadorned business suit . . . and setting up as instant peasants in New Mexico, the Cotswolds or Tolmers Village (Reyner Banham, *New Society*, 26 June 1975).

136. Roof repairs.

Sadly there is only space for a few examples. I could also mention the two junkies who found a squat in Tolmers Village the only place they could remain free from harassment; the girl who turned up with only a handbag and a baby, took a squat and then disappeared; the alcoholic with one leg who lived above the TVA for several months; and the Bengali family who took a house, nine of whom had previously been living in two rooms.

There were many foreigners, in particular a number of Israeli students who were unable to return to their own country because of draft. During the summer the population was swelled by an influx of visitors from all over the world, who preferred to accept hospitality in squats rather than pay for friendless hotels. As a result, many international links were established, especially with squatting communities in other parts of Europe.

Several radical groups established themselves in the area. In particular many squatters were members of the International Marxist Group. Later an International Socialist women's group squatted an office in the area, and the Wages for Housework Campaign set up its headquarters in an old Bank, and later took over the Gorilla bookshop.

Tolmers Village was not without its drug scene. There were a few acid freaks, and some squatters grew their own marijuana on the roof of their house until they got busted. (Rumour has it that M I 5 and the Special Branch have offices in the Euston Tower, and spotted the plants with binoculars.)

As the numbers increased, the squatting community developed its own dynamics. It was insecure, changing daily, and there was a sense of energy and enthusiasm which is seldom found in the centres of our cities.

Reversing decline

Squatters did not merely provide housing for themselves; they also gave a boost to the whole area. Derelict buildings, which were previously a fire and damp hazard as well as being an eyesore, were now inhabited, and in many cases cleaned up. The squatters also revived the faltering trade of many small shops and businesses. Above all perhaps, they re-established Tolmers as a place with a 'community', albeit a very different kind of community from the one of the past.

An elderly lady, commented 'I think the squatters have introduced the only communal element we have ever had in this district. I've lived here 23 years and there's been nothing but backbiting, and now the squatters have brought a friendly atmosphere in' (Dorothy Norden, *Tolmers: Beginning or End?*). And a local restaurant owner wrote:

> As a direct result of the influx of squatters and the establishment of the Tolmers Village Association I have seen a community re-established in these streets which is unique in my experience of London in the last 22 years. . . . They have contributed an enormous amount of life and activity to the community which would never have happened without them. I believe in a modern community it is essential that people should have contact with their neighbours and organise themselves in communal activities. Without this kind of structure people in cities are cut off from their neighbours and remain friendless and lonely. . . .
>
> I have made more friends among these people in the last 18 months than I have in the 22 years I have lived in London (Jeyant Patel, affidavit).

It was extremely important for the general campaign that the squatters should have the support of the established community. As already mentioned, squatters played a key role in the running of the TVA, both in organising political action and in providing manpower for community events. Although in theory the TVA had little connection with squatting, in practice if squatters were unpopular the TVA would lose support. Also there was the question of Council support. When the squatters eventually faced eviction from Stock Conversion, they would be in a much stronger position if the Council was behind them. And Council policy on squatting was largely determined by the relationship between the squatters and the long-term residents. If the squatters lost the support of the long-term residents they would lose the support of the Council also. There were in fact a number of minor conflicts between squatters and tenants, mostly resulting from a clash of values and attitudes. Inevitably, a few squatters behaved antisocially by holding late-night parties and so on. But in general these conflicts were resolved, and with the exception of a few dedicated right-wingers, the long-standing population were prepared to accept, if not actively support, the new occupiers.

Avoiding eviction

If the squatters were to play a role in the campaign against Stock Conversion, it was imperative that they should avoid being evicted. Throughout the first two years of occupation, the squatters were living under a constant threat of eviction. At any time, Stock Conversion, who owned most of the squatted houses, could have started possession proceedings and evicted everyone within weeks. But they did not. It was 1.5 years after the first squatters had occupied one of their houses that Stock Conversion finally issued summonses for possession, and even then they were not very successful. By using a variety of tactics, the squatters were extremely skilful in avoiding eviction, and it is interesting to examine these tactics in some detail.

The 'reasonable' approach

The first house owned by Stock Conversion to be openly squatted was No 12 Tolmers Square which four friends and I occupied in September 1973, during the Stop the Levy Deal Campaign. Almost immediately we wrote an 'ultra reasonable' letter to Stock Conversion:

> Dear Sir, Twelve days ago we occupied number 12 Tolmers Square. . . . All of us in the house study or work in central London and have been unable to find suitable accommodation. Your house seemed almost ideal and as it was not being used for any other purpose we took the liberty of occupying it. We are improving the house and keeping it in good condition with our own money, and we are quite prepared to pay rates. When you require the house for redevelopment purposes we will move out without fuss. Until that time we hope you will let us stay. In any case, we are more than willing to discuss the situation.
> Yours faithfully . . . (27 September 1973).

Three and a half weeks later we received a reply from one of the Directors:

> I am sure you will appreciate that in taking unauthorised possession of our premises at No 12 Tolmers Square you are trespassing, an act which we cannot possibly condone. Moreover, your action could result in this Company being unable to carry out its obligation to the London Borough of Camden, to whom we have undertaken to deliver vacant possession of No 12 Tolmers Square. In these circumstances, we have no alternative but to seek our Solicitor's advice on our remedies (22 October 1973).

There was no more to be said and we merely wrote back restating our position and added for luck 'I hope you will not take any unnecessary action against us prior to consultation' (12 December 1973).

Whether this 'reasonable' approach had any beneficial effect will never be known. However for several months no action was taken against us, and a number of other houses owned by Stock Conversion were squatted without any trouble. Nothing more was heard from them until January 1974 when a commercial building was squatted at 142 Drummond Street. This occupation sparked Stock Conversion into action. Almost immediately the occupants were told they would be evicted, and a few days later I received a letter from the same Director, saying 'I think it would be useful, if you agree, that you and I should have a meeting at my office in Jermyn Street' (23 January 1974).

It was with a good deal of trepidation that two of us sat down at the conference table in Stock Conversion's offices one week later, faced by a Director and another executive. The executive opened the meeting with scathing moral condemnation of people who trespassed on private property. We replied by pointing out that Stock Conversion's morals were not above question; their policies amounting to legalised vandalism on an unprecedented scale. After a few minutes of bickering the meeting was started in earnest. It appeared that they were concerned at the rapid increase in squatting and in particular the occupation of 142 Drummond Street, because these were 'commercial' premises. They wanted it stopped. They were clearly confused about the relationship between the TVA and squatters but felt that by virtue of my own position as co-ordinator of the TVA I could 'control' the squatting in the area. They rejected any form of licence and said that the squatters would have to leave 142 Drummond Street and refrain from squatting any other buildings. If not they would evict all the squatters. We should meet them again in a month.

It was a difficult dilemma. If the squatters took any notice of Stock Conversion's threats it would look like weakness, yet on the other hand they could not afford to ignore them. It was essential for the TVA that the squatters remain, and at that time there was not enough strength or solidarity to fight off an eviction attempt. It was tactically a bad time for a confrontation. After some bitter disagreement the TVA decided to try and conform to Stock Conversion's demands for the time being and ask the squatters to vacate the commercial premises.

This policy came under a lot of attack. As one underground newspaper reported:

> It then transpired that the TVA had come to an agreement with Mr Levy. They were to be allowed to stay, unmolested for the time, in Mr Levy's houses as long as they promised not to implement any further squats in Mr Levy's houses and ensure that no other group squatted Mr Levy's empty fucking houses. This was a low blow. Whereas previously, anybody wishing to squat had had free option, now the TVA were setting themselves up as an effective police force for Mr Levy. Yes sir! The campaign was bowing down at the altar of compromise. . . . The Tolmers Village Association had SOLD OUT (*International Times*, May/June 1974).

The policy never became operational as one hard-liner refused to leave the commercial building, and the situation was aggravated even further when Stock Conversion fixed a new padlock to the building thinking that it had been vacated. The sole remaining occupant returned from work, ripped off the lock, and accused the TVA of having put it on in order to intimidate him. He threatened to kill anyone who tried to get him out.

A hint of strength

The second meeting with Stock Conversion was less congenial than the first. One of the Directors opened the meeting by telling us that we had lost all credibility. We had failed to vacate 142 Drummond Street and to add insult to injury we had ripped their padlock off the door. Furthermore we had squatted another house in the area. (In fact it was already squatted before the first meeting but they had not noticed.) There was no further use in our meeting, and they would start eviction procedure immediately. We replied by pointing out that we had no control over the squatters and re-emphasised the absurdity of throwing people out of the houses which would then lie empty. It was this moral absurdity, combined with the organisational strength of the squatters and the TVA which would determine the press and Camden's reaction to any eviction attempts. It was the squatters only weapon and we made it as clear as possible, that if they tried to evict the squatters, there would be a big fight. It was partially a bluff but it seemed to work. Stock Conversion took no immediate action.

A show of strength

But a few months later an investigator came round to the squats, asking for names, the first step in possession proceedings. The squatters immediately held a meeting, revived the Tolmers Square Squatters Action Group, and started making preparations for a campaign. A public meeting was organised in the local school on property speculation. The squatters' demands were militant:

> We are not prepared to hand over these houses to the bulldozers of the profiteers. . . . Faced with a new Levy offensive we therefore demand an end to the dithering of the Council. The Council must immediately declare that it has broken off negotiations with Levy and CPO all his property at minimal cost. It must embark on a programme of rehabilitation and rehousing. If Levy attempts to carry out any evictions before the CPO process is completed, we demand that the Camden Labour Party and Camden Council organise a campaign throughout the labour and tenants movement to resist any attempted eviction *by all means necessary* (Leaflet of TSSAG, June 1974, original emphasis).

It may be that this show of strength made Stock Conversion reconsider their position. In any case they took no further action for nine months, during which time the squatters increased in strength and numbers.

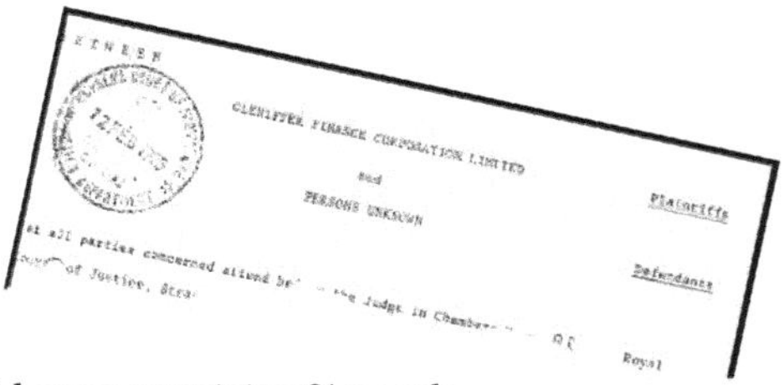

Anti-eviction campaign

But eventually, on 11 March 1975, 26 houses containing 81 people received summonses to appear at the High Court in ten days' time. The long-awaited threat had finally materialised. That evening the squatters held a meeting, formed the Tolmers Village Squatters Action Group (TVSAG), and launched a campaign.

There was no apparent reason why Stock Conversion should have decided to evict the squatters at this particular moment. Stock Conversion, despite repeated approaches from the press and the Council, gave no clues; 'We have no comment to make, and we have never made any comment in the past. That is our policy' (*Guardian*, 21 March 1975). Or, more explicitly, 'We never comment on anything' (*Building Design*, 28 March 1975). Whatever their motives it clearly represented a renewed attack by Stock Conversion on the area, and the TVSAG declared that it would fight all the way: 'We shall prevent ourselves being made homeless by all possible means' (Press statement, 18 March 1975).

The Leader of the Council was contacted immediately. He expressed his surprise, promised it was nothing to do with the Council, and said he would do everything he could to prevent it. Camden Council policy on squatting depended on the circumstances of each particular case. From past experience in the Borough it appeared that they would support squatters in private property if there was sufficient pressure for them to do so, and provided that the squatters were not a nuisance to neighbours and were not preventing the occupation of accommodation by people on their housing waiting list. While the Council had no legal power to prevent the granting of possession orders, they might be able to use their influence with Stock Conversion. It would in any case be a test of their sincerity, as many squatters thought that Camden might actually be in league with Stock Conversion over the evictions.

This theory was not without foundation, as shown by some correspondence between the Council and Stock Conversion which had been leaked from the Town Hall. The Council were at the time engaged in moving some of the older residents out of houses owned by Stock Conversion into new flats nearby. The Director of Housing wrote to Stock Conversion informing them of this: 'As this step will be to the advantage of Stock Conversion Ltd., I must ask you as agreed at meetings last year with the Council's officers not to allow the houses concerned to be filled up again' (3 January 1975). In reply, Stock Conversion said that they could not undertake to prevent the properties being occupied by squatters, partly because 'the buildings you mention in North Gower Street are Listed ones and it is very difficult to prevent illegal occupiers entering the buildings when there is a restriction on our carrying out any alterations to the fabric'. In other words they could not vandalise them enough to prevent squatters. But they added that if the Council told them when the houses were to be vacated 'we will arrange for our builder to be present to secure the premises as best we can' (8 January 1975). A memorandum from the Director of Housing a month later stated that 'despite all the difficulties, liaison must be maintained with Stock Conversion to try and ensure an orderly transfer' (13 February 1975). The squatters were quite rightly suspicious.

81 TO BE EVICTED HERE
FIGHT PROPERTY SPECULATION NOW!
Haven't you seen this poster somewhere before?

But faced with having to make a public stand one way or the other, the Council came down on the side of the squatters. The Leader of the Council issued a press statement reaffirming the Council's commitment to obtaining the ownership of the land, and pledging support for squatters faced by 'unnecessary' eviction. He also instructed the Town Clerk to contact Stock Conversion and urge them to adjourn the cases for 28 days. Stock Conversion agreed to this and the cases were in fact adjourned for five weeks.

This gave the squatters a breathing space in which to organise their opposition. The squatters' action group was democratic, with all decisions being made at meetings of all the squatters, held at least once a week with a revolving chairperson and secretary. A number of smaller committees were set up to carry out the work: publicity, legal, intelligence, fund-raising, 'networks' (for investigating physical defence systems), and 'other places' (a pessimistic committee searching for alternative squats in the eventuality of the squatters losing).

By this time, the squatting community contained within it most of the ingredients necessary for organising a campaign. The printing press was able to print leaflets and other material within hours, silk screen equipment was available for making posters, and there were plenty of musicians (and a disco) for organising benefit concerts and other events to raise money. An elaborate press statement was circulated to the press and local radio, leaflets were distributed throughout the Borough, and letters sent to Trade Union branches, other tenants' associations and squatters' groups, colleges, MPs and the local Labour Parties asking for their support. Pickets were held outside Camden Town Hall, and outside the offices of Stock Conversion, and a public meeting was organised in a nearby hall.

The primary objective of the campaign was to obtain as much support as possible from all quarters, in order to force the Council and the Government to take a stand both over the present evictions and over property speculation generally. Although neither of these bodies had the power to intervene in the legal process of eviction, it was hoped that they might requisition the property or speed up the compulsory purchase orders.

Although there were inevitably ideological divisions among the squatters, the mainstream of the campaign was left wing.

> The machine of the law is moving into motion to protect the interest of capitalism against the homeless. The Labour Council, the Labour Party and trade union leaders of the working people of Camden must throw everything into a campaign against the speculators. They should show that they will stand squarely behind those threatened with being thrown on the streets. They should immediately:
>
> 1. Mobilise large-scale support throughout the labour movement to resist any evictions.
>
> 2. Demand that the Labour Government take over Gleniffer Finance [subsidiary of Stock Conversion] and other companies that reaped fortunes out of the misery of the homeless. (Campaign leaflet)

The campaign received verbal support from all sides, but sadly this support had little effect on the plight of the squatters. It appeared that neither the Council nor the Government were prepared to take sufficient action to prevent Stock Conversion going ahead with the court proceedings.

138

139

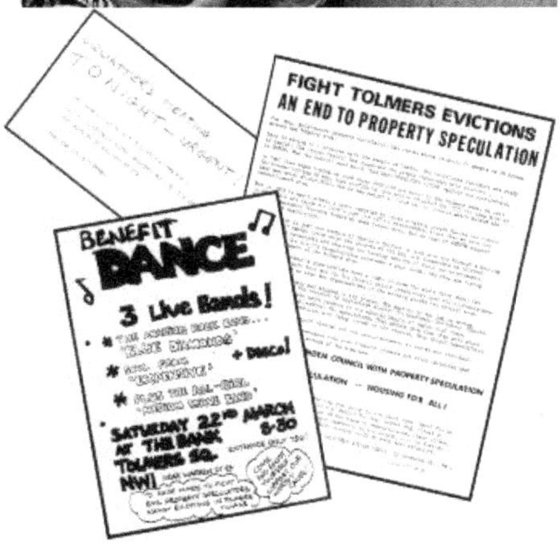

140

141

142

Tolmers eviction battle

SQUATTERS WIN A REPRIEVE

81 squatters told to go

Resist evictions — tenants call to unions

Tolmers squatters demonstrate at Levy office

Camden Journal, 11 April 1975, *City Press*, 27 March 1975, *Hampstead & Highgate Express*, 27 March, *Workers Press*, 19th March 1975

Stalling in court

Although there was no chance that the squatters would be able to win in court eventually, it was possible that they could stall long enough to give the political opposition time to build up greater strength, or for the development situation to change so that Stock Conversion no longer found it necessary to continue with the proceedings. From the moment the summonses were received considerable effort was spent on preparing a legal defence.

The laws relating to squatting would appear to be completely absurd. Whether an owner can obtain a possession order against squatters or not has nothing to do with whether he has any alternative use for the property, or whether the squatters will become homeless as a result. Moral and political questions do not enter into it. The owner merely has to fulfil a number of legal technicalities. Before 1970, owners wishing to gain possession of their houses from squatters had to obtain the names of all the occupants. It was a tedious process, so in 1970, the Rules committee of the Supreme Court introduced Order 113 which made it possible to evict unnamed persons and speed up the whole process, Under this Order the owner could automatically obtain a possession order from the Court providing, first, that he served the summonses correctly; second, that he could prove that he owned the property; third, that he could show that the occupiers were there without a licence or consent (i.e. that they are unlawful occupiers); and fourth, that he could convince the judge that he had taken ‘reasonable steps’ to find out the names of the occupiers. There is no defence against the granting of a possession order other than by challenging these procedural technicalities. (This whole situation is likely to change if the Criminal Trespass Bill becomes law).

The majority of squatting cases are not defended and go through at the drop of a hat, with the squatters not even bothering to go to court. Only a few of the cases which are defended involve lawyers, as preparing a case requires organisation, time, and money, with very little chance of success. But if squatters are organised it is possible for them to use the law to their advantage and at least gain time.

No money was spared by Stock Conversion in preparing their case. A renowned firm of solicitors handled the case and they hired one of the leading property barristers who would not normally deal with such minor affairs as proceedings to evict squatters.

The squatters’ defence was prepared by the legal committee set up by the TVSAG. They were fortunate in having a trainee solicitor squatting in Drummond Street, and his firm (Offenbachs) agreed to act as solicitors. David Watkinson, the most experienced lawyer in squatting cases in the country, agreed to act as barrister. The case was unique in that the lawyers and squatters acted as a team. During the five weeks prior to the court hearing, the legal committee worked night and day, meticulously analysing the affidavits prepared by the opposition, and drafting 45 affidavits in response.

143

On the morning of the court case, everyone gathered in the Square with banners and then marched in procession the twenty-minute walk to the High Court in the Strand.

The cases were heard in Chambers in front of Justice Croom-Johnson. The squatters' barrister initially asked for an adjournment on the grounds that the cases were unnecessary as Camden would soon be acquiring the properties by CPO. The chairman of Camden's housing committee presented an affidavit to back this up, but the request-was turned down after Stock Conversion's barrister had objected, criticising Camden for conspiring to trespass along with the TVA. The squatters' barrister also requested that all the cases be heard together but this too was rejected, and only one household was allowed in court at any one time. The remainder of the squatters waited outside.

144. Demonstration outside the High Court in the Strand.

The first case ridiculously hinged around a doorbell. The private investigator hired by Stock Conversion to take 'reasonable steps' to find out the names of the squatters, claimed he had knocked on the front door of this particular house on seven occasions, and received no reply. The two squatters concerned claimed that one of them was in on at least three of these occasions, and produced an affidavit from an elderly lady who was having dinner with them on one of them. Also, they claimed that their flat, one of several in the house, has an independent doorbell which the investigator should have rung, instead of knocking on the door. A knock would not be heard in their flat. Other discrepancies in the investigator's affidavit were pointed out. For one thing, he claimed to have visited three other squats in a neighbouring street at precisely the same time as he knocked on their door.

After well over an hour, the judge adjourned the case pending further information about the precise location of the bell, and clarification from the investigator (who was not present in court) about his movements. He was following the law to the letter, playing it straight down the middle. It seemed that although not renowned for being particularly sympathetic towards squatters, the judge was keen not to be seen railroading the case, undoubtedly because of all the publicity it had received.

In the second case, there was again conflicting evidence between the evidence of the investigator and that of the squatters. One squatter accused the investigator of telling lies, and gave evidence on oath contradicting his evidence. When the judge eventually granted a possession order, the squatter asked 'Does this mean you think I'm a liar?' the logical corollary. The judge denied this and was about to adjourn for lunch when he suddenly cancelled the order that he had just made, adjourned the case for a week, and asked the plaintiffs to ensure that the investigator was present in court at that time to be cross-examined. A successful first morning in court – the squatters had gained another week.

A week later, the court reassembled and the investigator came to the witness box. He turned out to be an ex-policeman: polite, smart and professional. He claimed that when he said 'knocking' he meant 'knocking and ringing' and managed to explain a number of other anomalies to the satisfaction of the judge. The key issue then became whether the judge would believe the investigator or the squatters, who gave conflicting evidence. He finally decided to believe the investigator and granted the first order with £50 costs against the squatters. One down, but it had taken over six hours of court time.

Stock Conversion were clearly surprised at the effectiveness of the defence and at this point a small incident occurred which indicated just how rattled they were. Their barrister made an application to the judge to have the squatters' solicitor's clerk thrown out of court on the grounds that he was known to be a squatter. The squatters' barrister complained bitterly: 'My learned friend has a whole army of people to assist him, while I have only my solicitor and a clerk.' The judge let the clerk stay.

Stock Conversion did indeed have an 'army' of people in court. They had 2 barristers, 4 solicitors, 2 private investigators plus 4 representatives from Stock Conversion itself. Even one of the directors was seen in court at one stage. The wages of these people for one day must have been hundreds of pounds.

The day continued. Three more cases were lost and the squatters waiting outside the court room began to lose heart. In each case the evidence given by the investigator was disputed by more than one squatter, and each time the judge decided to believe the investigator rather than the squatters. Then the case of 217 North Gower Street came up. The occupants – two medical students, a music student at the Royal Academy, three local authority social workers and housing surveyor – claimed that the investigator had not visited the house at the times he said he had, and each of them swore on oath that they were in at certain times and would have answered the door had someone knocked. There was endless argument about whether a knock on the door could be heard if someone was practising a flute on the second floor; all very amusing, if the homes of 81 people had not depended on it. The squatters' barrister argued forcibly that these were not the kind of people who would come to court to tell lies just for the sake of a few weeks. They were indeed middle-class, educated, articulate and good-looking. The judge was clearly in a dilemma and after two hours announced that this was the last case he would hear. The rest would have to wait for another judge. The atmosphere was electric and he adjourned for ten minutes. He was clearly tired and did not like the prospect of having to continue disbelieving middle-class squatters in favour of the investigator even if the latter was an ex-policeman. When he returned he spent twenty-five minutes summing up. He went to great pains to stress that he thought the investigator was reliable and trustworthy, but he also thought the defendants truthful. He thought there might be some 'innocent confusion' on both sides and because of this confusion, he had no option but to throw the case out, and to award costs against Stock Conversion.

A great cheer went up from outside the court room as the waiting squatters went ecstatic with elation, before rushing across the street to ring the press and have a drink. It was indeed a major victory. The squatters' barrister described the whole case as his 'victory of the year'. In the morning the judge himself had said that he would sit late, and continue the next day in order to hear all the cases, yet at the end of the day only four cases had been lost, and the remainder were unlikely to be heard for at least five weeks because of court pressure. By skilfully handling the technicalities of the law, the squatters had gained valuable time.

Preparing for physical defence

The time was used to advantage. A further ten houses emptied by the Council were squatted, so building up strength. The film *Tolmers: Beginning or End?* was updated, and shown twice on BBC 2, providing more publicity and support.

But the squatters could not hope to win in court, and it was only a matter of time before Stock Conversion would obtain possession orders. Therefore they started organising a defence system for physical resistance against eviction.

It was generally felt to be a waste of time to fortify the houses completely; past experience elsewhere showed that the bailiffs and police could get in anywhere eventually and there would inevitably be violence and bad publicity. Also the siege mentality which develops in such circumstances can be disastrous, leading to many people leaving anyway. The only real defence against eviction is lots of people and publicity. So they set up a dawn patrol, an alarm bell system, a phone-tree and portable ten-minute barricades on the doors of the houses. Evictions generally happen in the early morning. The theory was that three people would get up every morning at dawn and patrol the streets. If they saw any police or bailiffs in large numbers they would set off the alarm bells which would get 180 squatters plus friendly tenants onto the streets within minutes. At the same time the phone tree would be triggered, rousing the press and other people prepared to help (mainly nearby squatting groups). The portable barricades would hold for several minutes, during which time people would swarm into the house being attacked via an adjacent house, so that by the time the door was down, the bailiffs would be confronted by a mass of humanity. The remainder of the protesters would harass them from outside. The tactics were similar in many ways to those employed unsuccessfully in other areas of London, but the scale was unprecedented. Quite recently 6 bailiffs and 120 police had been used to evict one house in Camden High Street. The prospect of a mass eviction involving up to 40 houses was daunting.

Press attack

Throughout the court case period, local and national press provided coverage of the events. Although it was not passionately pro-squatter, this coverage did publicise what was happening, and made it easier to generate support. But in the middle of the campaign, the press started a general attack against squatting which by this time was flourishing all over London.

The housing situation by this time had become even more critical as a result of the 1974 Rent Act, which gave security of tenure to furnished tenants. This had the effect of drastically reducing the number of tenancies available, as landlords often preferred to leave houses empty rather than let them. The government still refused to introduce legislation to enable empty property to be requisitioned, with the result that both homelessness and the amount of empty property increased. Squatting itself had become demystified. With a wealth of information on what to do and what not to do, it had almost become institutionalised. The net result was a boom in squatting. The Advisory Service for Squatters – the only organisation with an overview at all – estimated that there were 30,000 squatters in London alone.

It was inevitable that the Establishment would react to this increase, and the Law Commission was in the process of drafting its proposals for a law which would make squatting a criminal offence. The anti-squatter press campaign paved the way for this Bill by attempting to isolate squatters, discredit them and turn public opinion against them. The attack originated in a series of highly distorted 'investigations' by the Mirror group published in the *Sunday People*: Squatting, 1975, is highly organised, nationwide, spreading rapidly – and DANGEROUS . . . it is not only a social problem, but a sinister political threat" (*Sunday People*, 8 June 1975). The articles went on to show how squatters were 'parasites', 'grabbers' and 'revolutionaries' who were in fact causing the housing crisis, and living off everyone else.

The Tolmers squatters, being one of the largest and best organised groups, received considerable attention. Three 'investigators' were sent to the area: a middle-aged man who claimed he was writing a series on the creative aspects of squatting in developing new forms of community; a fake left-wing freelance journalist; and finally a girl who claimed she was homeless, and spent four days squatting in the area. Naively the squatters were taken in by all three.

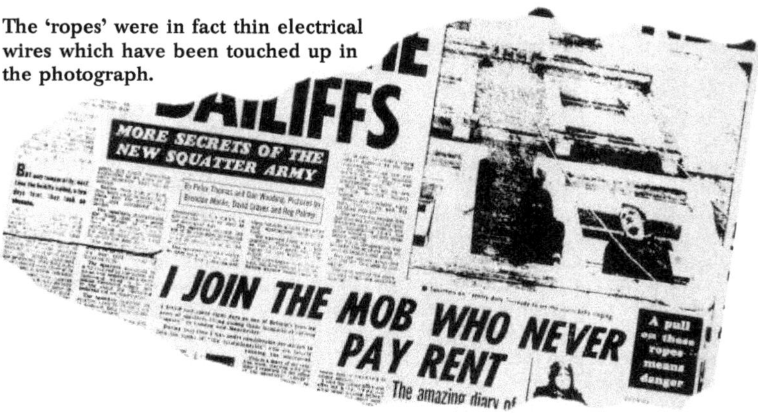

The 'ropes' were in fact thin electrical wires which have been touched up in the photograph.

Whether these articles and the ensuing hysteria in all the media caused any long-term damage to the squatting movement remains to be seen. It may even have had the reverse effect by politicising many squatters who had personal experience of the press lies. In the short term it was certainly harmful and in Tolmers Village relationships between tenants and squatters deteriorated. Several elderly residents sent a letter of protest to the Council listing a number of specific complaints. A few of these complaints (such as excessive noise) were quite justified, though little to do with squatting *per se*. But the majority merely reflected a paranoia which had been instilled by the press; for instance 'Most of the tenants will not go on holiday this year – afraid to. Might find squatters in' (Letter from a tenant to the Town Clerk, July 1975).

As a result of these complaints the Ward Councillor called a public meeting, which resolved most of the conflicts. After some violent exchanges, both sides became quite humorous and ended up going to the pub together.

Saved

Fortunately the press campaign and ensuing events came too late to affect the outcome of the eviction battle. Just as the squatters were returning to court, the Council announced that Stock Conversion had agreed to sell all their land to them. The court proceedings were suspended indefinitely, and the barricades were never tested. The squatters were safe for the time being.

The squatters played a unique role in the struggle against Stock Conversion. An important part of the developers' strategy was to run down the area so that redevelopment became absolutely essential. The Council, having certain responsibility for slum areas, would then be forced to deal with them on their own terms. The Council was almost powerless to prevent this decline, and there was little opposition from the people within the area, partly because they did not understand the causes of the problems, and partly because the most able people got out while they could. As the population dwindled, the possibility of local opposition dwindled also.

It was only by taking direct action that anyone could intervene. By occupying empty buildings, squatters were able to halt the decline, revive the community, and provide leadership in the struggle against the developers.

Evening Standard, 5 June 1975,
Hampstead & Highgate Express, 6 June 1975.

9.

Council take control...

On 5 June 1975, Camden Council announced that they were going to buy all Stock Conversion's land in the Tolmers area. The news was sensational. After years of struggle it seemed that the people had won. The developers would be out for good, and Camden would be able to build a socially desirable development.

Why did Stock Conversion sell out to Camden Council at this time? Could the victory be attributed to the efforts of Labour Councillors, or to the fierce resistance of the squatters and the TVA? Or was it entirely due to economic and political changes at national level? To answer these questions we have to examine the events of the twenty months leading to this announcement, following on from the Council's rejection of the Levy Deal in October 1973.

Although the Council rejected the Levy Deal and the Claudius Offer in 1973, they did not immediately commit themselves to any other method for carrying out a development. However a majority of the Labour Group were determined to bring the whole area into public ownership and carry out a development themselves. The question for them was how this could be done within the existing framework of legislation and balance of political power.

Initially the Council took several courses of action designed to pressurise the Government into giving them additional powers which would strengthen their position. It was decided to 'make representations to the Government to grant Compulsory Purchase Orders for Tolmers Square and to authorise a system of financing a commercial development which would return profits to the community' (Council Minutes, 10 October 1973). The local members of Parliament were asked to arrange a meeting with the Conservative Minister of the Environment, and discussions were held with other London Boroughs and the GLC 'to secure a joint campaign to redress the balance of advantage between developers and local authorities' (Council Minutes, 21 November 1973).

Although nothing concrete came out of these discussions for Tolmers Square itself, they played a significant part in the general change in government attitude towards property speculation. In

December 1973, the Tories did in fact bring in a complete ban on the issue of Office Development Permits in an attempt to stem the flows of funds into speculative development. This in itself affected the possibility of any immediate scheme for Tolmers Square, as both the Levy and Claudius schemes depended on such a permit, and it is difficult to imagine an economically viable scheme without one.

Tolmers Square was firmly fixed in the political arena. A solution depended on changes at national level.

While waiting for these changes, the Council produced a revised planning brief for the area. It was restated that housing was of the utmost importance. 'As the Council's original and continuing interest in the area is the provision of housing for people in housing need, the housing requirements represent an irreducible minimum without which no scheme is acceptable.' (The housing requirements were 1500 bed spaces plus a 40-person home for old people.) There was also an indication, however, that quick results in the housing field would no longer overrule a socially and politically desirable scheme. 'Every effort should be made to secure this at the earliest opportunity but the timing may be subject to lower priority than the planning and financial criteria.'

There was also an indication that the arguments being put forward by the TVA about maintaining the community had been heard: 'The maximum amount of the existing fabric should be retained.' This was the first clear indication that the Council was no longer dedicated to comprehensive redevelopment.

In addition there was a hint that the Council would not look kindly on a Claudius-type alternative. The scheme should 'if possible, leave financial control in the hands of Camden rather than any other body and dispense with intermediaries' (Planning brief, 17 December 1973).

The architects were then asked to undertake a further study based on the new 'planning' criteria. This study particularly related to the area not owned by Stock Conversion to the east of North Gower Street. The architects proposed a number of immediate remedies including rehabilitation of housing in Drummond Street and North Gower Street, the closing of Drummond Street to traffic, the establishment of a street market, the planting of trees, and the building of social facilities such as a community hall, play area, sitting out spaces and so on. As a result of the study, the Council resolved to make a CPO (no.5) on a number of houses in the area.

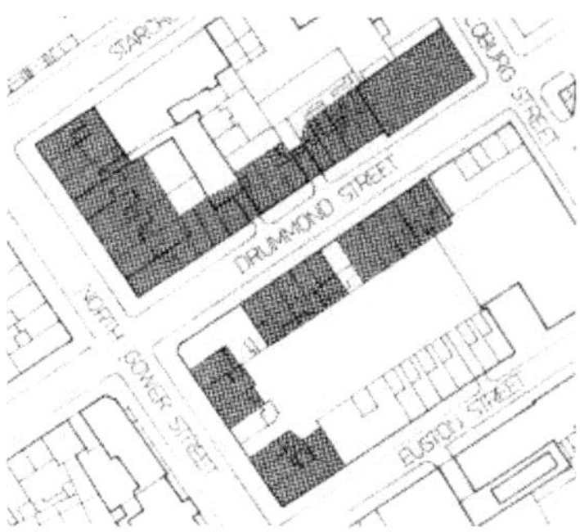

Compulsory Purchase Order, April 1974. (Source: Council Minutes, 24 April 1974)

This action by the Council was important because although they were still avoiding the basic and most contentious issue about what to do with land owned by Stock Conversion, they were slowly undermining the basis on which the original Levy Deal was founded. By independently buying up the surrounding land, this land could no longer be used as a bargaining piece for a deal. It also provided a degree of stability for those people in the area concerned, and was reflected by a burst of activity by the owner-occupiers and small businesses in starting long overdue repairs, conversions and repainting of their premises. It was a turning point; the end of years of uncertainty.

A new Labour Government

The most important single event in 1974 for Tolmers was the election of a Labour Government. Labour were elected back to power in February, following the miners' strike. Property speculation featured highly in their election manifesto and it seemed fair enough to assume that the problems of Tolmers – one of the most publicised victims of speculation – would soon be over. The Party manifesto stated clearly: 'Land required for development will be taken into public ownership, so that land is freely and cheaply available for new houses, schools, hospitals and other purposes. Public ownership of land will stop land profiteering' (Labour Party Manifesto, February 1974). New legislation was promised shortly.

The change in government enabled Camden to take a bolder stance. Renewed approaches were made to the Government to see if in view of the restriction on Office Development Permits (maintained by the new Government), they would reconsider proposals to acquire the land for housing. In April, several Councillors had talks with members of the Labour Government, and although they made no comment, it was reported that the Government were suggesting that Camden should await new legislation before making any decisions. (Throughout this period the TVA was maintaining constant pressure on the Council to make a Compulsory Purchase Order immediately. Deputations were taken to Council meetings, public meetings were held and other publicity generated.)

In June, the Council commissioned the consultant architects to carry out a study on the area owned by Stock Conversion to find out if the premises should be redeveloped or rehabilitated. They refused to make any decision on how to acquire this land but they did hint that 'it will be our intention to promote a Compulsory Purchase Order under the Housing Act on all the existing housing in this part of the Tolmers Square area' (Council Minutes, 17 July 1974).

Stock Conversion on the run

True to style, Stock Conversion had never responded publicly to Camden's rejection of the Levy Deal. However, a few paragraphs appeared in their shareholders' report for 1974.

> Now. . . it seems for political reasons the Council has refused to implement its freely negotiated agreement. The consequence is that the Council has delayed, if not lost the opportunity of building some 600 badly needed low rent dwellings, thus prolonging the problems of its [sic] homeless and creating a position where when the much needed homes are built, they will cost the Camden ratepayers and public funds an unnecessary additional amount of some £6 million.

Their response to the proposed CPO's was optimistic: 'Your Company is confident that such Orders can be successfully resisted'.

In order to increase their chances of resisting a CPO, and perhaps hoping for some favourable publicity, they drastically altered their plans, and in September at their Annual General Meeting disclosed their ideas for a new scheme. They would go it alone without waiting for Camden to do a deal with them. There would only be 100,000 square feet of offices instead of the previous 250,000 and the emphasis would be on rehabilitation. It was a scheme to please the conservationists and was accompanied by an attempt to change their whole image. Chairman Robert Clark announced:

> If the architects declare the buildings in Tolmers Square to be safe, we hope to refurbish and modernise them, restoring the Square to what it was when it was built in the early 19th century. . . . It is a job of which we will be proud. Our hope is that it will be a very beautiful square, with a fair amount of green and pleasant land (*Evening Standard*, 9 September 1974).

Camden Journal, 11 October 1974, *Daily Telegraph*, 10 September 1974, *Evening Standard*, 9 September 1974

A very beautiful square, but for whom? The question was raised by the small number of TVA members who had become nominal shareholders for the specific purpose of attending the Annual General Meeting. 'We must remember that it was not always what is now known as working-class', replied Mr Clark. 'The rents charged if this scheme materializes will depend on the cost of rehabilitation and conversion' (*The Times*, 10 September 1974). Clearly what Stock Conversion had in mind was gentrification, with rents far above anything that the present tenants could afford. (In fact the Square had always been working-class - see Appendix.)

Council commit themselves to going it alone

But the odds by this time were against Stock Conversion. Camden ignored their much publicised turn of face, and less than a month later publicly announced that they would make a CPO on the whole of the Levy triangle and carry out the development themselves.

The announcement was given a lot of publicity and was carefully timed to occur two weeks before the October General Election, in the hope that it might favourably affect the outcome.

Times, 30 September 1974.

HOME NEWS

Camden issues new purchase order for Tolmers Square and pins hope on Labour victory

ello little joe
bet yer feelin peeved
shifty shifty is our joe
but we aint bin deceived

(*Tolmers News*, No.15, 14 October 1974)

The Council also declared its intention of using the new powers, as outlined in a Government White Paper, for acquiring the land at existing use value. These powers, later incorporated in the controversial Community Land Bill, would eventually require councils to take all land needed for development into public ownership, and also give them the power to do so. By publicly announcing these intentions, Camden were exerting a certain amount of pressure on the Labour Government to live up to its earlier promises.

The Council also approved new proposals put forward by the architects for a mixed rehabilitation and redevelopment scheme for the whole area (see p. 137). This scheme differed from earlier proposals in that it contained a massive reduction in office content (from 250,000 square feet to 85,000 square feet), an increase in the amount of housing to be rehabilitated (from 40 units to 13.0 units) and an increase in the total number of persons to be housed (from 1,464 to 1,707) (Council Minutes, 23 October 1974).

Stock Conversion's hopes were finally dashed with the re-election of a Labour Government on 10 October. It was now merely a matter of time before the Community Land Bill became law giving the

Council powers to acquire land. Their only remaining hope was that either the Government would fall before the Bill could be introduced (a possibility not that remote given the general instability), or that the new powers would not be sufficiently strong to cater for land of such a high value.

Stock Conversion decided it was not worth hanging on. Late in 1974 they approached Camden offering to open discussions for the sale of the whole of the company's interests in the area. Negotiations then started in strictest secrecy to agree upon a price. For some reason Stock Conversion stipulated secrecy as one of their conditions for negotiating at all. If it was leaked that they were involved in negotiations they would back out.

It was of course because of these negotiations that Stock Conversion were trying to evict squatters from their property. A vacant house has a higher value than an occupied one. In the case of statutory tenants this may be as much as 40 per cent higher, although with squatters it is likely to be less, depending on the anticipated difficulties of getting them out and the prospects of damage. Disregarding their newly discovered 'social conscience' Stock Conversion considered it to be worth spending several thousands of pounds on eviction proceedings in order to increase the value of the houses. It was therefore in Camden's financial interest that the squatters resisted eviction; by doing so the squatters may have saved Camden many thousands of pounds. (Ironically, by supporting the squatters publicly, the Council may have lost out financially as they could no longer claim that the squatters were a liability. For this reason the Labour leadership was strongly advised by the officers not to support the squatters; advice which fortunately they ignored.)

After several months a price of £4 million was agreed by both parties. Stock Conversion were originally asking £5 million, but Camden were not prepared to pay more than the price they would have to pay if they waited until the Community Land Bill became law, estimated by the District Valuer to be £4 million. It would have been politically unacceptable to the Camden public to pay more, and Stock Conversion eventually had to accept this.

The price itself was significant because of the implications for the Community Land Bill as we will see later. £4 million for 6.07 acres (gross) is on average approximately £660,000 per acre. In fact it was worked out at roughly £300,000 per acre for the housing land and £1 million per acre for the commercial sites. It was based on existing use value except for completely empty sites which of course had no existing use value. These sites were valued by assuming a 'reasonable planning use'.

After agreeing upon a price, Camden then had the problem of trying to raise the money, still a considerable amount despite the supposed 'collapse' in the property market. Letters were written to Reg Freeson and Anthony Crossland, reminding them of their earlier commitment, and asking how much the Government would be prepared to provide. After this arm-twisting the Government indicated that they would give loan sanction for approximately £1 million for just over 3 acres of housing land. The other £3 million would have to be borrowed from the City at normal rates of interest. Eventually an arrangement was made with merchant bankers Morgan Grenfell. The bank would buy the land for Camden immediately, and Camden would then pay them a sum of money each year (roughly equivalent to interest on the money) which would guarantee them the option of buying the land from the bank at some time in the future. Camden would thereby obtain effective ownership of the land.

The agreement was announced publicly on 5 June 1975 and on 12 June contracts were exchanged with Stock Conversion.

Why it happened

There were three factors which enabled Camden to buy out Stock Conversion, all of which were to a certain extent interrelated. First, the general economic crisis which was reflected by a slump in the property market, beginning in November 1973. Demand for offices decreased and rents fell, and Stock Conversion could no longer hope to carry out such a profitable development.

The second factor was the existence of a Labour Government who were committed to bringing in legislation to enable local authorities to acquire development land. It would only be a matter of time before the Community Land Bill would become law, and Stock Conversion's chances of being able to prevent Camden acquiring their land compulsorily were decreasing. In addition, the Government was determined to prevent new office building in central London, so that even supposing Stock Conversion could resist Camden buying their land, they might find it difficult to obtain an Office Development Permit.

These two factors both affected the value of the land. Before the slump, Stock Conversion's holdings were valued at between £8 million and £12 million, whereas a year later they were valued at only £4 million.

The third factor was undoubtedly the momentum of the political opposition over Tolmers Square itself. Although the slump and the new legislation were vital components, there is little doubt that Camden would not have bought out Stock Conversion had it not been for the sustained pressure of the TVA and the squatters, and the commitment of almost all the Labour Councillors and party workers. It is also probable that this affected Stock Conversion's willingness to sell. It was better to get out while they could. Most Councillors admitted privately that there were no financial or even planning reasons for buying Stock Conversion out at that particular time. As we will see later, Camden would be unable to start on any non-residential development before the property market picked up again, and until that time the purchase was a liability. But the Labour Group had committed themselves to buying out Stock Conversion, and they could not politically afford to refuse the opportunity when it was offered to them. It is also probable that had there not been such pressure, and had Reg Freeson and other senior members of the Labour Party not committed themselves earlier, the Government would have stepped in and prevented the spending of such a vast sum of public money at a time of economic crisis.

146. Council proposal, April 1976.

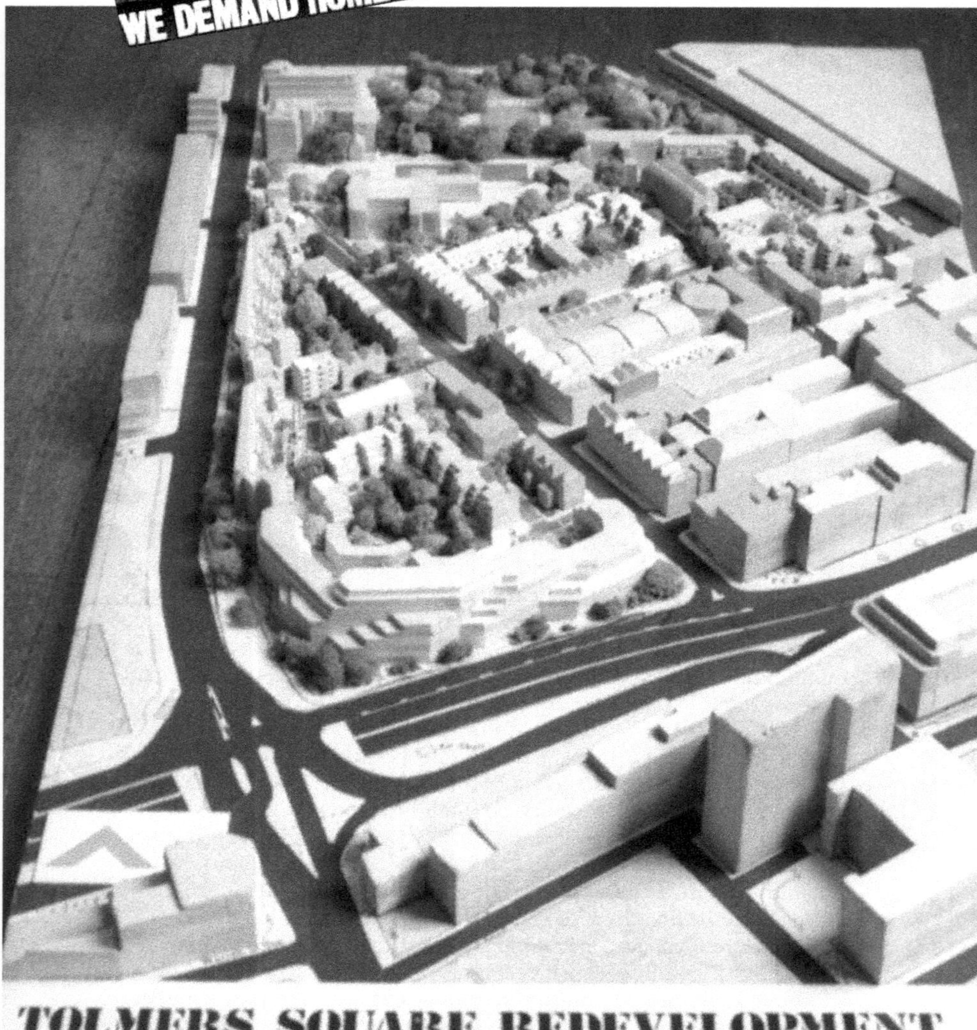

10.

.... or do they?

We believe we can do the scheme with fewer offices and more homes than proposed by the developers, and gain the advantage of owning the property (Frank Dobson, *Evening Standard*, 5 June 1975).

The way is now open for Camden Council to try a 'profits to the people' experiment in property development in Tolmers Square, after a 10-year battle for ownership of the strategic site in Euston. Alternatively, the Council's announcement yesterday that it is to buy the six acres of land owned by Mr. Joe Levy's Stock Conversion and Investment Trust for £4 million, could mean that Camden is buying into a massively expensive white elephant (*Hampstead and Highgate Express*, 6 June 1975).

A monstrous proposal

Unfortunately Camden obtaining ownership of the land has not ended the problems.

In April 1976, less than one year after they had bought Stock Conversion's land, Camden Council approved new proposals for the land it had just acquired, now known as site 1. The proposals were approved by the full Council without any dissension, as it was claimed that they were in line with proposals which had been approved in principle 1.5 years previously, and which had received public support including that of the TVA (p. 137, 191). 'Considerable public consultation has already been held on the broad principles of the Tolmers Square development, from which the present proposals *are no departure*' (Council Minutes, 22 April 1976).

But far from being 'no departure' from the previous proposal, the new proposals are almost a complete reversal:

1. The office content is increased by over 200 per cent, from 85,000 square feet to 300,000 square feet - 50,000 more than was contemplated under the 'Levy Deal'. It is significant that the increase in the office content is not mentioned in either the four-page Council report,

or in the model and plans displayed at the Town Hall. The figures are only contained in officers' reports to committees, which are not readily available to the public.

2. The housing is reduced by more than a quarter, from 894 bed spaces to 610 bed spaces. In addition, a hostel for 75 people is left out. The Council blames the reduction in the amount of housing on the new government policy to reduce densities of new developments (incidentally, a policy which shows little understanding of the real problems relating to quality of life in cities). But in fact, complying with government's new directives accounts for less than half of the housing loss.

3. The 2,000 square feet of light industrial space is left out and there is no provision at all for any industry or manufacturing.

4. The 57,500 square feet of public building is left out.

5. The cinema is left out.

6. The whole of Tolmers Square itself is to be demolished instead of only the south side.

The reason for these preposterous proposals is that Camden consider that the development of the site must be self-financing, and also that it must be sufficiently profitable to pay back the money it borrowed to buy the land from Stock Conversion.

The Council in effect paid £4 million for the 6 acres of land formerly owned by Stock Conversion. All this money had to be borrowed and the interest payments on these loans are just over £1.5 million per year (£512,000 in 1976/7). At the time the transaction took place, the revenue from rents was only around £60,000 per year, leaving a short-fall of approximately £450,000 which can not possibly be met even if rents are raised a little, empty buildings put to use, and empty sites built on. In order to be able to pay the interest payments, let alone pay back the loan, the Council will have to redevelop the site for far more profitable uses than exist at present.

The Council's main objective is to build as much housing as possible on the site. As housing on its own would not provide anything like enough revenue, the non-housing part of the development must provide most of the income, while at the same time using as little land as possible. This inevitably leads to the choice of office development, as offices provide the maximum income from a given amount of building space. Yet with the current depressed state of the property market, a massive amount even of office space will be required to provide the necessary income.

> A viability study prepared by the Chief Valuer last July [1975] demonstrated that 300,000 square feet of offices would be required to subsidise the land for housing development and an application for an Office Development Permit with that amount of floor space was submitted to the D.O.E. on the 28th July 1975. An up-to-date valuation could well show that a figure in excess of 300,000 square feet would be required (Report by Town Clerk to Committee, 1 April 1976).

If the need for these offices is accepted, then this largely determines the content and physical layout of the remainder of the development. There will be no room for the more socially useful and productive activities of industry and manufacturing, nor for public buildings or places of entertainment, and there will be less room for housing. There will also be less flexibility for rehabilitation. North Gower Street almost certainly has to be retained as parts of it have been listed by the DoE as being of architectural importance (p. 4). There are also a couple of more recent buildings, the demolition of which it would be difficult to justify. But Tolmers Square itself will have to be demolished. It would be almost impossible to locate 300,000 square feet of offices on the site and retain the Square; there simply is not enough room.

There are however powerful reasons for arguing that Tolmers Square should be retained as a whole. Although fairly dilapidated at present, it could still be rehabilitated and restored for an equivalent or

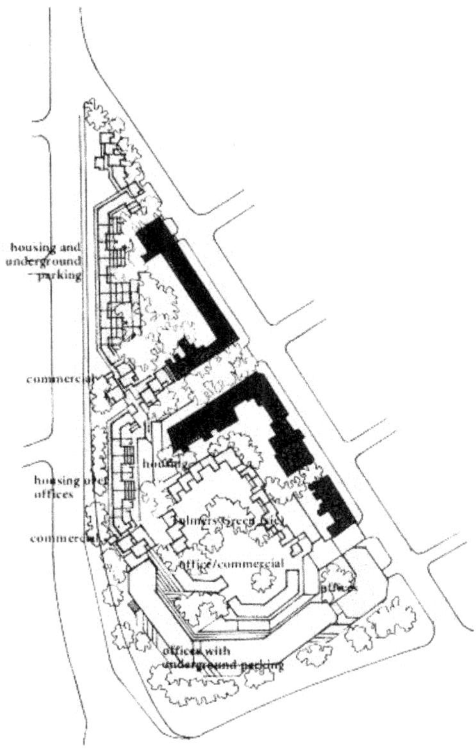

Council's proposals, April 1976.

retained buildings (existing use maintained)

new buildings

(Source: Report by Town Clerk to Community Planning and Resources Committee, 1 April 1976) even lower cost than rebuilding, and the quality of the accommodation would almost certainly be higher than that obtained with new buildings. The Square is interesting from an architectural point of view and it has become a landmark of historical importance, if for no other reason than by virtue of the events described in this book.

As well as requiring the demolition of the Square, the proposed scheme will also require the demolition of the western end of Drummond Street and the whole of the Hampstead Road frontage. The new proposals make no suggestions as to what will happen to the shops, industries and restaurants currently leasing space in these buildings; it appears there will be little room for them in the new development.

The nature of the whole scheme then is determined by the financial need to build a massive number of new offices. And yet the arguments against having more offices in the area are still as powerful as they ever were. It would indeed be against GLC, Camden Council and central Government policy: all Labour-controlled. Yet the Labour Council itself is forced into the hypocritical position of advocating this monstrous scheme.

There is of course another option open to the Council. They could decide not to insist that the development be self-financing. They could decide to build a scheme which they consider to be socially desirable for the people in the area, the people of Camden, and the people of London as a whole. If, as is likely, there proved to be a financial loss, they could then charge this to the rates, or put pressure on the government to make up the difference.

There is already some support for this kind of approach within the Labour Group, but at a time when both the Council and the Government are attempting to cut public expenditure, a lot of political pressure will be required to make the Council accept it.

So much for the Community Land Act

The current situation in Tolmers Square highlights one of the most fundamental problems faced by all those who are attempting to obtain a rational and socially equitable use of land in the centres of cities: the inflated value of land.

Public ownership of land is of little use in itself if the cost of buying that land and the methods of arranging finance are such that the public authorities are forced to develop it in line with the dictates of private financiers. It would appear that there will never be a rational and socially equitable determination of land use without the social ownership of finance capital as well as all land and property. Only then will it become possible for democratically elected bodies to decide the appropriate use of land and arrange finance accordingly. Only then will it be possible to take action on the basis of an evaluation of all the costs and benefits of any particular scheme to different sections of society.

Unfortunately the present position in Tolmers Square largely dispels any hopes that the new Community Land Act will solve the problems faced by local authorities in the centres of cities. It appears the Act will do little to curb socially unnecessary office development, and little to enable councils to build housing and other community facilities where they are most needed. Although the land in Tolmers Square was not bought under the Community Land Act legislation, the price paid for the land was roughly equal to the price that would have been paid had the Act been in force. The powers available to the Council to develop are also roughly equivalent. So as the *Evening Standard* reported, 'the scheme will be a test case for Government optimism about councils' abilities to carry out commercial development under the Land Bill proposals' (5 June 1975).

Sadly, the Act will only be a partial form of land nationalisation.

Louis Hellman, May 1976.

It fails to deal with the vital issue of financial speculation in the location of land and property. Despite being able, indeed being compelled, to buy land needed for development at existing use value, councils will have no powers to build community facilities and housing on this land. They will still have to obtain government approval to spend money for social uses, and with the prospect of the government's attempts to hold down public expenditure, this is unlikely to be forthcoming. Instead councils will be obliged to obtain the maximum return possible. (Under the Act, councils will not even have the power to charge part of the purchase cost to the rates, as Camden could do on Tolmers Square.) As there is no provision in the Act for ending the free market in rents and leases, obtaining the maximum return can only be achieved by building commercial developments. Furthermore, councils are not being given powers to carry out this kind of development themselves; there is no provision for additional grants or subsidies. So the land acquired will be leased out to developers who will behave in much the same way as they have in the past. Instead of changing the system by which land is exploited for the maximum profit, the Community Land Act will push councils right into the middle of the market system. They too will be taking profits from land, and are likely to behave in much the same way as developers.

The developers themselves will hardly be affected. As an illustration of this point it is interesting to note that the sale of all their land in Tolmers Square for the supposed Community Land Act price of £4 million had little appreciable effect on Stock Conversion. The calculation of the price took little account of the amount that Stock Conversion paid for the land, but the scanty information available indicates that it represented more or less the price they originally paid plus interest and management charges during the years that the land was standing under-used. Certainly Stock Conversion did not suffer unduly. Brokers continued to recommend their shares as being some of the most attractive on the market, and Stock Conversion themselves forecasted that their pre-tax profits would actually increase to £3.25 million for the year 1975/6, an increase of almost £1 million over the 1974/5 figure of £2.4 million.

The sad fact is that Tolmers Square was relatively insignificant in relation to the overall size of their operations. The £4 million sale merely eased their liquidity problem (which in any case was not very serious), and represented the end of any prospect of them obtaining massive profits on this particular site.

Stock Conversion and Investment Trust continue to thrive. Despite the supposed collapse of the property market, the impending Community Land Act (frequently described as 'the most radical single measure to be introduced during this Parliament'). and their final frustration over Tolmers Square (and incidentally Piccadilly Circus), the Investors Chronicle was able to report 'the shares remain a safe long-term hold' (11 July 1975).

Maybe when the office market picks up again, Camden Council will actually be inviting Stock Conversion to develop and manage the 300,000 square feet of offices on Tolmers Square – under the Council's close control, of course.

The struggle continues

Achieving a rational system of land use allocation will take many years. It will require massive changes in legislation, attitudes and values which can only come about by continuous campaigning at all levels of the political system. The seventeen years of campaigning in Tolmers Square have made a small but significant contribution to this process.

At the same time the campaigns have drastically affected the life and the future of the area itself. At the time of writing (April 1976), building work has started on several small infill sites to the east of North Gower Street where the Council is building new housing. The Council has committed itself to retaining several areas containing housing, shops, restaurants, industry and warehousing, which were formerly threatened with demolition. A CPO on the area to the east of North Gower Street has still to be approved by the Minister, but if, as is likely, it is approved, it should go some way to removing the threat of private speculation in the future, and provide the occupants with a certain measure of security. Council ownership of former Stock Conversion property has provided both tenants and squatters with immediate security, a few of the empty buildings have been let on a short-term basis, and the centre of Tolmers Square has been landscaped, even if it is only 'temporary'.

But there are still a number of problems. One of these relates to the site owned by British Rail near Euston Station (p. 46). Although not requiring the site for its existing use (warehousing and a derelict area) British Rail are objecting to Camden's proposal to use it for housing. Instead they want to build, of all things, a *multi-storey carpark*. Camden rejected their planning application, and the future of this site now depends on the result of British Rail's appeal to the Minister.

There are many other unresolved issues. Will rents continue to rise and drive existing businesses out? Will the Asian community be able to survive? What will happen to the squatting community? Will those residents who were forced to leave be able to return if they want to? Will the social amenities which feature so large in the Council's earlier plans actually materialise? And of course the biggest question of all: What will be the future of site 1? Will the Council continue with its current proposals or will they think again? Will they choose to build a development which caters for the needs of the community at large, or will they build an office development which differs little from the proposals of the private developers? And if Camden Council does try to continue with its present proposals, will the government and the GLC grant its request for an Office Development Permit and the necessary planning permissions?

The answers to these questions largely depend on whether people, both inside and outside the area, can sustain a sufficient level of political activity to combat the continual search for profits. The struggle continues. The battle for Tolmers Square is not yet over.

147. 'temporary'?

Appendix-A little local history
by Tim Wilson

(Tim Wilson was born in 1950. He is currently a graduate student in Renaissance cultural history at the Warburg Institute, and has been squatting in Tolmers Square since 1974.)

The Tolmers Square Development Area lies in what were the grounds of the large old manor of Tottenhall, or Tottenham Court, in the Parish of St Pancras. Until the end of the eighteenth century the whole area was rural: a newspaper of about 1761 described it as 'a pleasant village situated between St. Giles and Hampstead'. Development came with the great expansion of London, in the second half of the eighteenth century. A brief history of the area will help to fill in the background to the main story of the book. (1)

The Manor of Tottenhall

At the time of the Doomsday Book, the manor of Tottenhall was the property of the Canons of St Paul's Cathedral. The land of the manor covered five 'hides' - that is, about 600 acres – and was valued at £4 a year. It was recorded that eight men were living on the land to work it, the whole population of St Pancras in the eleventh century being probably under 300. (At the end of the nineteenth century it was just under a quarter of a million.)

Under the Tudors and early Stuarts the land was leased to the Crown and occupied by royal servants. In 1649, at the establishment of the Commonwealth, the leasehold of the manor, together with other Crown land, was expropriated, and bought by a Londoner called Ralph Harrison for £3,318 3s. 11d. In 1660, at the Restoration of Charles II, it reverted to the Crown and a few years later was made over to the young Isabella Bennet, who also inherited from her father, the King's favourite the Earl of Arlington, the family seat of Euston in Suffolk. She was married in 1672, when both were still children, to Henry Fitzroy, who was the second son of Charles II and his mistress Barbara Villiers. (The name Fitzroy was often used for the illegitimate children of a King.) On the marriage, Henry was made Earl of

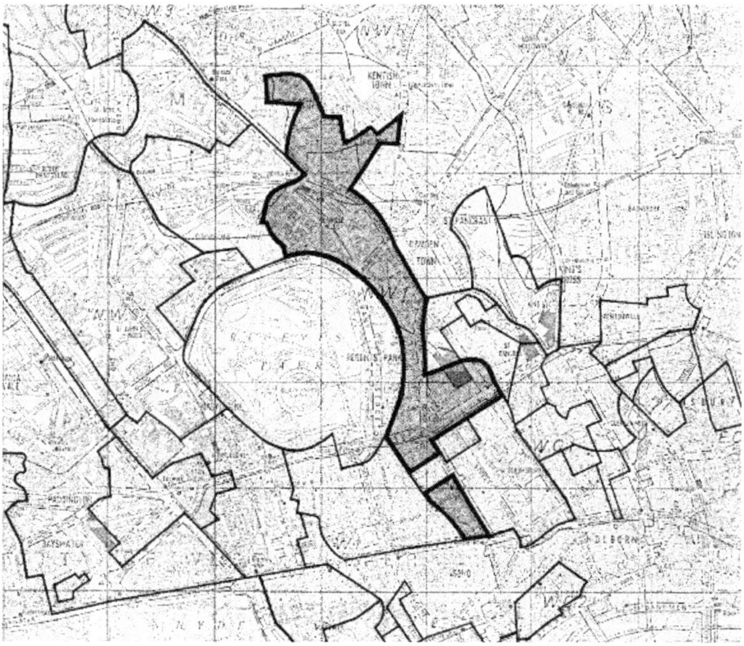

The Fitzroy Estate (the old manor of Tottenhall) and the other great estates at the end of the eighteenth century (Source: *London Street Names* by Gillian Bebbington).

Euston, and three years later first Duke of Grafton. Three generations later, the third Duke's younger brother, Charles Fitzroy (b. 1737), created first Baron Southampton in 1780, inherited the lease on the manor of Tottenhall, while the elder (Grafton) branch of the family inherited the seat at Euston in Suffolk, which they hold to this day.

When inherited by Charles Fitzroy, the manor was still on a lease, periodically renewable, from the Canons of St Paul's. A remarkable piece of aristocratic sharp practice in 1768 transformed this lease into a freehold. The transaction is described by a writer in the *Morning Chronicle* in 1837:

> 'In the year 1768 the Duke of Grafton was Prime Minister. His brother, Mr. Fitzroy, was lessee of the Manor and Lordship of Tattenhall, the property of the Dean and Chapter of St. Paul's, London. Dr. Richard Brown, the then prebendary of the stall of Tattenhall, having pocketed the emolument attending the renewal of the lease, and there being very little chance of any further advantages to him from the estate, readily listened to a proposal of Mr. Fitzroy for the purchase of the estate. The thing was agreed, and the Duke of Grafton, with his great standing majority, quickly passed an act through Parliament, in March 1768, diverting the estate, with all its rights, privileges, and emoluments from the prebend, and conveyed the fee - simple, entire, and without reserve, to Mr. Charles Fitzroy and his heirs for ever. The Act states it to be with the consent of Richard, Lord Bishop of London, and the privity of the Dean and Chapter of St Paul's. (2)

The writer goes on to deplore the irresponsibility of the churchmen's alienation of the enormously valuable freehold in return for a relatively paltry payment of £300 a year. Much of the estate, including most of the Tolmers area, stayed in the hands of the Southampton family until this century. By 1900 the estate had been built over from end to end.

The origin of the name Tottenhall is unclear: it is perhaps derived from a Saxon owner called Totta. The original form Totehele, or Tottenhele, was later corrupted into Tottenhall. and eventually to Tottenham Court. A writer in 1748 noted a tradition that: 'The elegant village of Tottenham Court belonged to Edward IV. There he kept his beloved Jane Shore.' (3) It is said that the name 'Court' derives from this supposed royal connection.

The extent of the manor varied at different times during its history, but consisted basically of a long strip of land along the old Hampstead Road, stretching from Kentish Town, Chalk Farm and Primrose Hill in the north, to Fitzroy Square and down Tottenham Court Road almost to the junction with Oxford Street in the south. To the west the estate bordered on the Crown estate (formerly Henry VIII's Marylebone Park); to the south-east it bordered on the Bedford Estate and its fashionable development in Bloomsbury.

The Manor House

The manor house itself stood to the east of Hampstead Road, between the present sites of Tolmers Square and Euston Road. The position is marked on a plan made by William Necton on 6 April 1591, when the manor was in the hands of the Crown. Necton added a memorandum with some remarks on the building, which was then occupied by Daniel Clarke, Master Cook to Queen Elizabeth. He calls it 'a very slender building of timber and brick', which 'hath been of a larger building than now it is. For some little parte hath been pulled down of late to amend some part of the houses now standing.' (4) The surveyor also noted that part of the building was 'very greatly decaied'. From another survey (of 1649) we learn that the house and gardens were 'moated round'.

148. Tottenhall, 1743.

This is a water-colour of the house from the Heal Collection made in 1801. The painting is captioned as a copy of a painting of the house done in 1743; and the Elizabethan building was pulled down at about this time. The older (fifteenth-century?) building shown to the left of the Elizabethan block is what was known as 'King John's Palace', though there is no evidence of any actual connection with King John: it was pulled down in 1808. The site of the manor house is now (1976) ingloriously covered by a temporary car park.

An ancient Structure, denominated in various Records KING JOHN'S PALACE; lately situated near the New River Company Reservoir, TOTTENHAM COURT. 149

The South View of Tottenham - Court. 150

Wine, Wenching and Wickedness

While these buildings were still standing, Tottenham Court, as it had come to be generally known by the seventeenth century, became a favourite place of excursion for Londoners. George Wither in 1628 wrote,

> And Hogsdone, Islington and Tothnam-Court,
> For cakes and creame had then no small resort. (5)

The name was well enough known for Ben Jonson in 1633 to characterise a country squire in his play *A Tale of a Tub* as 'Squire Tub of Totten-Court'. In 1645 'Mrs. Stacey's maid' and two others were fined one shilling apiece for the enormity of drinking on the Sabbath day at Tottenham Court. (6)

The best evidence for the character and reputation of the place in the seventeenth century is to be found in a play by Thomas Nabbs, called *Totenham-Court, a pleasant comedy*, published in 1639. Here Tottenham Court seems to be more than anything else a good place for a cheerful dirty weekend. One character says: 'A maid at your years, and so near London! . . . The park here hath fine conveniences: or Totenham-Court's close by: 'tis suspected that fine Citie ladies give away fine things to Court Lords for a country banquet.' And a little later: 'A wench is grown a necessary appendix to two pots at Totenham-Court.' A few pages later we hear of an elopement, and someone comments: 'The parson of Pancras hath been here.' The answer is: 'Indeed I have heard that he is a notable governor. And Totenham-Court pays him store of tithe. It causeth questionless much unlawful coupling.'

On either side of the Hampstead Road, south of the turnpike on the road north, were two celebrated pubs, the *Adam and Eve* on the west (first mentioned in 1718, but possibly a good deal older), and the King's Head on the east. The *Adam and Eve* was particularly famous for its tea gardens and the boxing matches that took place there, as well as for its cakes and ale. Both pubs are shown in Hogarth's engraving below.

151

A REPRESENTATION of the MARCH of the GUARDS towards SCOTLAND, in the YEAR 1745.

This century both pubs have been the victims of road-widening schemes – the *King's Head* in an LCC scheme in 1906, the *Adam and Eve* in the Euston Centre scheme. In the 1930s the Adam and Eve was said to have the best beer and the cheapest girls in the West End – so the great tradition lived on.

To the south-west of the present road junction, near where Warren Street is now, were the grounds of the Tottenham Court Fair, famous for its boxing matches and theatrical booths, as well as for the chaos it generated every summer, to the great distress of respectable citizens. In the eighteenth century, various attempts were made to suppress the fair, but it proved tenacious, and not till the nineteenth century was it finally suppressed. The writer of a manuscript in the Heal Collection dated 1808, describes the fair and its suppression with puritanical sternness:

> Tottenham Court was a place of resort for the lower orders of society, and their successors even now presume at Easter and Whitsuntide to set order and magistracy at defiance. Information having been given upon oath to his majesty's Justices of the Peace for the County of Middlesex that several lewd and disorderly persons and players of interludes had erected booths and stalls at Tottenham Court in the County of Middlesex aforesaid, wherein was used a great deal of prophane swearing together with many lewd and blasphemous expressions, as also several rude, riotous and disorderly actions committed; eleven of his Majesty's Justices, having duly considered the evil tendency of such wicked and abominable practices, for suppressing thereof and for preventing the like for the future, granted a warrant . . . for the apprehension of several of the persons concerned in the management of the said interludes, which hath since been put into execution, and the same have been suppressed accordingly and the said booths and stalls pulled down and taken away.

152

The New Road

In 1756, the first London bypass road, the 'New Road from Paddington to Islington', now the Marylebone, Euston and Pentonville Roads, was built. It crossed the Hampstead Road a little to the south-west of the cluster of buildings that was Tottenham Court. This grandiose new project was sponsored by the Duke of Grafton, and opposed by the Duke of Bedford on the grounds that it would spoil the view from his house and create dust. It seems that the Duke of Grafton was the first to travel on what is now the Euston Road, and, moreover, on a Sunday. One account described the Duke as 'accompanied by a great company as little sensible of religion as himself', and another commented that 'he and his jovial crew on horse back' passed along as if in triumph over everything sacred. (7)

The Southampton Estate development

The building of the New Road (so called until 1857) speeded up the development of the area by the Southampton family. The part of the estate to the west of Tottenham Court Road was the first to be developed, in the last years of the eighteenth century (Fitzroy Square was begun by the Adam brothers c. 1793). In the same period was built Southampton Place, a row of elegant houses fronting the north side of the New Road a little to the east of where North Gower Street now is; these houses lasted until the Second World War, remaining socially a cut above the streets to the north. By the turn of the century, new terraces were going up at speed to the west of the Hampstead Road, and soon afterwards the main terraces in our area were built – George Street (now North Gower Street) and Euston Square in about 1810, the smaller houses in Drummond Street and the other streets in the years immediately following. Most of these streets, like other streets on the estate, got their names from members of the Southampton family and families they intermarried with. (8)

The system on which the Southampton Estate, like most of the great London estates, was built over was one that enabled the landowners to develop their land at no financial risk to themselves and with the certainty of a substantial profit only in the very long term.(9) The land to be developed would be divided up into building plots and leased to a contractor, or directly to a builder, for a long period of time – usually 99 years – at a low ground rent, say £5 a year for each house. The builder or contractor built the houses at his own expense, and then normally tried to make his profit by selling the lease. It was a perilous business for the builder, in a flourishing but irregular market; he had to sink a lot of capital into building the houses and took all the risk. At least one of the builders who took a building lease from the Southampton family – a certain George Brown, who built several houses at the south end of what is now North Gower Street – ended up in the bankruptcy courts. At the end of the 99-year term, the land and the houses on it reverted to the ground landlord, who might then renew the lease (at a much higher rent) or else redevelop the now urbanised land to make a further profit. What tended to happen in poorer districts was that towards the end of the original lease term, the houses would degenerate as the tenants ceased to have much interest in spending money to maintain them. This may have happened on the Southampton Estate in the early years of this century. (10)

The streets in the area were built up on this system between 1800 and 1830, and were probably intended for middle-class people – George Street and Euston Square certainly so. But the houses never had the social status of the exclusive Bedford Estate to the south-east: revealingly, among the first tenants of Drummond Street were two coal merchants. The original leases stipulated that the tenants were:

> not to follow the trade or business of a brewer, bagnio keeper, distiller, pipeburner, melting tallow chandler, working hatter, baker, sugar baker, butcher, poulterer, fishmonger, fruiterer, herb-seller, vintner, victualler, coffee house keeper, dyer, brazier, pewterer, smith, farrier or any other offensive or obnoxious trade . . . on or upon the said demised premises.

This looks like an attempt to establish for the new houses a similar kind of social exclusiveness to that enjoyed by the nearby Bedford Estate (which had gates at the northern entrances to keep out undesirables and tradesmen); but it never worked and apparently no serious attempt was made to enforce these regulations.

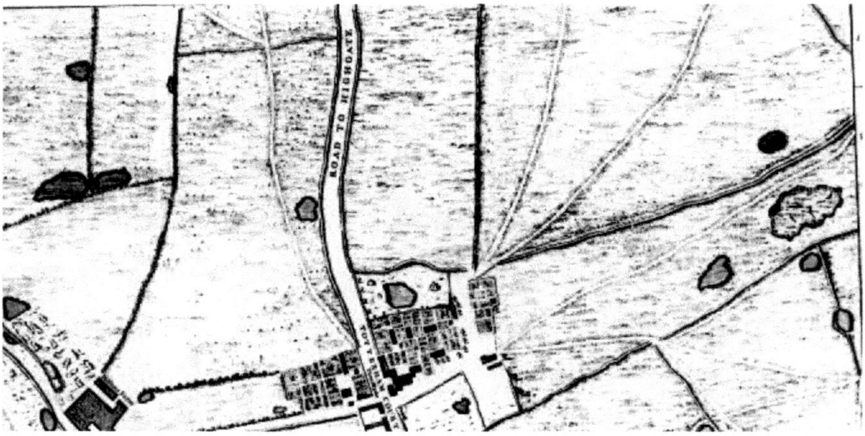

1746

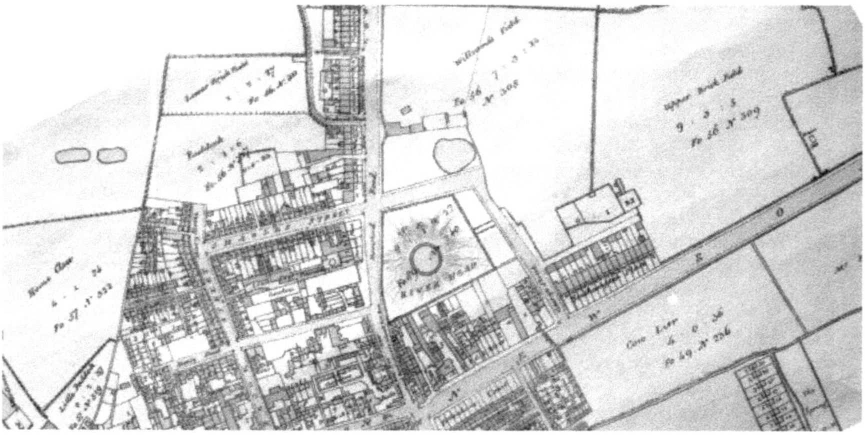

1790

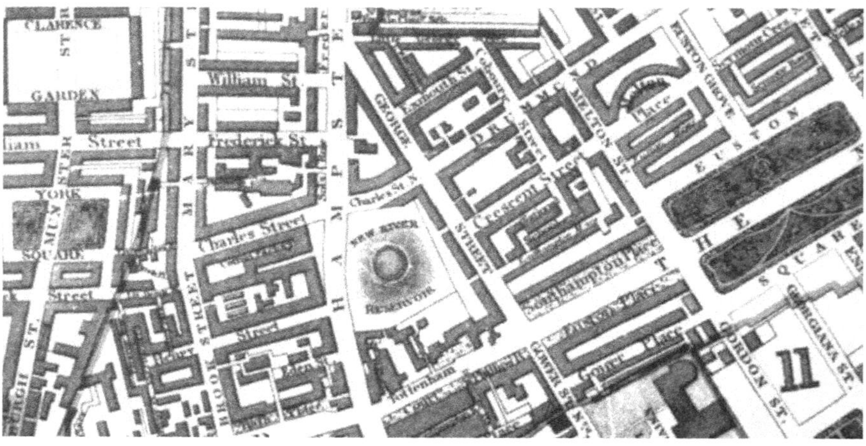

1834

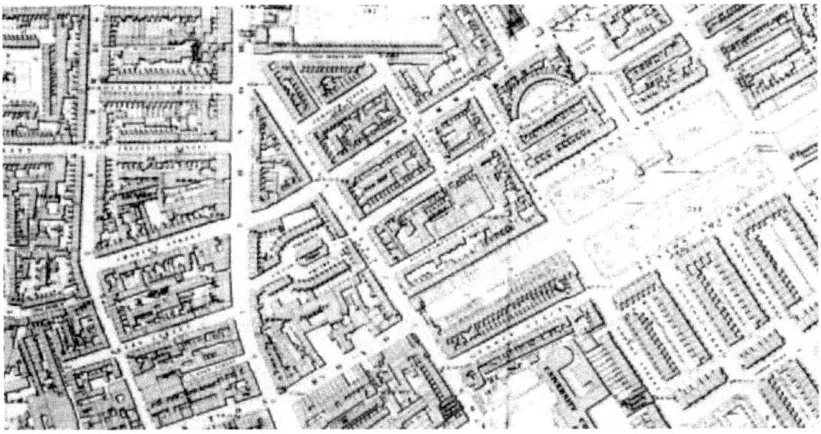

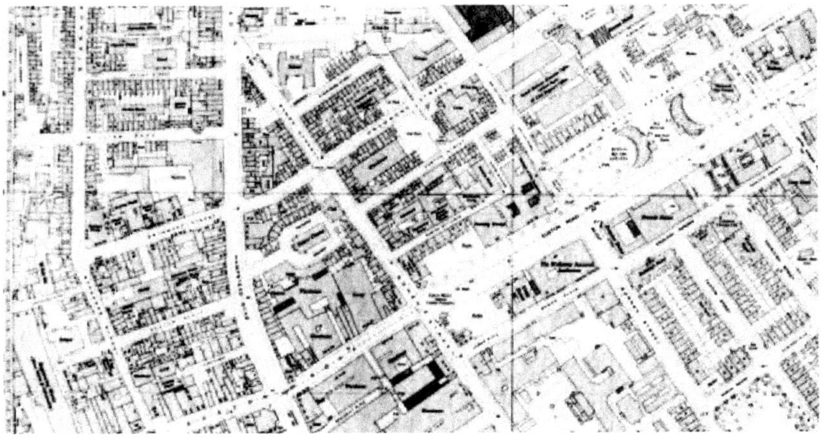

153. From Roque's map of London, 1746.

154. From an un-named map of St Pancras, c. 1790.

155. From Davies' map of St Pancras, 1834.

156. From Ordnance Survey map, 1880.

157. From Ordnance Survey map, 1954.

Social decline

Such gentility as there may once have been, vanished in the social decline that hit all the housing north of the New Road in the middle of the nineteenth century. The decisive factor was the coming of the railways: first, Euston Station (London and Birmingham Railway, 1836), then a little later, King's Cross (Great Northern, 1851-2), and finally St Pancras (Midland Railway, 1868 –74). The great stations made the areas close to them less salubrious, created a need for housing for the large numbers of men employed in the railways, and above all displaced thousands of people from their homes in the path of the stations and the lines leading into them. St Pancras alone made thousands of people homeless, virtually wiping out the densely populated Agar Town area.

> By the end of the century it is estimated that over 100,000 people had been uprooted from their homes by the coming of the railways. . . Modern Londoners, accustomed to the exhaustive compensation and re-housing provisions of publicly controlled comprehensive redevelopment, would find it hard to imagine the impact the railway boom of the 1860's had on the social and physical environment of the city. It was not only Dickens and his 'smoke, and crowded gables, and distorted chimneys, and deformity of brick and mortar pinning up deformity of mind and body.' It was also the migration within the city of a population itself the size of a small city, a population uncontrolled, at the mercy of the laws of the free market and for the most part poverty-stricken in the extreme. . . . Railway building in London simply crowded neighbouring slum properties even more densely and forced up their rents.(11)

Such feeble statutory provision as there was for re-housing of tenants displaced was easily and regularly evaded.

Thus between, and to the west of, the stations a belt of poor and over-crowded housing grew up along the north of the New Road, stretching from King's Cross almost as far as Regent's Park. Tolmers Square was towards the west end of this belt. To the north and west, approaching the luxury housing of Regent's Park, conditions were rather better. To the east was Somers Town, one of the most notorious slum areas of Victorian London. The present isolation of Tolmers Village is a modern phenomenon resulting from the destruction of all the surrounding housing (p. 18).

Tolmers Square

The history of the Tolmers Square site is rather different from that of the surrounding streets. (12) One story says that there was a burial pit on the site at the time of the Great Plague, but there is no real evidence to support this story. In 1802 the New River Company, a company which worked an artificial waterway from Hertfordshire to the New River Head in Islington, took a lease on the land and converted it into a reservoir for the supply of water to west London.(13) In the 1830s an Artesian well was sunk on the site: the appearance of this was a large grass-covered mound.

In the 1840s a complex of public baths and wash-houses for the poor was built on the north-east corner of the site, served by water from the reservoir. A writer in a contemporary newspaper was enthusiastic:

Pent up by their occupations in the midst of London, a large proportion of its vast population can only on rare occasions find time to go to the necessary distance to obtain the advantage of a bath and the comfort of a clean skin: and when they do so they find the greatest impediments in their way. They are now prohibited from bathing in the Thames. The Lea and Serpentine Rivers are only open to them at particular hours. The comfort of a warm bath is placed out of their reach by its costliness, and to procure a warm bath at home, which is never thought of except when disease make it necessary, is almost an impossibility. Under these circumstances it is not surprising that they scarcely ever indulge in a practice so essential as bathing to the health and to the full enjoyment of life. . . . The corporations of Liverpool have lately built baths and wash-houses for their poor. . . . It is proposed to carry out in London on an extensive scale the plans of which the success and usefulness have thus been confirmed. . . . (The first of these model establishments has just been completed in St Pancras. In that populous district the Society for Establishing Baths and Wash-houses for the Labouring Classes has been enabled by the liberality of the directors of the New River Company to procure at a nominal rent an excellent site for their establishment on a portion of vacant ground at the base of the reservoir in the Hampstead Road. We have visited the baths and wash-houses and have pleasure in bearing witness to the excellency of the arrangements. (14)

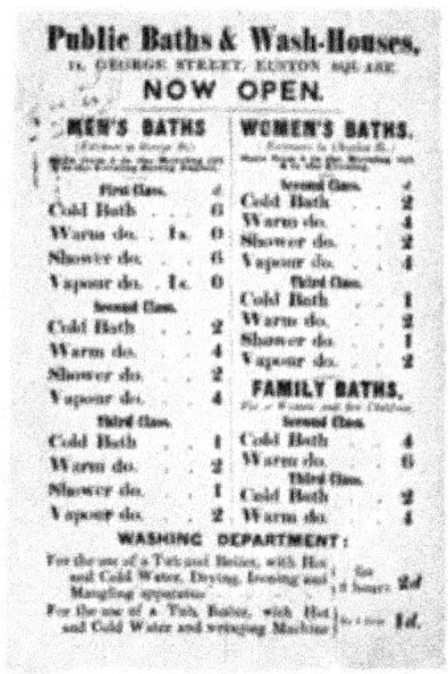

159

However, in spite of the worthy efforts of the Society for Establishing Baths and Wash-houses for the Labouring Classes, it seems that the Labouring Classes were not altogether eager to take advantage of the excellent arrangements offered to them. In 1859 the wash-houses were closed. A little later the mound above the reservoir was levelled and the earth was carted to Regent's Park.

The houses in the Square were built by a builder called William Sawyer between 1861 and 1864. Simultaneously the Tolmers Square Congregational Church was built in the middle of the Square; this was a Gothic edifice designed by John Tarring (an architect known as 'the Gilbert Scott of the Nonconformists' from the large number of Nonconformist Gothic churches he built in London). The church, which had a spire at the west end some 120 feet high, was highly praised by the contemporary press: one newspaper described it as in a style 'somewhat after that of the House of Commons'. The name 'Tolmers' was taken from a small village in Hertfordshire, near the source of the New River.

It is fairly clear from the architecture that the houses in the Square were intended to be rather more 'genteel' than the streets to the east: in fact it is said that originally there were gates at the entrance on the east side to the scruffier Drummond and Euston streets, the main entrance being from the rather more affluent Hampstead Road. But this did not really achieve its intended effect of isolating the Square from the poorer housing to the east, and within a few years of being built, though some 'posh-ish' people did live there the tall houses in the square had mostly degenerated into multi-occupation and overcrowding nearly as bad as the rest of the area. In the 1871 census almost all the houses are in multi-occupation and there are 364 people recorded as living in the 28 houses.

160. Tolmers Square church, 1903.

Tolmers at the end of the nineteenth century

Charles Booth at the turn of the century wrote of the church that it 'finds it something of a struggle to exist in so unpropitious a neighbourhood'.(15) The area attracted a variety of charitable institutions, such as a large-scale soup kitchen in the Euston Road, a Salvation Army post in Tolmers Square and a Baptist Mission in Drummond Street. The most notable of these was the Tolmers Square Institute, an appendage of the church built in 1877 for meetings and good works. A contemporary press cutting gives some idea of the character of the area at the time in a way that was probably only a little melodramatic;

> Thousands of young men and women are living in the large houses of business very near to Tolmers Square Institution, also thousands of men employed on the Midland, London and North Western, North London and Metropolitan Railway live about here, and it is to gather such and influence them for good that the Tolmers Square Institute, People's Cafe and schools have been erected. . . . The scene of the Euston Square murder is within a few minutes of the Institute, and recently, within a few yards, a man hacked his wife to death with a hatchet. More than one child has been found dead within the railings of the church, one with its throat cut. Wickedness abounds, and Tolmers Square Institute has been built to try and stem this torrent of iniquity. (16)

161. Tolmers Square Institute, Drummond Street, c. 1879.

At the end of the last century the area was certainly rough, increasingly so towards the east. In Booth's general survey of north-west London he wrote:

> By far the worst area of poverty is that between St. Pancras Station and the Hampstead Road, extending in places to Albany St. Any improvement here is due to displacement by railway extensions. The people are low rough labourers mixed with costers and prostitutes. . . . The missions have maintained a stream of charity, and the railways, with the growth of the great furnishing shops in Tottenham Court Road, have helped to provide work. Thus supported, and clinging to their accustomed surroundings, the people have crowded every house within reach, and filled from cellar to roof whatever new buildings have been provided. The result has been to raise site values, and of late there has been little or no fresh building. Extravagant claims are made by the owners of slum property, and every scheme of improvement hampered. Crowding is chronic, and the instances of excessive overcrowding that have come to light are appalling. (17)

Of the overcrowding we have statistics: in the streets comprising what is now the Tolmers Square development area, according to the census of 1871, were living some 5,200 people. (Compare with this a population of about 600 in 1971.)

Not all streets were equally bad; Booth gives the following breakdown:

Well to do: Hampstead Road, Southampton Row (Euston Road), Euston Square.
Fairly comfortable: George Street, Euston Buildings.
Poverty and comfort mixed: Tolmers Square, parts of Euston Street, Drummond Street.
Moderate poverty: Exmouth Street, Coburg Street, and various sites tucked in behind the main streets.
Lowest class: Little Exmouth Street, Little George Street.

This is in fact a rather better picture than some of the other evidence might lead us to expect. It seems that some quite well-off people continued to live in the area, which was never socially completely homogeneous. In some of the houses in George Street and to the west the 1871 census notes the presence of servants. This photo of Tolmers Square, taken in 1903, certainly does not seem to show a slum.

To sum up, we may describe the social composition of the area as predominantly rather poor but with a scattering of more prosperous families towards the west. People who grew up in the area early this century certainly remember a sharp contrast between the 'posh end' and the 'rough end'.

The main sources of employment at the end of the century were the railways (including the Metropolitan line, built along the line of the Euston Road in the early 1860s), the furniture shops in Tottenham Court Road, and the rag trade: a very high proportion of the women in the 1871 census described themselves as seamstresses - though considering Booth's remark about prostitutes that may have been something of a euphemism in many cases. As well as these major employers there were a lot of small businesses and craftsmen flourishing in the area – bookbinders, jewellers and so on.

162. 8-18 Hampstead Road, 1906.

163. The Orange Tree pub at the corner of North Gower Street and Hampstead Road, 1904. Demolished in the 1960s for road widening.

164. Looking north up the Hampstead Road from the junction with Euston Road, c. 1903.

The twentieth century

In most respects the history of the area this century is one of a slow disintegration, accelerating around the time of the Second World War and afterwards. The land passed out of the hands of the Earls of Southampton and the New River Company and into those of a variety of landlords, big and small, more or less anonymous. Some of the worst streets – Little George Street and Little Exmouth Street – were cleared for an LCC school. Extensions to Euston Station wiped out others. Everywhere the population slowly declined as commercialisation spread into what were formerly residential areas. The housing stock was further reduced by Second World War German bombing.

In Tolmers Square, half of the south side was taken over by a pharmaceutical company and converted to factory and warehouse use. The church finally gave up the struggle to exist and closed just after the First World War. The building was converted into a popular and lively, but not at all elegant, cinema (1923), which lasted until 1972, when it was bought by Stock Conversion and closed. (Local legend has it that the church had to be deconsecrated after the minister of the church hanged himself over the altar. This would explain the famous ghost of the cinema. Two of the staff claimed to have seen a bright light appear at four in the morning behind the screen where the old altar used to be. The light moved up the aisle to the foyer and disappeared. As a result of this the night watchman used to go for a cup of tea at Euston Station at this time.) The spire was pulled down at the end of the 1920s and the trees which used to surround the church disappeared. All this finally put paid to the Square's pretensions to gentility.

Physically, the area continued to evolve in a piecemeal fashion. Buildings were converted for new uses, extensions were added, and backyards filled in to cater for increasing numbers of commercial and small industrial firms. Several new buildings were erected where old ones failed to cater for new needs, or to fill in bomb sites. Most of the new units were for commercial purposes: architectural studios, a TGWU headquarters, a London Transport generating plant, company offices. The only new housing built this century was the Cecil Residential Club, a charitable hostel for girls. This building, designed by Maxwell Fry in the late 1930s, actually won an RIBA architectural award. (18)

165. 1903 houses converted to shops 166. 1976

167. 1903 houses and shops replaced by transport facilities 168. 1976

169. 1903 houses and shops replaced by offices 170. 1976

171. 1903 houses and shops replaced by commerce 172. 1976

173. 1903 light industry replaced by offices 174. 1976

From about 1920 onwards, many of the long-established residents started to move out to more spacious parts of London. They were replaced by immigrants of many nationalities. It seems to have been an area where newcomers to London would come and live for a few years, then, as they became established, they would move out to (literally) greener pastures. After the Second World War there was a strong Greek and Cypriot population, then from about 1950 some Asians began to move in, transforming Drummond Street with their grocery shops and restaurants into a colourful and lively commercial street.

Socially there were tensions and divisions. In general the western end was the 'posh end', as opposed to the east (by the station, and towards Somers Town). In addition, there were several owner-occupiers, in North Gower Street in particular, struggling to maintain a 'respectable' existence in a declining area. There were divisions between the nationalities, and between tenants and owner-occupiers. Between the wars, children from the south side of Tolmers Square (where there were owner-occupied houses) were forbidden to go to the houses on the north side, where the people were mostly tenants. A woman who grew up in Tolmers Square remembers as a child being so ashamed of her address that she would tell people she lived in North Gower Street. People who are asked to give their memories of what the area was like in the 1930s, 1940s and 1950s tend to come back to the same themes: it was a rough area with regular fights which the local children would stand round and watch; it was full of alcoholics, prostitutes, and gambling clubs – an atmosphere like that of the areas round other major stations; conditions were often squalid and the people generally poor. By the mid-1930s the buildings were already falling into disrepair, and little was spent on their upkeep. On the other hand, especially for people who lived there between the wars, it was a 'place with atmosphere', a place full of colour and variety: 'Railway, shops. Market. Self-employed. You name the trade or service and you would find it in this area.' And when people are asked how it has changed, there is one metaphor that keeps recurring. In the words of the policeman whose beat it was in the 1960s, 'the area sort of died'. Whatever else the 1970s have done to Tolmers, they have brought it back to life.

Notes to appendix

(1) There is not much original research in this account, although the history of the manor of Tottenhall has never been thoroughly treated. The indispensable sources are the relevant volumes of the LCC Survey of London, the Heal Collection of manuscripts and documents in Swiss Cottage Library, and the records of the manor in the Greater London Record Office. I have not seen the private records of the Southampton family.

(2) Quoted from W. Howitt, *The Northern Heights of London* (London, 1869). On the transaction see also *Commons Journals*, vol. 31, 1766-68 (1803), pp. 639, 647, 655, and *Survey of London* (London, 1900 etc), vol. 19, p.12.

(3) Stukely, manuscript volume of memoirs, quoted from C.H.Denyer (ed), *St Pancras through the Centuries* (London, 1935), p.24.

(4) *Survey of London*, vol. 21, p.120.

(5) In his *Britains Remembrancer* (London 1628), fol. 120 b.

(6) See W. Wroth: The London Pleasure Gardens of the eighteenth Century (London, 1896), pp.77–80.

(7) C. Lee in *Camden Journal* (Libraries and Arts) April/May 1972.

(8) See G. Bebbington: *London Street Names* (London, 1972) pp. 132-3. There are articles by John Stansfield on the local streets in *Tolmers News*, no. 8 and 10. On the Fitzroy/Grafton family see B. Falk, *The Royal Fitzroys* (London, 1950).

(9) See John Summerson: *Georgian London* (Harmondsworth, 1962), ch. 3.

(10) Compare Charles Booth, *Life and Labour of the People in London* (London 1902–3) series III, vol. I, p.189:'When a lease nears its termination no money will be spent that can possibly be avoided, and when it is anticipated that the site will shortly be wanted, coming events cast their shadows before them. It may be for the extension of a business premises such as Maple's, or for the further enlargement of Euston Station, or by the local authority for widening a street or opening up a slum. But though all in themselves good objects, their shadow is the shadow of death.'

(11) Simon Jenkins: *Landlords to London* (London, 1975), pp.107–8.

(12) See also Simon Hodgkinson: *History of Tolmers Square*, unpublished manuscript essay (copy in Swiss Cottage Library).

(13) Information kindly supplied by the archivist of the Metropolitan Water Board, Mr G.C. Berry. See also F. Miller: *St. Pancras Past and Present* (London, 1874) p.164.

(14) Cutting in the Heal Collection.

(15) Booth: *Life and Labour*, series III, vol. I, p.185.

(16) Cutting in Heal Collection.

(17) Booth, *Life and Labour*, Series III, vol.I, pp.195, 187-8.

(18) See N. Pevsner, *London II* (Buildings of England, Harmondsworth, 1952) p.372.

Sources

Published books and pamphlets

Ambrose, P. and Colenutt, B., *The Property Machine*, Penguin, 1975.
Bailey, R., *The Squatters*, Penguin, 1973.
Burn, D., *Rent Strike St Pancras*, Pluto Press, 1972.
Counter Information Service, *The Recurrent Crisis of London*, 1973.
Greater London Council, *London; The Future and You*, 1973.
London County Council *Administrative County of London Development Plan Statement*, 1962.
Marriott, O., *The Property Boom*, Pan, 1969.
Schlaffenberg, B., *Camden Scene; Planning Survey 1975*, London Borough of Camden, 1975.

Unpublished Sources

Baldrey, J., Britton, E., George, P., Henshaw, P., and Wates, N., *Tolmers Square, third year planning project*, University College London, School of Environmental Studies, 1973.
Camden Labour parties, minutes of meetings.
Herbert Fitch & Company Limited, *Euston Centre*, (undated, c.1964).
London Borough of Camden, minutes of meetings, reports, correspondence, press statements, survey material, planning applications.
Morgan, K., *Tolmers Village: Evolution or Revolution*, Oxford polytechnic, School of Architecture, 1974.
Read, Hurst-Brown & Co., *The Stock Conversion & Investment Trust*, 1973.
Renton Howard Wood Levin, Tolmers Square Area reports no. 1 (1973), 2 (1974), 3 (1974).
Stock Conversion and Investment Trust, *Report and Accounts*, 1973, 1974, and 1975.
Tolmers Village Association, minutes of meetings, reports, correspondence, survey material, affidavits, *Tolmers News* no. 1–20 and other material. Also *Tolmers Destroyed*, ed. Wates, N., 1974 (available from TVA, 102 Drummond Street, London, NW1).

Newspapers and Periodicals

Architects Journal (1973: 26/9, 10/10; 1974: 30/10), *Building Design* (1973: 8/6; 1975: 28/3), *Built Environment* (Nov. 1973), *Camden Tenant* (no. 9, 11, 12, 17, 20, 23, 24, 26), *City Press* (1975: 27/3), *Construction News* (1973: 14/6), *Community Action* (no. 11, 14), *Daily Worker* (1962: 25/9, 20/10), *Economist* (1973: 8/9), *Estates Gazette* (1974: 14/9), *Evening News* (1973: 9/10,13/10), *Evening Standard* (1959: 18/11; 1962: 24/9; 1973: 26/6, 13/9, 20/9, 21/9, 26/9, 2/10, 3/10, 8/10, 9/10, 13/10, 19/10; 1974: 9/9, 27/9; 1975: 3/4,14/4, *Financial Times* (1973: 4/6, 14/9, 27/9; 1976: 9/1), *Guardian* (1973: 13/9, 14/9, 27/9, 11/10; 1975: 21/3, 26/4, 3/5, 4/12), *Hampstead & Highgate Express* (1968: 16/2, 22/3; 1970: 25/9, 27/11; 1971: 5/2, 10/4; 1973: 16/2, 18/5, 25/5, 8/6, 15/6, 22/6, 29/6, 14/7, 27/7, 3/8, 17/8, 14/9, 21/9, 28/9, 5/10, 12/10, 19/10, 26/10, 2/11, 7/12, 21/12; 1974: 15/2, 1/3, 3/5, 17/5, 28/6, 27/9; 1975: 27/3, 2/5, 6/6, 13/6, 5/12), *Investors Chronicle* (1974: 13/9; 1975: 11/7; 1976: 9/1), *Inside London* (1973: 11/10), *International Times* (May 1974), *Morning Star* (1973: 27/9; 1974: 21/6; 1975: 5/4), *New Civil Engineer* (Oct. 1973), *New Society* (1975: 12/6, 26/6, 14/8), *New Statesman* (1973: 22/6), *North London Press - Camden Journal* (1957: 23/8, 13/9; 1959: 3/7, 6/11, 13/11, 4/12, 25/12; 1960: 22/1, 25/3, 1/4, 24/6; 1961: 17/2, 24/2, 3/3, 21/7, 11/8, 1/12; 1962: 28/9, 19/10; 1963: 8/11; 1964: 30/10; 1965: 23/7, 6/8; 1968: 16/2, 29/11; 1969: 14/2; 1971: 10/4; 1972: 24/3; 1973: 25/5, 8/6, 22/6, 13/7, 27/7, 3/8, 10/8, 14/9, 21/9, 28/9, 5/10, 19/10; 1974: 18/1,12/4, 3/5, 10/5, 24/5, 7/6, 28/6, 19/7, 27/9, 11/10; 1975: 28/2, 11/4), *Peace News* (1975: 13/6), *Private Eye* (1973:

9/2), *St Pancras Chronicle* (1959: 20/11, 4/12; 1960: 8/4, 24/6, 29/7, 12/1; 1972: 24/3; 1973: 17/3, 8/6, 6/7, 21/9, 12/10, 19/10; 1975: 28/3, 6/6, 13/6), *Sunday Observer* (1973: 9/9, 14/10; 1975: 25/5, 30/11, 7/12, 14/12, 21/12), *Sunday People* (1975: 15/6), *Sunday Telegraph* (1974: 20/10), *Sunday Times* (1973: 22/4, 3/6; 1975: 18/5, 27/7), *Telegraph* (1970: 30/10; 1974: 10/9; 1975: 3/5, 24/5, 6/6, 12/7), *Time Out* (1973: 9/2, 6/7, 14/9, 21/9, 5/10; 1974: 10/5, 28/6; 1975: 9/5, 15/5, 13/6, 7/11), *Times* (1971: 15/4; 1973: 4/6, 14/9, 27/9, 9/10, 12/12; 1974: 10/9, 30/9, 16/10; 1975: 14/2), *Workers Press* (1975: 19/3).

Films

Who owns Britain? Money Programme, BBC 2, 16 June 1972.

Sitting on a Fortune, Man Alive, BBC 2, 28 November 1973.

Tolmers; Beginning or end? dir. Phillip Thompson, 1974, 16 mm bw/col/opt, 30 minutes, (available from Cinegate, 70 Portobello Road, London W.11, tel. 01727 2651, or from Thompson Films, 1325 1/2 Princeton Avenue, Santa Monica, CA 90404, USA).

Interviews

Peter Best (councillor), Christopher Booker (journalist), Gavin Brown (resident), Jill Burke (Labour Party worker), Leila Campbell (councillor), David Christie (GLC architect), Frank Dobson (councillor), Martin Early (Labour Party worker), James Ferman (film director), Reg Freeson (Minister of Housing), Jane French (resident), David Goldhill (councillor), Frank Goodingam (resident), Bennie Gray, (journalist), Alan Greengross (councillor), Mrs Hall, (ex-resident), Dick Hobin (lecturer), Mr Jammilly (business owner), Brian Jeffreys (valuer, Camden Council), Lena Jeger (MP), Alec Kazantzis (councillor), Andrew Keeshan (cinema manager), Gerald Levin (architect, Renton Howard Wood Levin), Mrs Livermore (ex-resident), Brian Loughran (councillor), Alix Maxwell (Labour Party worker), John Mills (councillor), Frank Nickson (Deputy Town Clerk, Camden), Paddy O'Connor (councillor), Jim Palmer (ex-resident), Mr Pomson (cinema owner), PC Charles Russell (police officer), Mike Searle (valuer, Camden Council), Roy Shaw (councillor), Dianna Sherston (Housing dept, Camden Council), Jock Stallard (MP), Mike Stratton (architect, Renton Howard Wood Levin), Rachel Syers (co-ordinator, TVA), Mr Thomas (Health dept, Camden Council), Ivor Walker (councillor), David Watkinson (barrister), Teresa Wootten (ex resident). In addition, I have had informal discussions with numerous people who at some time have lived or worked in the Tolmers area.

NB. The Directors of Stock Conversion and Investment Trust declined an invitation to discuss the issue, as did also the Director of Planning for Camden Council, Dr Schlaffenberg.

Photograph sources

Except where otherwise credited, the photographs are the property of the author. Thanks are due to the following for permission to reprint photographs as listed:

Cover photograph, 1976
1. 1976
2. 1976
3. Alex Smith, 1974
4. Michael Anne Mullen, 1974
5. Pedro George, 1973
6. Michael Anne Mullen, 1974
7. Michael Anne Mullen, 1974
8. Michael Anne Mullen, 1974
9. Michael Anne Mullen, 1974
10. 1976
11. Martin Slavin, 1974
12. Michael Anne Mullen, 1974
13. 1975
14. 1976
15. 1976
16. 1976
17. 1976
18. 1976
19. Ken Morgan, 1974
20. 1976
21. Caroline Lwin, 1976
22. 1976
23. 1976
24. 1976
25. Martin Slavin, 1974
26. Aerofilms, 1932
27. Aerofilms, 16 October 1968
28. 1976
29. *North London Press*, 23 August 1957
30. Steve Palmer, 1960
31. *Northb London Press*, 28 September 1962
32. Teresa Wootten, c.1960
33. *Euston Centre*, brochure, c.1964
34. Mann Brothers, 5 January 1961, @ Greater London Council Photograph Library
35. 1976
36. Martin Slavin, 1974
37. Caroline Lwin
38. Steve Palmer, 1960
39. 1976
40. Local History collection, Camden Public Libraries
41. 1976
42. 1974
43. *Camden Journal*, 7 June 1974
44. Martin Slavin, 1974
45. Martin Slavin, 1974
46. Pedro George, 13 October 1973
47. *New Civil Engineer*, 1973
48. Local History collection, Camden Public Libraries c.1955
49. 1976
50. Alex Smith, 1974
51. Greater London Council Photograph Library
52. Local History collection, Camden Public Libraries
53. 1976
54. 1976
55. *Time Out*, 1972
56. Martin Slavin, 1973
57. Martin Slavin, 1973
58. Martin Slavin, 1974
59. 1976
60. 1976
61. Martin Slavin, 1974
62. Alex Smith, 1974
63. Alex Smith, 1974
64. 1976
65. Angela Deane-Drummond, 1973
66. *Man Alive*, 28 November 1973
67. *Man Alive*, 28 November 1973
68. *Man Alive*, 28 November 1973
69. *Man Alive*, 28 November 1973
70. *Man Alive*, 28 November 1973
71. 1976
72. 1976
73. 1976
74. 1976
75. Phillip Thompson, 1974
76. 1974
77. Michael Anne Mullen, 1974
78. 1976
79. 1976
80. 1976
81. 1976
82. Pamla Toler, 1974
83. Phillip Thompson, 1974

84. Phillip Thompson, 1974
85. 1975
86. Phillip Thompson, 1974
87. 1974
88. 1974
89. Pamla Toler, 1974
90. 1974
91. 1973
92. Barry Shaw, 1974
93. 1974
94. Atalia Avrahami, 1974
95. Caroline Lwin, 1974
96. Caroline Lwin, 1974
97. Atalia Avrahami, 1974
98. Atalia Avrahami, 1974
99. Atalia Avrahami, 1974
100. Caroline Lwin, 1974
101. Ken Morgan, 1974
102. 1974
103. 1974
104. Pamla Toler, 1974
105. 1974
106. 1975
107. Atalia Avrahami, 1974
108. 1974
109. 1976 (painting 1974)
110. Arthur Chesney, 1974
111. Barry Shaw, 1974
112. Barry Shaw, 1974
113. 1976
114. Arthur Chesney, 1974
115. 1976
116. Phillip Thompson, 1975
117. Phillip Thompson, 1975
118. 1976
119. 1976
120. 1976
121. 1976
122. Barry Shaw, 1973
123. Phillip Thompson, 1975
124. 1976
125. 1976
126. 1976
127. 1975
128. Atalia Avrahami, 1975
129. Ken Morgan, 1974
130. 1975
131. 1976
132. Ken Morgan, 1974
133. 1975
134. 1975
135. 1975
136. Ken Morgan
137. Pedro George, 1975
138. 1975
139. Atalia Avrahami, 1975
140. 1975
141. David Turner, 1975
142. Caroline Lwin, 1975
143. Moyra Ashford, 1975
144. Caroline Lwin, 1975
145. Phillip Thompson, 1975
146. 1976
147. 1976
148. Local History collection, Camden Public Libraries
149. Local History collection, Camden Public Libraries
150. Local History collection, Camden Public Libraries
151. Local History collection, Camden Public Libraries
152. Local History collection, Camden Public Libraries
153. Local History collection, Camden Public Libraries
154. Local History collection, Camden Public Libraries
155. Local History collection, Camden Public Libraries
156. Guildhall Library
157. Senate House Library
158. Local History collection, Camden Public Libraries
159. Local History collection, Camden Public Libraries
160. Local History collection, Camden Public Libraries
161. Local History collection, Camden Public Libraries
162. Greater London Council Photograph Library
163. Local History collection, Camden Public Libraries
164. Local History collection, Camden Public Libraries
165. Local History collection, Camden Public Libraries
166. 1976
167. Local History collection, Camden Public Libraries
168. 1976
169. Local History collection, Camden Public Libraries
170. 1976
171. Local History collection, Camden Public Libraries
172. 1976
173. Local History collection, Camden Public Libraries
174. 1976
175. 1975

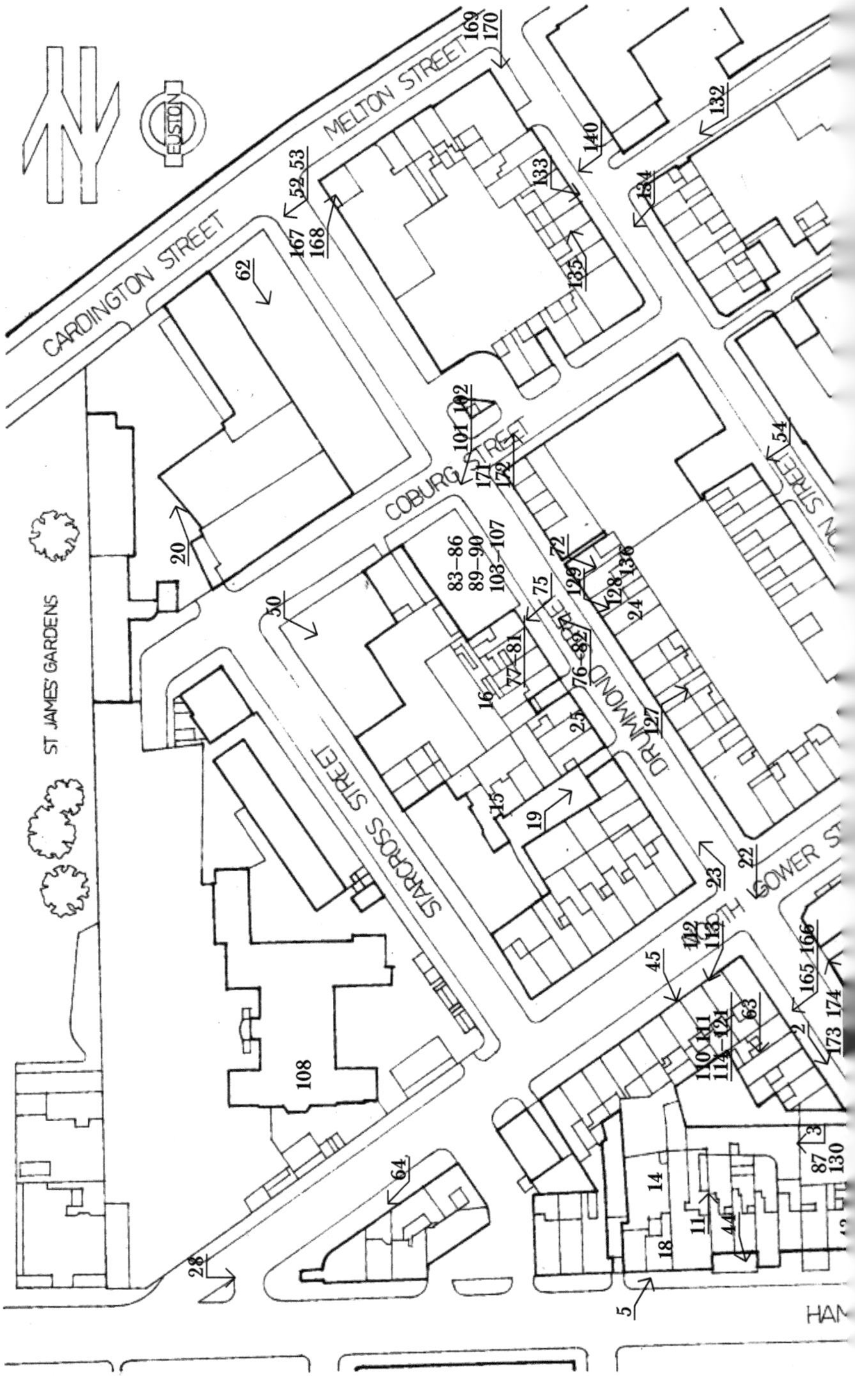
EUSTON
CARDINGTON STREET
MELTON STREET
COBURG STREET
STARCROSS STREET
DRUMMOND
ST JAMES' GARDENS

Photograph location map

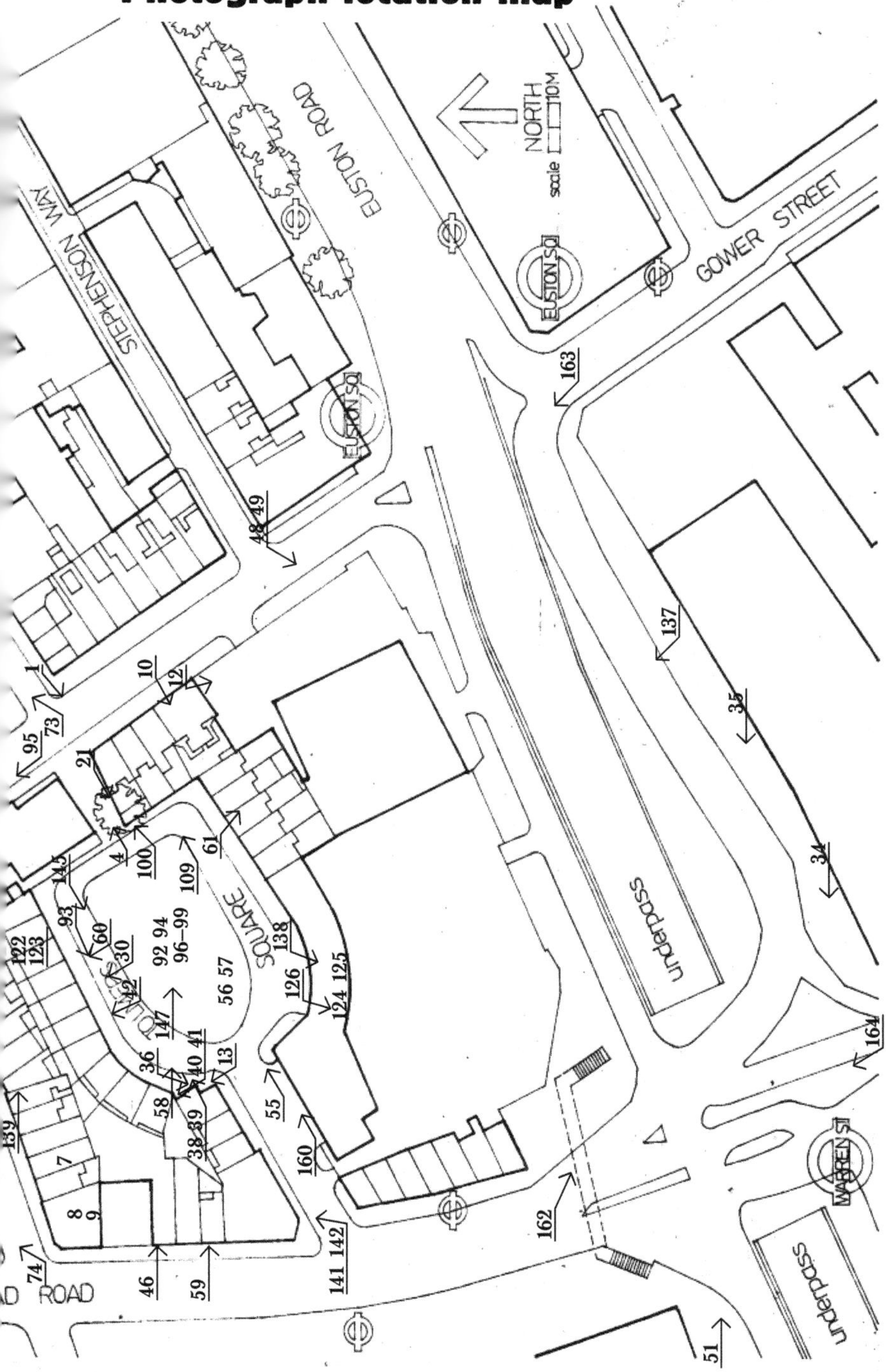

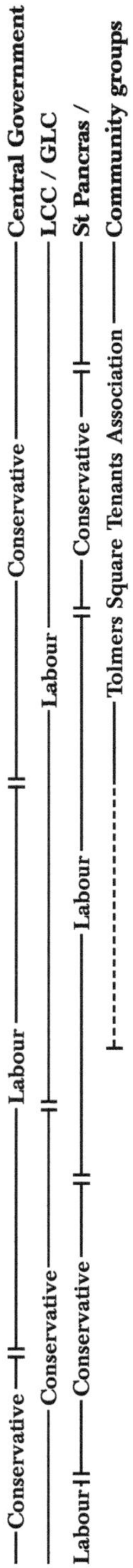

Chronology of events

	Government/Council/Developers	Community groups / Other
1957	Rent Act.	Tolmers Square Tenants Association formed.
1958		
1959	Private developers submit planning application for office development.	TSTA anti-office campaign.
1960	LCC reject planning application for office development, and start preparing plans for comprehensive housing development.	
1961		
1962	Stock Conversion start buying land in the Tolmers area.	TSTA campaign for tenants displaced by the Euston Centre development.
1963	LCC start trying to demolish 'unfit' houses.	
1964		
1965	Reorganisation of London government. LCC replaced by GLC and St Pancras amalgamated into Camden. Central Government refuses to give Camden permission to buy land or to build offices.	
1966	Camden Council start negotiations with Stock Conversion for the island site.	
1967	Camden Council continue to demolish 'unfit' housing.	
1968	Camden Council submit CPO for a small area of housing, and start negotiations with Stock Conversion for the Levy triangle.	
1969		
1970	Central Government reject CPO. Camden Council start negotiations with Stock Conversion for the whole Tolmers area.	
1971	The beginning of opposition from some Labour councilors.	
1972		

Central Government: Conservative — Labour | GLC: Labour | Camden Council: Labour | Community groups: Tolmers Village Association; Squatters action group

	Government / Council / Developers	Community groups / Other
1973		
Jan		The issue starts receiving considerable publicity.
Feb		First squatters move in.
Mar		
Apr		
May	Camden Council approve the Levy Deal.	Student project from University College London.
Jun		Claudius Offer.
Jul		
Aug		Tolmers Village Association formed.
Sep		Stop the Levy Deal campaign.
Oct	Camden Council reject the Levy Deal.	House collapses in Hampstead Road.
Nov		
Dec		
1974		
Jan		
Feb	General Election.	TVA hold exhibition.
Mar		
Apr	Camden make a CPO on a few buildings.	
May		TVA publish *Tolmers Destroyed.*
Jun		TVA hold first carnival.
Jul		
Aug		
Sep	Stock Conversion disclose new plans to develop without the Council.	
Oct	Camden Council decide to submit a CPO for all of Stock Conversion's property. General Election.	
Nov		
Dec		
1975		
Jan		
Feb		
Mar		Squatters summonsed by Stock Conversion.
Apr		Squatters' anti-eviction campaign.
May		*Tolmers: Beginning or end?* shown on television.
Jun	Camden Council buy Stock Conversion's property.	
Jul	Camden Council apply for an Office Development Permit for 300,000 square feet.	
Aug		
Sep		
Oct		
Nov		
Dec		
1976		
Jan		
Feb		
Mar		
Apr	Camden Council approve new scheme.	

TOLMERS
RULES
O.K.

www.ingramcontent.com/pod-product-compliance
Ingram Content Group UK Ltd.
Pitfield, Milton Keynes, MK11 3LW, UK
UKHW021955180926
475701UK00003B/43
* 9 7 8 0 4 1 5 6 5 8 9 3 5 *